PUBLIC EXPENDITURE HANDBOOK

A Guide to Public Expenditure Policy Issues in Developing Countries

edited by
Ke-young Chu and Richard Hemming

Government Expenditure Analysis Division
Fiscal Affairs Department
International Monetary Fund
Washington, D.C.
1991

Library of Congress Cataloging-in-Publication Data

Chu, Ke-young, 1941–
Public expenditure handbook: a guide to public expenditure policy issues in developing countries/edited by Ke-young Chu and Richard Hemming.
p. cm.
Includes bibliographical references.
ISBN 1-55775-222-2
1. Government spending poilicy—Developing countries.
2. Developing countries—Appropriations and expenditures.
I. Hemming, Richard.
HJ7980.P83 1991 91-27924
CIP

336.3'9'091474—dc20

Price: $22.50

Address orders to:
International Monetary Fund, Publications Services
700 19th Street, N.W., Washington, D.C. 20431, U.S.A.
Telephone: (202) 623-7430
Telefax: (202) 623-7491
Cable: Interfund

Foreword

Over many years, staff members of the Fiscal Affairs Department have undertaken studies on numerous aspects of public expenditure policy. The *Public Expenditure Handbook* is the outcome of an effort to bring together the various strands of these studies and related outside work.

Public expenditure issues have become increasingly important in the context of both stabilization and structural adjustment programs. Yet rather little systematic guidance is available on these issues for those who must formulate public expenditure policy recommendations. The *Handbook* is intended to fill this gap. In so doing, it provides a blend of macroeconomic and microeconomic analysis. The aggregate level of public expenditure has to respect an economy's overall resource constraint if macroeconomic imbalances are to be avoided. But the impact of public expenditure on the efficiency of resource use, and its equity implications, raise microeconomic issues concerning the composition of spending and the design of individual expenditure programs. Distinguishing productive from unproductive programs is central to improving the economic and social returns to public expenditure, and the basis for such a distinction—albeit a difficult one to make—is explored in many of the *Handbook* chapters.

I hope that the use of the *Handbook* will result in a better informed discussion of public expenditure policy with country authorities. I should stress, however, that the views expressed are the responsibility of the authors and are not necessarily those of the Fund.

VITO TANZI
Director
Fiscal Affairs Department

Acknowledgement

The Handbook papers were prepared mostly by the staff members of the Government Expenditure Analysis Division of the Fiscal Affairs Department. Other staff members contributed in various ways. Peter Heller, who as Chief of the Division coordinated the Handbook project in its initial stage, has continued to be interested in the project after moving to the African Department and contributed a paper. Jack Diamond, Kalpana Kochhar, and Sandy Mackenzie cooperated actively after moving to other Divisions; Robert Holzmann even after leaving the Fund. Henri Lorie and Claire Liuksila, of the Fiscal Review Division of the Fiscal Affairs Department, also contributed papers.

Anamaria Handford and Leda Montero typed and read successive drafts and revisions of the Handbook. Theresa Garrison also read the drafts and made editorial suggestions. Alicia Etchebarne-Bourdin helped with typesetting. David Driscoll, of the External Relations Department, provided editorial advice.

The Handbook papers have benefited substantially from the comments and suggestions of many colleagues in the Fiscal Affairs Department and other Departments throughout the Fund. Having found those comments too numerous to credit customarily in footnotes in individual papers, the editors, on behalf of the authors, would like to express here their gratitude for those extremely helpful and constructive suggestions.

The editors are also grateful to Vito Tanzi, Alan Tait, and Teresa Ter-Minassian for their guidance and support.

KE-YOUNG CHU and RICHARD HEMMING

Table of Contents

Analysis of Major Expenditure Categories

Policy Issues

Introduction

Ke-young Chu and Richard Hemming

Public expenditure is one of many forms of government intervention designed to compensate for the failure of competitive markets and to secure distributional equity. But while its justification lies in microeconomic concerns about resource allocation, public expenditure has wide-ranging macroeconomic implications, and is therefore used also as a macroeconomic policy instrument. The *Public Expenditure Handbook* represents an attempt to discuss policy issues within a framework that combines both the macroeconomic and microeconomic aspects of public expenditure. It should be emphasized, however, that public expenditure is only part of a larger set of policies designed to achieve a country's economic objectives. Where appropriate, the *Handbook* stresses the links between public expenditure and other policy instruments.

Macroeconomic and Microeconomic Considerations

The level and composition of public expenditure can have conflicting implications for growth, inflation, and the balance of payments. Balance of payments and inflation problems often require a fiscal contraction to contain aggregate demand, and the experience has been that adjustment has tended to affect the expenditure side of the budget more than the revenue side. Moreover, in face of the constraint imposed by high interest payments—especially in the heavily indebted countries—and the resilience of some other current outlays—such as defense and social spending—capital spending in general and infrastructure projects in particular have borne the burden of expenditure adjustment. While halting or delaying public investment projects may offer sizeable immediate dividends for public finances, the balance of payments, and inflation, a price could be paid in the longer term in the form of lower growth, especially if more productive investments are affected.

By the same token, efforts to promote growth may threaten stabilization objectives. For example, an increase in foreign-financed public investment that benefits primarily the nontradable goods sector may lead to higher growth in the short run but at the same time could undermine balance of payments viability if the increase in capital goods imports outweighs the contribution of additional import-substituting or export activities to growth. To resolve these conflicts requires an appropriate blend of macroeconomic stabilization policies and microeconomic structural policies.

Structural policies are a response to the need to ensure that, while stabilization measures may be harmful to growth in the short term, the longer-term growth objective is not jeopardized. While this clearly requires sound stabilization policies, it is also dependent upon policies to stimulate the supply side of the economy. As regards public expenditure, the challenge is to secure a level of spending consistent with macroeconomic stability, and then restructure expenditure as part of a systemic reform package aimed at raising the sustainable growth rate by promoting domestic saving, productive investment, and the efficiency of resource allocation. However, the notion of sustainability extends beyond macroeconomic stability; growth may be stable, but if little progress is made in terms of equity gains—which are also a function of public expenditure—this may undermine the social and political sustainability of growth.

Positive and Normative Issues

Restructuring public expenditure is a complex process. To be carried out effectively, a strategy is required, including an assessment of the objectives of government intervention, the policies needed to attain such objectives efficiently, and an evaluation of the broader implications of these policies. Thus, while it may be relatively easy to determine, for example, whether a highway has been constructed cost effectively, it is more difficult to assess whether the highway will meet transportation needs or whether such needs could be met more efficiently through some other public program. Similarly, allocating scarce resources to highway construction rather than education (or another program) involves difficult comparisons, as does choosing between public and private provision. As one moves from strictly positive to more normative questions, the answers become increasingly judgmental.

Moreover, positive and normative questions are often linked. For example, allocating resources between highway construction (physical capital) and education (human capital) has both positive and normative aspects. It is a positive question because a severe imbalance between physical and human capital can cause economic inefficiency. And it is a normative question because the benefits provided by a new highway accrue to different people than education expenditure benefits. While the intertwining of positive and normative questions makes public expenditure policy issues complicated, this complexity can be exaggerated. If it is simply assumed that resource allocation decisions are too difficult, many opportunities to reach reasonably unambiguous conclusions and offer useful advice will be missed.

Productive and Unproductive Expenditure

What are the principles and criteria that should be used in assessing the level and composition of public expenditure? It is clearly necessary to distinguish productive from unproductive expenditure. This will be straightforward if the question is to choose between two expenditure programs that share an identical objective (e.g., meeting the transportation needs of an area) and the same implications (for growth, inflation, balance of payments, and equity); the government should choose the more cost-effective project. In practice, however, competing programs are not directly comparable, and setting normative priorities cannot be avoided. Moreover, productive expenditure should be distinguished from unproductive expenditure by reference not only to the cost and wider implications of achieving program objectives, but also by assessing whether the objectives are appropriate.

Overview of the Handbook

The opening section of the *Handbook* describes the analytical framework that provides a background to public expenditure analysis. In part, this addresses the link between expenditure and macroeconomic aggregates, which principally determines the appropriate level of public expenditure. While identifying relevant structural reforms focuses on microeconomic issues concerning efficiency aspects of public expenditure, the formulation of public expenditure policy does not lend itself easily to analysis within a unifying microeconomic framework, beyond the broad arguments for government intervention associated with traditional welfare theory. This contrasts with the discussion of tax policy, which benefits from the consistent application of principles deriving from more modern tax theory. The heterogeneity of expenditure, and its use to pursue a much wider range of objectives than tax policy, has yet to yield an operational framework for expenditure policy analysis. However, recent work on the role of shadow prices in assessing policy reform in the public sector provides a potential basis for the development of such a framework.

The second section of the *Handbook* turns to an analysis of major expenditure categories. Although the breakdown of expenditure broadly corresponds to standard economic (as distinct from functional) categories, its motivation derives more from the issues that arise most frequently in discussions of expenditure policy with country authorities. As a result, the categories are not exhaustive. Moreover, no attempt has been made to impose a uniform structure on the notes, although each is meant to convey a clear impression of policy objectives, the problems and issues that arise in meeting them, and reform possibilities.

Distributional aspects of public expenditure are addressed in the following section of the *Handbook*. While major social expenditure programs such as health, education, and pensions are usually justified by reference to the failure of the market mechanism to guarantee adequate provision, they also have distributional consequences. In many countries, the poor are not well served by such programs. Part of the longer-term strategy to reduce poverty lies in raising health and education standards of the poor, together with the provision of effective social insurance; however, short-term concerns relate more to efficient means of guaranteeing adequate consumption standards—and especially food availability—for the poor.

The final section of the *Handbook* is somewhat more eclectic than the rest, drawing together notes on a group of policy issues which, although not all entirely expenditure related, do have a significant expenditure implications. These include notes on privatization and cost recovery, both examining the extent to which these policies can relieve the burden of expenditure on the government and promote increased efficiency. Another note reflects newly emerging concerns about the environment. There are also notes dealing with expenditure arrears, debt relief, and the fiscal activities of nongovernment public institutions, issues that have arisen in the context of a number of Fund-supported programs.

It is hoped that the *Handbook* can provide a useful input into future policy discussions with country authorities. As such, each of the notes is intended to be a concise and self-contained briefing of key issues that can be used as background to discussions where extensive preparation is not possible. It is clear that short notes cannot provide the solution to the problems that are likely to emerge in each and every individual case. The content of the notes has to be adapted to circumstances as they emerge. At the same time, however, the recurring themes of the *Handbook* should remain the guiding principles in formulating public expenditure policy. The **appropriate level of expenditure** is constrained by the scope to raise revenue and to finance the fiscal deficit. The **composition of expenditure** should be consistent not only with the microeconomic objectives that justify intervention but also with macroeconomic objectives. The **productivity of expenditure** should be assessed by reference to program goals, the direct cost of meeting them, and wider policy implications of the program.

Finally, it is important to note that expenditure problems derive not only from an inappropriate level and structure of expenditure, but also from administrative difficulties in controlling expenditure. Inadequate expenditure monitoring and control has been responsible for the failure of a number of Fund-supported programs to achieve their objectives. Issues relating to expenditure management are not covered in the *Handbook*; interested readers are referred to *Government Financial Management—Issues and Country Studies*, ed. by A. Premchand (Washington: International Monetary Fund, 1990).

Framework for Public Expenditure Analysis

I. Public Expenditure and Sustainable Fiscal Policy

Richard Hemming and G.A. Mackenzie

What factors determine whether public expenditure is too high?

What are the macroeconomic consequences of taxation and alternative forms of deficit financing?

How are judgments about the sustainability of fiscal policy affected by public debt accumulation?

That public expenditure should not exceed 60 percent of national income may seem a surprising conclusion to those who have had to argue the case for reductions in expenditure from already much lower levels. Yet it is a conclusion for which Milton Friedman is well known, and other commentators on the limits to public expenditure in a number of countries have been guided by it. However, the most surprising aspect of this conclusion is not so much the number quoted or the arguments used to defend it. Rather, it is the fact that such a rule of thumb has been suggested at all, since it must use as its benchmark the level of public expenditure that can be sustained in the context of broad growth, inflation, and balance of payments objectives. Given that these objectives are country specific, so is the sustainable level of public expenditure.

The following discussion abstracts from a number of issues. First, public expenditure can be measured in a variety of ways, and in the presence of a wide range of measures the notion of a sustainable level of public expenditure is necessarily an uneasy one. The discussion proceeds on the basis of an agreed and clearly understood measure of public expenditure. The note on *Public Expenditure Measurement* discusses some of the issues that arise in arriving at such a measure. Second, microeconomic concerns related to economic efficiency are not fully taken up—these are covered in detail in the note on *Public Expenditure and Resource Allocation.* Clearly, if the rate of return on public expenditure is sufficiently high, the question of sustainability is virtually defined away. It is, however, assumed that the macroeconomic constraint is binding. It nevertheless remains the case that the microeconomic impact of public expenditure has a significant bearing on its macroeconomic sustainability. The link between the microeconomic and macroeconomic implications of public expenditure is discussed in the note on *Public Expenditure, Stabilization, and Structural Adjustment.*

Paying for Public Expenditure

The issue of the sustainability of public expenditure cannot be separated from questions related to how it is paid for. These are questions that are usually considered in two alternative but closely related ways. The first alternative focuses on the **government's (or public sector's) financial balance**, which can be written

$$-(T - C^g - I^g) = B^{gp} + \Delta H + B^{gf}, \qquad (1)$$

where T = tax revenue, C^g = government consumption, I^g = government investment, B^{gp} = government borrowing from the private sector, ΔH = the change in the stock of high-powered money, and B^{gf} = government borrowing from foreigners. The left-hand side of equation (1) is the fiscal deficit. If the government wishes to increase expenditure, this can be paid for with higher taxation without affecting the fiscal deficit. If a higher deficit results, this has to be financed by a combination of borrowing from the private sector, money creation and borrowing from foreigners. There are also other sources of financing, some of which do have a bearing on the analysis of sustainability. For example, if the government were to run down foreign reserves, this may be indicative of an impending foreign exchange crisis. In most respects, however, the economic impact of depleting reserves is the same as that of increased foreign borrowing, and the former possibility is not discussed in its own right below. Two other sources of financing with less obvious implications are discussed in subsequent notes: these are financing through the sale of public sector assets (see the note on *Privatization*) and financing through the accumulation of arrears (see the note on *Expenditure Arrears*).

While equation (1) lists the options available to pay for public expenditure, some aspects of the economic impact of these options are more readily analyzed in the context of the second alternative, the **economy's savings-investment balance**. This can be written

$$-(T - C^g - I^g) = (S^p - I^p) + (M - X), \qquad (2)$$

where S^p = private saving, I^p = private investment, M = imports, and X = exports. $(M - X)$ corresponds to the external current account deficit. Equation (2) then indicates that the fiscal deficit is the sum of the private sector's saving-investment gap and the external current account deficit. The link between (1) and (2) is seen by noting that

$$S^p - I^p = B^{gp} + \Delta H - B^{pf}, \qquad (3)$$

$$\text{and } M - X = B^{gf} + B^{pf}, \qquad (4)$$

where B^{pf} = private sector borrowing from foreigners. Equation (3) says that the private sector's excess saving is measured by the extent to which it lends to the government and holds additional high-powered money less its foreign borrowing. Equation (4) says that the external current account deficit is financed by government and private sector foreign borrowing, or foreign savings. Substituting (4) and (3) into (2) yields (1).

Taxation

An increase in expenditure matched by an equivalent increase in taxation leaves the fiscal deficit unchanged. According to the **balanced budget multiplier** this will have a positive impact on aggregate demand and output. In a closed economy, aggregate income rises by an amount exactly equal to the expenditure increase; in an open economy, the increase is lower as part of the increase in expenditure leaks out of the economy through imports. The expansionary consequences of balanced budget expenditure increases on output are, however, limited. In particular, aggregate supply may fail to keep pace with aggregate demand. For example, this may be the case if there are capacity constraints. It may also arise if increasing taxation is associated with disincentives to work and save. At a theoretical level, the behavioral response of labor supply and saving to higher taxes is ambiguous, being the net outcome of the disincentive effect of higher marginal tax rates and the usually offsetting income or wealth effect of higher average tax rates. At the empirical level, labor supply responses have in general been found to be small. However, important dimensions of labor supply, such as work effort and employment in the underground economy, are not reflected in these estimates, which may underestimate damaging supply responses. Similarly, tax-induced changes in interest rates generally have a small impact on the level of savings but significantly influence the composition of savings, with a possible bias against activities with the highest rate of return. An emerging mismatch between aggregate demand and aggregate supply, with its adverse implications for inflation and balance of payments, would point to a level of public expenditure that is unsustainable despite being paid for entirely by higher taxation.

Deficit financing

If higher expenditure results in larger fiscal deficits, then the issue of sustainable expenditure coincides with the issue of a sustainable fiscal deficit. The commonly held view is that this latter issue rests on the impact of the associated financing, be it borrowing from the private sector, money creation, or foreign borrowing. There is, however, an alternative view that financing does not matter.

Debt neutrality

According to the **debt neutrality (or Ricardian equivalence) hypothesis**, borrowing is no more than deferred taxation, and insofar as the private sector recognizes this, it will adjust its consumption/savings behavior accordingly and the financial impact of borrowing will be reduced to that of the equivalent amount of taxation. While this argument is easy to understand in the context of borrowing from the private sector or foreigners, it less obviously applies in the case of borrowing from the central bank. However, the resulting money creation will lead to a higher price level which will require holders of money balances to increase their nominal money holdings to preserve their real balances. This phenomenon is often referred to as the **inflation tax**. If money creation is equivalent to taxation, the debt neutrality view is readily seen to extend not only to the prospect of borrowing financed by future taxation but also to the prospect of a future inflation tax. Notwithstanding the theoretical attraction of this view, it clearly assumes a degree of rationality on the part of private agents that is most unlikely to exist in practice. Moreover, the contention that taxpayer behavior is affected in the same way by different taxes—including one that is levied through higher inflation—is difficult to accept as an empirical proposition. Not surprisingly, the debt neutrality hypothesis gets little support from the available evidence in either industrial or developing countries. Despite its powerful theoretical implications, for all practical purposes it has to be assumed that the hypothesis is of limited relevance and that financing indeed matters.

Private saving

Equation (1) indicates that an increase in the fiscal deficit can be financed by increased borrowing from the private sector, while equation (2) points to the fact that this could reflect an increase in private saving of equivalent amount. However, as already indicated, the available evidence suggests that the elasticity of savings with respect to interest rates is small, making it difficult to raise voluntary savings substantially in the short run. In consequence, any adjustment in the private sector's savings-investment gap will tend to come from the **crowding out** of private investment. The precise mechanism by which this crowding out takes place can vary. If public and private investment are close substitutes then the latter may be directly displaced by the former. Alternatively, there may be financial crowding out as the availability of credit to the private sector to finance investment is rationed or the higher deficit forces up interest rates which, in turn, lowers investment. Crowding out is discussed in more detail in the note on *Public Expenditure, Stabilization, and Structural Adjustment*.

Money creation

While there is limited scope for increased voluntary saving by the private sector, there may be potential for increased forced saving. Money creation is the most direct way of achieving such an increase in saving—note from equation (3) that increased money holdings are part of private saving. Provided that the private sector's demand for real balances is inelastic with respect to inflation and the economy is sufficiently closed, the government can increase its spending power as the private sector accumulates nominal balances. There are two elements to this. First, the government collects seignorage revenue as real balances rise in response to changes in real income, interest rates, and financial structure. Second, it collects the inflation tax. Seignorage revenue is of limited potential. The standard quantity theory identity implies that

$$v\Delta\hat{H} = \pi + g, \tag{5}$$

where v is the velocity of circulation of high-powered money, which is assumed to be stable, $\Delta\hat{H}$ is the change in the stock of high-powered money relative to GDP, π is the inflation rate and g is the growth rate of real GDP. Rearranging (5) yields

$$\Delta\hat{H} = (\pi + g)/v, \tag{6}$$

indicating that seignorage revenue (which is defined at $\pi = 0$) is increasing in the growth rate but decreasing in income velocity. In developing countries v can be as high as 20 or more; therefore at a growth rate of 5 percent, seignorage revenue is unlikely to exceed 0.25 percent of GDP. With an inflation rate of 5 percent, revenue would double, and increase further with higher inflation rates. There are, however, limits on the feasibility of continued recourse to financing the fiscal deficit through the inflation tax.

In industrial countries, a generally low tolerance for high rates of inflation and the narrowness of the noninterest-bearing component of the monetary liabilities of the banking system in relation to GDP mean that inflationary financing could amount only to a small share of GDP. In developing countries, the share of monetary liabilities of the banking system that are noninterest bearing will be larger. However, increases in inflation may depress other tax revenues owing to collection lags. More importantly, the scope for inflationary financing will be limited by the elasticity of real balances with respect to inflation; the demand for real balances will tend to decrease over time as the private sector seeks alternatives to monetary assets. While there may be scope for collecting significant revenue in the short run through the inflation tax, in the longer term the impact of reduced money holdings will dominate. Moreover, in an open economy, foreign exchange can increasingly be used for domestic transactions.

Foreign saving

If there are limits to the extent to which higher public expenditure can be financed by domestic saving, equation (2) indicates that the only alternative is to rely more on foreign saving, or an increase in the external current account deficit. The link between the public sector deficit and the external current account deficit has tended to be a strong one, especially in heavily indebted countries. While there are examples of countries running large external deficits and fiscal surpluses—reflecting the strength of private sector imports, for example—these are exceptions that serve to illustrate that the link between the **twin deficits** is an imperfect one. Moreover, this link can be influenced by policy choices; in particular, the monetary policy that accompanies a fiscal expansion can, through its effect on the interest rate and the exchange rate, affect the resulting impact on the external current account deficit. But when there is a close link between the fiscal and external deficits, sustainability of the fiscal deficit requires an assessment of the external debt and debt service implications of running the implied external deficit. Indeed, if the government accumulated all the economy's external debt and no domestic debt or liabilities to the central bank, this would be all that is required. In reality, external debt and public debt do not coincide. Even if the accumulation of external debt is not threatening balance of payments viability, and deficit financing is not inconsistent with immediate growth and inflation objectives, rising public debt may create its own problems.

Public Debt

Public debt dynamics

The dynamics of public debt accumulation can be described by the following expression for the change in the debt-to-GDP ratio

$$\Delta\hat{D} = \hat{D}\,(r - g) + \hat{p} - \Delta\hat{H}, \qquad (7)$$

where r is the real interest rate, and $\hat{p}$ is the primary (i.e., noninterest) fiscal deficit relative to GDP; other variables are defined as above. A similar equation is derived in the note on *Interest Payments*; the principal difference is that equation (7) above allows for deficit financing through money creation, which does not add to public debt.

Equation (7) has a straightforward interpretation. The first term indicates that if the real interest rate exceeds the growth rate, rising interest payments will cause the debt ratio to increase; similarly, a primary deficit will also cause the debt ratio to increase. New debt need not be accumulated to the extent that the overall fiscal deficit (i.e., the primary deficit plus interest payments) can be financed by the creation of high-powered money. Otherwise, if the inflationary implications of money creation limit its acceptability, the debt ratio can be contained while running a primary deficit only if the growth rate of the economy exceeds the real interest rate; conversely, if the real interest rate exceeds the growth rate, containing the debt ratio without resort to money creation requires that the government run a primary surplus.

The dynamics of public debt are clearly sensitive to the relative magnitudes of the growth rate and the real interest rate. Prolonged periods with a growth rate higher than the real interest rate can accommodate an increasing level of debt. Although economic theory provides little guidance as to the general outcome, it is unlikely that a growth rate in excess of the real interest rate can persist indefinitely. In all likelihood, interest rates will rise and growth will be depressed as debt increases. Moreover, attempts to avoid such a result by maintaining interest rates at an artificially low level are likely to be counterproductive; this will either inhibit growth by fostering inefficient resource allocation, lead the government to borrow abroad at higher interest rates to maintain the growth momentum, or force increased reliance on money creation.

Public debt and inflation

A principal objection to rising public debt is that if there is an upper limit to the debt burden, deficits and debt will ultimately have to be financed through the inflation tax and that the required inflation rate will be unacceptably high. To demonstrate this, let the upper limit to the debt relative to GDP be denoted $\bar{D}$. At this upper limit, money creation necessary to finance the fiscal deficit is given by setting $\hat{D} = \bar{D}$ and $\Delta\hat{D} = 0$ in (7), which yielding

$$\Delta\hat{H} = \bar{D}\ (r - g) + \hat{p}, \tag{8}$$

which on substitution into equation (5) implies that the inflation rate can be written

$$\pi = v\ [\bar{D}(r - g) + \hat{p}] - g. \tag{9}$$

With $v = 20$, $r = 5$ percent, $g = 3$ percent, and a primary deficit equal to 1 percent of GDP, a permanent inflation rate of 37 percent is required to hold $\bar{D} = 50$ percent. A 1 percentage point higher primary deficit can be maintained with a 20 percentage point increase in the inflation rate. Conversely, eliminating inflation requires a shift to a primary surplus equal to 1 percent of GDP. Clearly, once the government is forced to rely on money creation to finance the fiscal deficit because public debt has reached its upper limit, the inflationary implications are potentially more costly than the measures needed to contain the primary deficit. A question, however, remains as to the maximum level of public debt that is sustainable.

Sustainability

The issues that arise in assessing the sustainability of public debt are taken up in more detail in the note on *Interest Payments*. In summary, it is shown that such an assessment should ideally be based upon whether the government (or public sector) is solvent. If the government's net worth, taking into account the present value of future receipts and payments, is negative then public debt—and by implication fiscal deficits and the stance of fiscal policy—can be regarded as unsustainable. This judgment is closely linked to the earlier conclusion that the sustainability of expenditure—and therefore fiscal deficits and fiscal stance—should be assessed by reference to its consistency with the stable evolution of growth, inflation, and the balance of payments. The continuous pursuit of fiscal policy that is unsustainable from a macroeconomic standpoint will likely result in insolvency, while an insolvent government is generally expanding aggregate demand at a rate that exceeds the economy's productive capacity.

Bibliography

Anand, R., and S. van Wijnbergen, "Inflation and the Financing of Government Expenditure: An Introductory Analysis with an Application to Turkey," *The World Bank Economic Review*, 3, 1989.

Buiter, W.H., and C.R. Bean, *The Plain Man's Guide to Fiscal and Financial Policy* (London: The Employment Institute, 1987).

Friedman, M., "The Line We Dare Not Cross: The Fragility of Freedom at 60 Percent," *Encounter,* 1976.

Tanzi, Vito, "Fiscal Management and External Debt Problems," in *External Debt Management*, ed. by H. Mehran (Washington: International Monetary Fund, 1985).

II. Public Expenditure, Stabilization, and Structural Adjustment

Richard Hemming

What are the implications of public expenditure for inflation, the balance of payments, and growth in the short term and the long term?

How are the macroeconomic consequences of public expenditure influenced by the stance of fiscal and monetary policy?

How should a given level of expenditure be restructured to raise the sustainable growth rate?

The note on *Public Expenditure and Sustainable Fiscal Policy* emphasizes that the reconciliation of a particular level of public expenditure with broad macroeconomic goals depends upon revenue-raising possibilities and how any associated fiscal deficit is financed. This note focuses more directly on the link between the level and composition of public spending and stabilization and structural adjustment objectives.

Stabilization and Structural Adjustment Policies

Stabilization

The objective of stabilization policy is to avoid and if necessary correct domestic and external imbalances that threaten disruption to the economy in the short term. A high inflation rate and/or a large current account deficit, which are often associated with losses of foreign exchange reserves and capital flight, signal the need for policy responses to restore financial stability. Stabilization is pursued through a combination of corrective fiscal, monetary and exchange rate policies. These policies are interdependent. A tightening of monetary policy alone is potentially damaging to the private sector as either interest rates rise (often sharply in developing countries) or, with interest rate controls, credit is rationed. A depreciation of the nominal exchange rate will have only temporary consequences if domestic prices rise and so appreciate the real exchange rate. In both cases, a supporting fiscal contraction is needed, in the first case to reduce the public sector's claim on available credit and prevent crowding out of the private sector, and in the second case to restrain aggregate demand. By the same token, fiscal policies alone are insufficient. A fiscal contraction will not result in lower inflation unless the money supply is constrained to a level consistent with the inflation target, and if wages and prices are relatively inflexible, a fiscal contraction will need to be accompanied by a nominal devaluation to achieve a real exchange rate depreciation.

Structural adjustment

Structural adjustment policies are directed toward the longer-term growth objective, by promoting efficient resource use. In one sense, the instruments of stabilization policy discussed above are also instruments of structural adjustment policy. Little progress is likely to be made on structural reform without the enabling environment provided by sound macroeconomic policies, while structural policies that are destabilizing cannot be sustained. But stabilization policies alone are not enough since of themselves fiscal retrenchment and monetary restraint can inhibit growth. However, these policies can be designed to fulfill their stabilization function while at the same time stimulating the supply side of the economy. In the case of fiscal policy, the focus shifts from the size of the fiscal deficit to the characteristics of the tax system and the composition of expenditure. In the case of monetary policy, the focus shifts from the rate of growth of money and credit to the process of interest rate determination and credit allocation. In other words, it is the structure of fiscal and monetary policies, rather than their stance, that has the more direct influence on growth, although the overall growth climate will be a reflection of both. Other policies will also be important. Liberalizing trade restrictions, industrial regulations, financial markets and price controls are central elements of most structural adjustment programs.

Public Expenditure, Inflation and the Balance of Payments

Public expenditure is a component of aggregate demand, affects private demand, and also influences aggregate supply. An increase in public spending will clearly change the composition of aggregate demand, but may not necessarily affect its level by the same amount. This depends upon the extent to which public spending crowds out private spending. Crowding out takes two forms. **Direct crowding out** arises when public spending displaces private spending which is a close substitute (e.g., education expenditure). It should be noted, however, that some types of public spending are complements to private spending (e.g., infrastructure investment). Generally, domestic spending will rise, but by less than public spending. Increased domestic spending will affect interest rates and the exchange rate, as a result of which there can also be **financial crowding out** of the private sector, and increased domestic spending will not translate fully into higher aggregate demand.

The extent of financial crowding out depends upon a number of factors: how the increase in public expenditure is financed; the stance of monetary policy and the interest elasticity of money demand; the mobility of international capital and the exchange rate regime; and supply responses. With an increase in expenditure paid for by higher taxes (i.e., no increase in the fiscal deficit), no change in the money stock, and interest inelastic money demand, interest rates will rise sharply, which—in tandem with higher taxes—will wipe out the initial impulse to aggregate demand. Relative prices will change, as interest-sensitive private expenditures are reduced, but the price level will not be affected. If money demand responds to interest rates, the increase in interest rates will be more modest—indeed, they may hardly change—and private spending will not adjust to fully offset higher public spending. There will be only partial crowding out. The impact on inflation will depend upon the extent to which the money supply is adjusted to contain further the rise in interest rates. In any event, relative prices will again adjust to reflect the changed composition of demand.

In an open economy, part of any additional domestic demand will be met through imports (i.e., the balanced budget multiplier will be less than unity) and the current account deficit will widen. The composition of imports will change to reflect that part of the additional expenditure which takes the form of government imports. Certain expenditures—defense, capital projects—are highly import intensive for most developing countries. This will influence the pattern of relative price changes associated with higher public expenditure. If the increase in public expenditure is accompanied by significantly higher interest rates, then with international capital mobility a flexible exchange rate will appreciate as additional capital inflows are attracted by the higher interest rates. The current account deficit will widen further, until eventually there is complete crowding out. But this can again be offset by monetary expansion to moderate the rise in interest rates, which will also determine the implications for inflation. With a fixed exchange rate, or if international capital is relatively immobile, there will be partial crowding out. Some of the net increase in demand will be met through higher domestic output, as long as there is some excess capacity in the economy. At full capacity, however, complete crowding out is unavoidable, at least in the short term.

Moving from taxation to deficit financing has similar crowding out implications, although the mechanism is more direct since the main forms of financing will be money creation, other private saving and foreign saving. In addition, accumulated debt will lead to additional pressure building up on interest rates and the possibility that future deficits may eventually have to be monetized (see the note on *Public Expenditure and Sustainable Fiscal Policy* for further discussion). In the longer term, the inflationary and balance of payments implications of a higher level of public expenditure depend significantly upon the extent to which this additional expenditure influences the underlying growth rate of the economy. The higher the growth rate, the lower the inflation rate associated with a given expansion of the money supply and the lower the burden of debt and debt service obligations associated with a given time path of current account deficits. The relationship between public expenditure and growth is a much discussed question.

Public Expenditure and Growth

It is a standard presumption that public expenditure supports the growth objective. Indeed, part of the economic rationale for intervention in terms of market failure and the resource allocation gains deriving from compensatory policies is predicated on this view. However, to the extent that the public sector engages in activities that can be more productively undertaken in the private sector, and given that the way in which expenditure is financed may have detrimental consequences, the link between aggregate public expenditure and growth is likely to be imprecise. Empirical evidence supports this: the data for a wide range of industrial and developing countries reveal no consistent correlation between aggregate public expenditure and growth.

It is more likely that growth is influenced by the composition of expenditure, since certain types of spending may have more of a growth orientation. Providing infrastructure to facilitate private investment, operations and maintenance to ensure that public infrastructure remains serviceable, education services to increase human capital, health services to increase labor productivity, and a general administrative and legal framework to support an increasingly complex economy should increase effective supplies of capital and labor, and thus promote growth. However, even apparently less productive expenditure—on defense, for example—may provide social and political stability that is necessary for growth, and reducing such spending could be counterproductive.

Empirical studies designed to resolve the expenditure and growth issue are mostly based upon the Denison growth accounting framework, according to which growth is explained in terms of changes in physical capital, human capital, technology, and efficiency in resource use. If public expenditure enhances any of these elements, a positive contribution to growth is expected. Studies to date provide some tentative support for a positive impact of capital expenditure on growth. Moreover, within capital expenditure it is education and other social sector spending that appears to have exerted the strongest influence. In addition, productive current expenditure—especially spending on social sectors and direct assistance to the private sector—also has a beneficial effect on growth. Overall, however, public spending is not among the most influential determinants of differences in growth rates either between countries or over time. External factors dominate most others, but much of the variation in growth rates remains unexplained. The main conclusions that can therefore be derived from these studies are that, to the modest extent public expenditure contributes to growth, it is indeed the composition rather than the level which is important and that, in the same context, the distinction between capital and current expenditure can be misleading; the focus should be on trying to distinguish productive from unproductive expenditure.

As indicated above, one possible explanation of the inconclusive empirical results is that while expenditure of itself may be growth promoting, the way the government chooses to pay for public expenditure has the opposite effect. This would occur when higher taxes constitute a disincentive to labor supply and savings while increased borrowing crowds out private investment. However, it has so far proved difficult to disentangle possibly stronger beneficial effects of public expenditure on growth from the offsetting influence of its financing.

Implications for Expenditure Policy

Adjustment programs typically call for policies directed toward both stabilization and structural adjustment objectives. The former comprises some combination of fiscal, monetary and exchange rate policies. In the fiscal area, an expenditure adjustment is often part of the policy package. However, as the preceding discussion illustrates, gauging the macroeconomic impact of an expenditure adjustment is complicated. Even in fairly simple models—of the type on which the macroeconomic framework underlying much of the Fund's country analysis is based—yield only limited conclusions. An expenditure reduction is generally consistent with lowering inflation (assuming supporting monetary policy), and if it is consumption rather than investment spending that is cut, then higher domestic saving should lead to increased investment and higher growth. But depending upon the type of consumption spending that is affected, the response of the private sector, and the stance of other policies, output growth could fall, at least in the short term. The impact on the balance of payments is in turn a function of the price and output responses, and is in general indeterminate.

Moreover, other stabilization and structural adjustment policies influence the level and composition of expenditure. Thus, changes in interest rates affect domestic debt service, external debt service and import costs depend upon the exchange rate, indexed and quasi-indexed expenditures (pensions, wages, purchases of goods and services) are a function of the inflation rate, and the demand for certain programs (health, education) is related to income. At the same time, changes in interest rates and the exchange rate, inflation and income growth affect revenues. The net outcome of other macroeconomic variables on expenditure and the fiscal deficit is therefore ambiguous, and an *ex ante* expenditure cut could easily translate into higher *ex post* expenditure and a larger deficit. These feedback effects complicate policy analysis even further.

In the presence of such uncertainty, it is clearly important that expenditure reductions are borne by unproductive programs, and that there is a more general reallocation from unproductive to productive programs. While it may be difficult to maintain the growth momentum in the short term, the economy's growth potential can then be more fully exploited over the longer term. Although there is widespread agreement as to the most obvious examples of unproductive expenditure—white elephants, overmanning, covering unlimited public enterprise losses—and productive expenditure—a high-quality public infrastructure investment program, supporting operations and maintenance funding, provision of education and health services—even in these apparently clear-cut cases the distinction between productive and unproductive spending is more elusive than it might at first appear. The note on *Public Expenditure Productivity* both discusses the principles that should be employed in making such a distinction, and provides some practical guidance as to how relatively unproductive expenditure can be identified.

Bibliography

Diamond, Jack, "Government Expenditure and Growth," *Finance and Development,* Volume 27, Number 4 (Washington: International Monetary Fund, December 1990).

Khan, M., "The Macroeconomic Effects of Fund-Supported Adjustment Programs," *IMF Staff Papers*, 37 (Washington: International Monetary Fund, 1990).

Tanzi, Vito, "Fiscal Policy, Growth, and the Design of Stabilization Programs," in *Fiscal Policy, Stabilization, and Growth in Developing Countries*, ed. by Mario I. Blejer and Ke-young Chu (Washington: International Monetary Fund, 1989).

World Bank, "Fiscal Policy for Stabilization and Adjustment," in *World Development Report* (Washington, 1988).

III. Public Expenditure and Resource Allocation

Richard Hemming

What economic arguments can be used to justify government intervention? Which activities should be undertaken by the public sector?

How can the government influence distributional outcomes?

Is the observed growth of public expenditure with income inevitable? What arguments have been offered to explain this growth?

Government intervention in the economy is motivated by a wide range of economic, social, and political objectives. The fact that the share of public expenditure in GDP, and the composition of expenditure, varies so much across countries reflects how much importance is or has in the past been attached to different objectives. This note focuses primarily on the economic justification for intervention, and discusses in particular the imperfections that typically characterize private markets and which give rise to a compensatory role for government. While many public programs can be defended by reference to market failure, others have to be justified using different arguments. In this connection, distributional objectives are important. Conclusions are also drawn about the link between microeconomic objectives and the size of the public sector.

The Optimality of Competitive Markets

The starting point for any discussion of government intervention is the voluntary exchange model of a competitive economy. According to this model, a competitive economy will result in an allocation of resources such that (i) inputs cannot be reallocated to yield a higher output of one good without reducing the output of another good, and (ii) total output cannot be reallocated to generate a higher level of welfare for one consumer without reducing the welfare of another consumer. This is referred to as **Pareto optimality**. A Pareto optimum is defined in terms of a set of marginal conditions, requiring equality between marginal rates of transformation in production and marginal rates of substitution in consumption. A corollary of these conditions is the **marginal cost pricing** rule (see the note on *Pricing and Cost Recovery*). However, these marginal conditions only support a Pareto optimal competitive equilibrium if a number of underlying assumptions are satisfied.

There are many different ways of characterizing these assumptions. For simplicity, they can be conveniently summarized as the following: (i) markets must exist for all goods—if market prices cannot be used to control supply and demand, or if economic agents do not share the same information, some goods and services may not be provided at all; (ii) there must be no externalities—prices must reflect all costs and benefits associated with production and consumption; and (iii) there must be decreasing returns to scale—unbounded scale economies lead to a noncompetitive economy dominated by a few large firms. To the extent that these assumptions are not satisfied, then there is market failure. Moreover, even if the marginal conditions do result in a Pareto optimal competitive equilibrium, this may not be socially optimal. There are many Pareto optima, each associated with a different distribution of factor ownership. For social optimality it must also be assumed that (iv) society judges the initial distribution of factor ownership, and therefore the final distribution of income and welfare associated with a Pareto optimum, to be acceptable.

Market Failure

The market failure that results when the assumptions of the competitive model do not hold takes a variety of forms. In its strictest sense, market failure results from the violation of assumptions (i), (ii), and (iii) above. The most common issues that then arise relate to the provision of **public goods** (for which market prices are inappropriate) and **collective goods** (which are characterized by externalities), the emergence of **natural monopoly** (when there are continuous economies of scale) and the need for **social insurance** (arising from information asymmetries). The inability of the free market to generate a socially optimal distribution of income and welfare, which violates assumption (iv), can also be regarded as an example of market failure. This issue, however, will be discussed separately.

Public goods

Public goods are characterized by **nonrivalry in consumption**. Nonrivalry in consumption refers to the idea that the benefits of a good can be enjoyed by more than one person simultaneously and that the cost of accommodating additional consumers is zero. **Nonexcludability** is also claimed to be a characteristic of public goods. Nonexcludability exists when a person can enjoy the benefits of a good whether or not there has been payment for its use. In other words, there are no clearly established **property rights** which can be assigned to particular individuals. The possibility of exclusion is to some extent a technical question; with rapidly changing technologies, there are increasing possibilities for limiting or charging for the consumption of goods heretofore considered as public goods. Nevertheless, it is undesirable on efficiency grounds to exclude access to nonrival goods, given that marginal cost is zero. It is therefore nonrivalry that primarily defines public goods. Generally, the private sector would tend not to provide public goods since market prices cannot be used to ration them. Therefore, if these goods are worth producing, it is up to the public sector to ensure their provision either directly, or by encouraging or contracting for private provision (see the note on *Privatization)*. In general, public goods are produced by the public sector. However, charging for public goods represents a problem for the public sector since individuals who cannot be deprived of consuming a public good have an incentive to minimize their potential contribution to financing its provision. The **free-rider problem** implies that public goods would be underprovided if the government tried to link charges to some indicator of consumer preference, because individuals would not reveal their true preferences. Such goods therefore tend to be financed from the budget. While the theory of public goods has a powerful conceptual appeal, when one looks to the real world there are not many examples of pure public goods. Defense and air pollution abatement clearly fit the technical characteristics of public goods (for further discussion see the notes on *Military Expenditure* and *Public Expenditure and the Environment*). Flood control, some public health services, weather forecasting, and lighthouses are also often-quoted examples.

Collective goods and externalities

While there may be relatively few pure public goods, there are many goods which have partial public good elements to them. These are goods which are largely rival in consumption and for which exclusion is possible, but where some of the benefits or costs associated with their provision accrue to or are borne by other individuals or by society as well. Goods exhibiting externalities in consumption or production are often referred to as collective or mixed goods. The existence of externalities forces a wedge between market prices and social valuation. Thus, although the private sector can and does provide goods and services characterized by externalities, the quantity provided will not correspond to the socially desirable level. The individual who demands education is not likely to consider or be willing to pay for the additional benefit derived by others, and private markets offer no mechanism whereby one individual's preferences for consumption by another individual can be readily expressed. In such situations, social benefits exceed the private benefits that a buyer would appropriate for himself; private markets would tend to supply too little compared with the amount that would emerge if all individual preferences could be fully captured by private markets. As a consequence, government action may be needed to help society approach the socially optimal level of output. Where there are external benefits—as in the case of education, vaccination, waste disposal, and certain forms of transportation, for example—the government can subsidize consumption and/or production. Where there are external costs—as in the case of air pollution and noise, for example—the government can levy compensating taxes. However, there are alternative strategies. For instance, the government could define the relevant property rights, thus establishing that polluters have to compensate the public who "own" clean air. But as with public goods, the government produces many collective goods directly. It also uses its regulatory powers to contain activities that give rise to external costs.

Natural monopoly

Natural monopoly describes a situation where one firm dominates an industry subject to continuously decreasing average costs of production. The incumbent firm can always expand capacity at a cost lower than that at which a new firm can create the same additional capacity. Efficient pricing requires that prices be set equal to marginal cost. However, under such circumstances, setting prices equal to marginal cost will result in losses, since marginal cost is necessarily below average cost. Therefore, if society is to benefit from the lower price and higher output than a profit-maximizing private monopolist would choose, either the private producer must be paid a subsidy, or the public sector must take over the industry and bear its losses directly. Examples of decreasing-cost industries include gas, electricity and water utilities, telecommunications, and mass transportation, all of which are characterized by extensive networks (gas pipelines, electricity grids, railway lines, etc.) that would be costly and inefficient for competing suppliers to replicate. Public production in these areas is commonplace.

Social insurance

Most types of insurance can be purchased on the private market; these markets are, however, very imperfect. The fact that the insured typically have more relevant information than the insurer gives rise to **moral hazard** and **adverse selection** problems. Moral hazard arises when the insured can affect the liabilities of the insurer without the latter knowing—with full medical cover, the insured will tend to demand too much medical care because the marginal cost is zero, the health care system typically has an incentive to provide it, and the insurance companies cannot monitor need. Insurers respond by using coinsurance and deductions. Adverse selection arises where low-risk individuals refuse to buy insurance at an actuarially fair price. Only high-risk individuals buy insurance, which forces up the price. In the end, only the worst risks would require insurance, and insurers would be reluctant to remain in the market. If they did so, they may attempt to discriminate against those in the greatest need. It is because complete private markets are unlikely to exist that government provision of unemployment insurance, health care for low-income families, and retirement pensions is often defended by reference to the benefits of risk pooling.

In these cases, however, **merit good** arguments are also used to justify intervention. Even if private insurance were generally available, it is argued that individuals would often not act in their own self-interest and purchase it. Government intervention is therefore justified on paternalistic grounds. It should be noted, however, that defending government intervention by reference to a paternalism motive involves the subordination of individual preferences. For this reason, arguments for public expenditure based on paternalism are uneasy ones for economists who otherwise argue for the efficiency of the market mechanism.

Toward Allocative Efficiency

Public goods, externalities, natural monopoly, and the need for social insurance provide government with an allocative role. However, the way in which the government influences the economy in pursuit of social efficiency is important. For example, **the theory of the second best** implies that when the conditions for optimality do not generally pertain, there should be no presumption that an attempt to correct for any one of many deviations from optimality will be welfare improving. In principle, the optimum associated with any compensated market failure is characterized by a completely new set of marginal conditions that can depart significantly from those that define a first-best optimum. Moreover, to move the economy to this new optimum, the government must use taxes, subsidies, regulatory controls, etc., that are themselves distortionary. Government policy has therefore to trade off the inefficiency of market failure against the inefficiency associated with the compensating policies, and the costs of administering them. The design of such policies is the principal challenge facing policymakers having to judge the appropriate role of government in influencing resource allocation.

Distributional Objectives

As indicated above, there exists a Pareto optimum associated with each initial distribution of factor ownership—the resulting distribution of income and welfare reflects the initial distribution of the capital stock and ability. If this distribution is unacceptable, society will sanction redistributive measures. While there are private agencies that can effect some redistribution—charitable organizations, for example—without the government's power to tax and transfer, the amount of coordinated redistribution that can be achieved is modest. Nevertheless, complicated issues still arise. Progressive taxation and cash transfers are the most direct redistributive instruments used by governments. But other policies are either intentionally redistributive or have redistributional implications. The public provision of health, education, housing, and other social services lies at the core of redistribution policy—there are, however, problems in assessing the amount of redistribution that takes place through the provision of public services. There is also a question as to whether the government should provide these goods and services directly, or provide income supplements and let people purchase the amounts they want in a market, if it exists or can be created. These issues are taken up at greater length in the notes on the *Distributional Impact of Public Expenditure* and *Poverty and Social Security*. In addition to its explicitly redistributive activities, governments affect the distribution of income and welfare in other ways. In particular, regulatory activities such as consumer protection, anti-monopoly legislation, and safety laws—many of which are justified by reference to problems associated with collecting, disseminating, and interpreting information, difficulties in organizing collective action, and the costs of establishing and enforcing minimum standards—have distributional implications. As in the case of policies directed toward improving resource allocation, measures aimed at addressing distributional objectives have an efficiency cost. There is therefore a trade-off between equity and efficiency that implies a limit to the amount of redistribution which can be undertaken.

Public Expenditure Growth

The preceding discussion provides a basis for government intervention by reference to its beneficial impact on resource allocation and equity. Public expenditure should therefore reflect the extent of market failure and the importance of distributional objectives. It is then interesting to ask whether the observed positive correlation between public expenditure shares and income, both between countries and over time, is linked to these factors (Table 1). The conclusion is unclear. It seems reasonable to conjecture that the richer a country, the more it can afford general redistribution. Also, as development proceeds income support is provided less by the extended family, and formal social security is needed in its place. Variations in social expenditure support such a conclusion. The link between other market failures and income is unclear, although it is often argued that poorer countries are characterized by more extensive market failure. Inadequate financial and capital markets are a case in point. Hence the dominant role of government in investment and production in many developing countries. But while market failure may be a bigger problem in poorer countries, they rarely have the resources to support all the necessary compensatory policies. On balance, market failure and distributional concerns probably suggest that public expenditure should increase with income and development. Specific theories of expenditure growth contribute a fuller explanation of expenditure trends.

Table 1. Public Expenditure as a Percentage of GDP, 1972–88[1]

	1972	1975	1980	1985	1988
Industrial Countries	36.7	42.1	46.0	48.3	48.9
Developing Countries	23.8	28.0	30.2	32.7	...
Africa	22.6	25.7	32.6	35.5	35.4[2]
Asia	27.3	24.8	30.3	29.3	27.0[3]
Middle East	32.2	50.7	44.6	43.1	42.7[2]
Western Hemisphere	21.8	24.1	24.6	29.1	30.0

Source: *IMF Government Finance Statistics Yearbook.*

[1] General government.

[2] 1986.

[3] 1987.

Wagner's Law—named after its nineteenth century originator—suggests that as a society becomes industrialized, the set of social, commercial, and legal relationships within it becomes more complex. Governments will occupy a more prominent role in establishing and running institutions to control this complexity. More recently, it has been argued that in a democracy there is a notion of the tolerable burden of taxation, and governments are severely constrained from increasing expenditure dramatically. However, during periods of social disturbance, such as war, famine, or some natural disaster, the level of tolerance for taxation is greater and, consequently, government expenditure is able to expand. After the social disturbance, the tolerable rate of taxation does not fully return to its original level; public expenditure therefore increases permanently due to the **displacement effect**.

Other approaches emphasize factors that influence the demand for public programs. For example, the role of **demographic factors** is particularly important in both industrial and developing countries. Aging populations in many industrial countries over the last three decades have been an important factor in explaining the growth of social expenditure on pensions and health care for the elderly. This is also expected to be the predominant demographic trend influencing social expenditure over the next forty years in these countries (see the note on *Pensions* for more detail). By contrast, developing countries have experienced high birth rates and declining infant and child mortality rates in the 1960s and 1970s, and many are still experiencing these trends. The result has been a rapid growth in their population as a whole and particularly the younger age cohorts. This has led to increased spending on education and health care. The role of supply-side factors in explaining the growth in public expenditure is emphasized in models of unbalanced productivity growth, which imply that the price of the goods and services provided by the government rises more rapidly than the price of privately produced goods and services (see the note on *Public Expenditure Measurement* for further discussion).

Much recent attention has focused on attempts to explain the growth of public expenditure in terms of political processes. Consumers reveal their preference for public programs through their voting behavior. The views of elected representatives are then mediated by the decisions of the bureaucrats responsible for policy and program implementation. Public choice theorists have advanced a number of hypotheses on the political and bureaucratic processes by which government decisions are made. It is argued, for example, that majority rule may lead to an over-provision of public programs because coalitions form to push expenditure above levels consistent with willingness to pay. Expenditure programs, however, do not come into existence merely because some interest group wants them. They must be provided by a government bureau. Thus, government expenditure may grow not because increasing expenditures are demanded by its citizens and interest groups, but because they originate with the bureaucracy supplying such programs, whose power and prestige is enhanced by larger budgets.

Analyzing Public Expenditure

A clear distinction needs to be drawn between normative rules describing the extent to which governments ought to intervene and positive explanations of the degree to which they actually do intervene. Market failure and distributional concerns constitute good arguments for public expenditure. Some of the theories of expenditure growth reflect such arguments. If the government has a regulatory role in the economy, the more complicated the economy becomes the greater the degree of regulation that may be needed. Similarly, if there is a compelling case for public provision of retirement pensions, then aging populations will put pressure on expenditure. But other theories are based upon bad arguments for public expenditure. There is little merit in public programs and high levels of expenditure that reflect misconceptions about the potentially damaging effects of increased taxation, low public sector productivity, the influence of pressure group politics, and the misconceived objectives of public bureaucrats.

The distinction between good and bad arguments for public expenditure is central to assessing the level and composition of public expenditure. In seeking to analyze a public expenditure program from a microeconomic perspective, the objective should be to distinguish between good and bad expenditures using arguments that derive from a clear view of the justification for government intervention. The focus of attention should be (i) the extent of market failure; (ii) distributional objectives; and (iii) the efficiency cost of compensating interventions. However, as the note on *Public Expenditure Productivity* reveals, the scope for clear-cut judgments may be rather narrow.

Bibliography

Atkinson, A.B., and J.E. Stiglitz, *Lectures on Public Economics* (New York: McGraw Hill, 1980).

Bohm, P., *Social Efficiency* (London: Macmillan, 1973).

Mirrlees, J.A., "Arguments for Public Expenditure", in *Contemporary Contributions to Economics*, ed. by M. Artis and A.R. Nobay (Oxford: Basil Blackwell, 1978).

Saunders, P., and F. Klau, *The Role of the Public Sector*, OECD Economic Studies, No. 4 (Paris: Organization for Economic Cooperation and Development, 1985).

IV. Public Expenditure Productivity

Richard Hemming, Daniel P. Hewitt, and G.A. Mackenzie

How can productive expenditure be distinguished from unproductive expenditure? What are the relevant concepts of efficiency?

To what extent can efficiency be increased by transferring public sector activities to the private sector?

What criteria should be used to judge whether the balance of expenditure between and within public programs is appropriate?

The motivation for restructuring the expenditure side of the budget is often found in macroeconomic imbalances that are judged unsustainable. In the absence of opportunities to secure increases in revenue, an expenditure adjustment is unavoidable. However, even when a clear case can be made for a cut in public expenditure, formidable difficulties remain. While it is uncontroversial to recommend the elimination of the least productive programs, reaching agreement on which programs are the least productive is normally quite difficult. The purpose of this note is to try and identify the characteristics and categories of expenditure that should be the priority targets in the event of either a need for expenditure cuts or a desire to accommodate new expenditure demands within the context of fixed resource availability.

Defining Unproductive Expenditure

The concept of **economic inefficiency in public expenditure** is central to any definition of unproductive expenditure. In what follows, attention is focused on four aspects of inefficiency. The first type of inefficiency arises from an **inappropriate assignment of activities to the public sector** as opposed to the private sector. Two other types of inefficiency arise from specific characteristics of public provision. **Allocative inefficiency** manifests itself as a mix of public programs that does not best meet the objectives that justify government intervention. **Productive inefficiency** describes a situation where goods and services are not provided by the public sector at minimum cost. It should be noted that allocative inefficiency is sometimes termed product mix inefficiency, in recognition of the fact that cost minimization involves decisions about the allocation of inputs. There is also a **macroeconomic dimension to unproductive expenditure**, related to the efficiency with which public expenditure serves broad macroeconomic objectives.

Public versus private provision

The note on *Public Expenditure and Resource Allocation* describes the contribution of welfare theory to the assessment of the appropriate role of government in a modern mixed economy. In essence, there is a clear case for intervention in the presence of market failure or when the distributional consequences of the market are considered unfair. Otherwise, competitive markets provide the incentive to seek economic efficiency, that is both allocative and productive efficiency. The product market guides prices and output—producers who do not sell what the public wants at a price they are willing to pay will not make a profit. The capital market constrains costs—producers who do not make adequate profit will go bankrupt or be taken over. If the distributional outcome is acceptable, there is also social efficiency.

To the extent that government intervention extends beyond those activities characterized by market failure or unacceptable distributional outcomes, the additional public expenditure that results could be regarded as unproductive. Private provision of goods and services that do not exhibit these characteristics will, in principle, be at least as efficient as public provision. Notwithstanding its theoretical attraction, the welfare-based minimalist approach to government intervention—which places the burden of proof on advocates of more extensive intervention—has to be applied with caution.

Clearly, government intervention varies widely in degree. In part, this reflects differences in the extent of market failure and the acceptability of distributional outcomes. In addition, political, social, and economic factors, largely unrelated to a welfare-based approach to intervention, are important. Moreover, not all of the arguments used to justify more extensive intervention are necessarily bad ones. For example, if governments choose to finance programs that benefit particular groups to preserve political stability, to support a declining industry so as to prevent widespread unemployment in regions dependent on that industry, and to maintain control of strategically important sectors (e.g., petroleum and air transportation), this is not necessarily misguided. But rather than debating the merits of each and every instance of intervention, the search for unproductive expenditure is better directed toward those activities where public provision is obviously wasteful and/or private provision is likely to be clearly superior. However, it is impossible to lose sight of the fact that every public program benefits some interest group, and proposals to cut even the most wasteful programs will meet vigorous opposition from the current beneficiaries.

The note on *Privatization* discusses the relative merits of private and public provision in more detail, and in particular the scope for devolving public sector activities—through asset sales, joint ventures, contracting out, and franchising—to the private sector. In summary, increased exposure to competition is likely to yield the largest gains in economic efficiency, and therefore the link between privatization and competition generally determines the strength of the case for privatization. Where a private market already exists, there is probably a case for privatization, although not necessarily an associated prospect of large efficiency increases. However, where the private sector is excluded from a particular market, and there is no reason to believe that public provision offers compelling political, social, or economic advantages, privatization accompanied by liberalization should increase efficiency substantially. There may also be scope, while retaining certain activities predominantly in the public sector, for allowing private sector involvement in some of the less central aspects of these activities.

Allocative inefficiency

It is difficult to comment on the extent of allocative inefficiency resulting from an inappropriate mix of programs in the absence of information about the **social welfare function (SWF)**. A SWF can be viewed as a representation of social preferences across the full range of public sector goods and services, and other public sector activities such as regulation. Society would prefer that mix of expenditure which maximizes social welfare as reflected in its SWF. It should also be the objective of government policy to achieve such a mix. However, the SWF the government uses in seeking to maximize social welfare may differ from that of society. This will arise when there are **preference revelation problems,** and society has no effective and/or efficient means of indicating its SWF to the government. Despite the best efforts of the government to reflect social preferences in its decision-making, there will be a loss of allocative efficiency in such circumstances.

The government may also override social preferences. On the basis of **paternalism**, the government could decide that individuals make inappropriate choices as far as **merit goods** are concerned—individuals choose to invest in too little education and consume too much alcohol and tobacco, for example—and the government will therefore seek to alter individual behavior. Whether there is a loss of allocative efficiency with a paternal government is the subject of debate. Much rests on the possibility of there being other justifications for intervention that is undertaken for ostensibly paternal reasons. For instance, persuading people to invest more in education and to limit their consumption of alcohol and tobacco can be defended by reference to externalities, in which case government intervention is intended to increase allocative efficiency. Only to the extent that paternal intervention cannot be justified by reference to market failure—and with some imagination most public programs can be so defended—could it reasonably be claimed that there is an associated loss of allocative efficiency.

The most serious allocative inefficiency reflects the failure of the government to provide a mix of goods and services consistent with any reasonable SWF (see below for further discussion). This would arise where other objectives compromise the ability to maximize social welfare. These objectives typically reflect the personal preferences of politicians, public sector managers and organized labor, who take advantage of their positions and the administrative complexity of public agencies to pursue activities that serve their own interests. The resulting loss of allocative efficiency is often said to reflect **state or government failure**.

Productive inefficiency

The efficiency of production has both a technical aspect—Is output maximized with given inputs?—and an allocative aspect—Does the input mix reflect opportunity costs? Numerous factors can contribute to high production costs in the public sector. Some of these need not in the strictest sense point to productive inefficiency, since they are a function of the objectives of government. For example, overmanning in the public sector may reflect a deliberate decision about employment generation and does not necessarily imply productive inefficiency. There is, however, a general presumption that the public sector does not use the least-cost production methods.

Productive inefficiency is often explained in terms of technical considerations (inadequate investment appraisal, low levels of research and development, etc.). However, while these can play a role, they are symptomatic of more general shortcomings in the internal organization of the public sector. These shortcomings give rise to what is often referred to as **X-inefficiency.** The root causes of X-inefficiency overlap with those that give rise to allocative inefficiency. These include the political and bureaucratic considerations that generate ever-increasing budgets; salary and wage-setting mechanisms that neither reward efficiency nor penalize inefficiency; and a fiscal illusion that leads the public to accept both increases in the number of public programs and the rising costs of running them. It will be recalled that these are essentially the basis of the bad arguments used to explain rapidly growing public expenditure that are discussed in the note on *Public Expenditure and Resource Allocation.* They provide the scope for inappropriate political manipulation of public agencies and lead to ineffective monitoring and control, poorly motivated management, and inflexible public sector labor markets. The resulting loss in productive efficiency is another aspect of state failure. That most other sources of high costs in the public sector would probably be eliminated if the organizational structure was improved is reflected in the fact that productive inefficiency is often equated with X-inefficiency.

Consistency between macroeconomic and microeconomic objectives

The note on *Public Expenditure and Sustainable Fiscal Policy* describes how the appropriate level of public expenditure can be judged by reference to its consistency with broad stabilization objectives. The note on *Public Expenditure, Stabilization, and Structural Adjustment* emphasizes the role of the composition of public expenditure in raising the sustainable growth rate. Expenditure switching that allows either (or some combination of) higher growth, lower inflation, and a greater debt servicing capacity without conceding another objective can be seen to imply an unambiguous reduction in unproductive expenditure. However, once objectives have to be traded off against one another, that is, growth vs. inflation and/or balance payments difficulties, normative judgments come into play in the same way as when the microeconomic aspects of efficiency are considered.

Matters become even more complicated when the macroeconomic and microeconomic aspects of efficiency are combined. Consider, for example, a SWF function that has growth, inflation, the balance of payments, poverty alleviation, and environmental protection as arguments. Again, if through expenditure switching one can do a little better with respect to one objective without conceding on others, then some unproductive expenditure can be said to be eliminated. But with an expanded SWF the possibility of conflict is increased, and the need to trade off objectives is a more likely occurrence. For example, growth vs. poverty alleviation and/or environmental protection may now be an issue. Normative judgments will have to play an even larger role. In general, the more carefully one attempts to characterize the SWF, the greater the possibility of a conflict between objectives and the larger will be the element of judgment in deciding whether an expenditure program is unproductive or not.

Widening the set of objectives also has consequences for the notion of sustainability. When discussing sustainable fiscal policy and sustainable growth, these have been judged so far by reference to stabilization objectives. However, it is clear that stability is not enough. If the pursuit of distributional objectives provides a compelling case for government intervention, sustainability should also be judged by reference to the consequences of policies and outcomes for equity. Indeed, when referring to sustainable growth, it is generally taken for granted that this refers to stable and equitable growth. It is also increasingly being argued that the rate of depletion of environmental resources be reflected in the concept of sustainability.

Identifying Unproductive Expenditure

Notwithstanding the formidable difficulties that are, in principle, involved in identifying unproductive expenditure, the aim of this section is to try to provide some practical guidance as to how such an assessment might, in certain instances, be made. However, it should first be noted that even if unproductive expenditure can be isolated, attempts to reduce it will tend to meet political resistance. As indicated earlier, such expenditure often serves the interests of political and other pressure groups who will be vocal in defense of their favored programs and projects. Across-the-board cuts, or those that concentrate on programs for which the beneficiaries are less powerful or well-organized, meet least resistance. It is often the case, therefore, that the programs which bear a disproportionately large share of cuts, especially in developing countries, are infrastructure investment projects and other programs with more diffuse benefits but relatively high economic and social rates of return.

Based upon the earlier discussion, the key questions to which the policy analyst seeks answers are: (i) Should a particular activity be undertaken in the public sector? (ii) Is the mix of public sector activities appropriate? and (iii) Are these activities being undertaken at minimum cost? As pointed out earlier, the considerations that bear upon the question as to the scope for efficiency gains from increased private sector involvement in activities currently undertaken in the public sector is discussed in the note on *Privatization*. Attention is therefore focused on allocative and productive inefficiency in the public sector.

The most obvious sources of allocative inefficiency are prestige projects that serve no apparent economic or social purpose. Examples are numerous: second airports where an existing facility is underutilized, multi-lane highways with capacity that far exceeds projected traffic flows; and public buildings which provide facilities that are never going to be in demand. The worst excesses are reflected in so-called **white elephants**, usually major civil engineering projects that serve to increase the prestige of those who order their undertaking. But even if unambiguously wasteful projects can be identified, reducing their number is quite another thing. The fact that ostentatious expenditure is often found to be largest in some countries that can least afford it, and where the opportunity cost in terms of forgone expenditure on essential infrastructure, social services, and anti-poverty programs is therefore higher, points to the entrenched nature of such expenditure.

Once white elephants and other obviously wasteful projects have been identified, further improvements in allocative efficiency require that expenditures be prioritized. This is difficult. It is necessary to take into account: the relevant characteristics of the SWF; the complementary nature of different activities such as the need for operations and maintenance expenditure to maximize the return from a particular investment; and substitution possibilities, given that any particular sector objective can be met in a variety of ways. It is likely that only sector experts will be able to rank expenditure programs in their particular sector.

Assuming that a reasonable ranking can be provided, the next step involves choosing between expenditure programs in different sectors. In principle, one is attempting to restructure the mix of expenditure until either cuts are equally distasteful in all sectors or a reallocation of expenditure can yield no further increases in social welfare. In practice, one ends up looking for proximate indicators of misallocation. Again, sector experts may be able to provide the necessary indicators. For example, low literacy rates combined with low mortality rates might point to too little being spent on education and too much on health care; an examination of teacher/pupil and doctor/patient ratios could provide support for this conclusion. Empty roads and crowded ports could indicate a similar misallocation of resources. Numerous other examples of expenditure imbalances can be constructed. Such indicators are frequently used in World Bank public expenditure reviews as the basis of arguments for a reorientation of spending to increase overall expenditure productivity.

Pricing policy may also provide an indication of misallocation. For example, theoretical arguments suggest that prices should be set equal to marginal cost for efficiency and therefore only public goods, which are nonrival in consumption, should be provided free and financed out of general revenue. To the extent that other goods are provided free—or, indeed, even if they receive any unjustifiable subsidy—the resulting overconsumption will imply allocative inefficiency. It would be more efficient to charge an appropriate price for such goods and services and either reduce distorting taxes and borrowing, or redirect resources to more productive expenditure programs. For a further discussion of charging for public sector goods and services, see the note on *Pricing and Cost Recovery*.

In the case of productive inefficiency, sector experts may also be able to provide guidance as to whether goods and services can be delivered at lower cost, say by using more efficient technology or combining capital and labor in different ways. Expenditure imbalances can also signal the presence of productive inefficiency. To this end, sector experts may be able to indicate whether there is an unnecessarily high doctor/nurse ratio in public health clinics, whether there is a high teacher/pupil ratio when basic teaching supplies are not available, or some other imbalance exists.

The above discussion has focused on exhaustive expenditure, reflecting the public sector's claim on the economy's real resources. In the case of subsidies and transfers, the distinction between allocative and productive inefficiency is blurred. For instance, consider a general food subsidy or a universal income transfer. While such programs are mainly intended to benefit the poor, they help everybody. Payments to the nonpoor give rise to both allocative inefficiency—it would be better to spend this money in other ways—and productive inefficiency—in that the poor could be aided at lower cost. If the programs do not in fact reach all the poor, this exacerbates inefficiency. Generally speaking, any measure designed to help a specific target group that also benefits others, except insofar as the spillover benefits can be justified by reference to this being necessary to ensure that the poor are indeed helped, should be judged inefficient. These issues are discussed further in the note on *Poverty and Social Security.*

Attempting to distinguish between good and bad expenditures by reference to their relative productivity—even if it is difficult to do—illustrates rather clearly that the normal distinction between current and capital expenditure is not especially helpful in this regard. There is just as likely to be wasteful capital expenditure as wasteful current expenditure. The fact that expenditure adjustment has been borne primarily by capital spending is not necessarily undesirable; there is only a problem if the affected projects are relatively productive. Similarly, calls to contain current expenditure may be counterproductive if it is the more valuable programs that are affected. An optimal expenditure structure will comprise a mixture of capital and current spending that reflects, among other things, the government's objectives (i.e., its SWF), the relative productivity of different public expenditures, and the expenditure activities of the private sector. Reasonable objectives can be met by an expenditure structure that is justifiably biased toward current, but highly productive, expenditure.

Unproductive expenditure is an elusive concept. It is not easily defined, and the definition offered here, while deriving from some notion of the success with which the objectives of government intervention are met, does not readily lend itself to direct practical application. Relying instead on proximate indicators of inefficiency requires detailed information, and specialized skills to interpret it. The most obvious source of both information and the necessary sectoral expertise is the World Bank.

Bibliography

Heald, David, *Public Expenditure* (Oxford: Martin Robertson, 1983).

Tait, Alan A., and Peter S. Heller, *International Comparisons of Government Expenditure*, Occasional Paper No. 10 (Washington: International Monetary Fund, 1982).

V. Public Expenditure Measurement

Richard Hemming

How is measured public expenditure affected by the choice of definition of the public sector?

Which activities should be included in measures of public expenditure?

Is the size of public expenditure a good guide to the role of the public sector in the economy?

No single measure of the size of government can serve every purpose for which such a measure might be needed. Government activity takes a variety of forms—consumption, production, redistribution, regulation—and each influences the economy and society in different ways. Ideally, a measure of government size should be tailored to the activity that is of interest. In practice, however, there has been a tendency to describe the size of government by reference either to the level of public expenditure or its share in national income. The purpose of this note is to show that a number of problems arise with this approach. As a result, comparisons of expenditure levels and ratios across time and between countries have to be treated with caution.

The Level of Government

For most countries, data are readily available on expenditure by the central government. But expenditure is also undertaken by local (and regional) governments and public enterprises. Expenditure can therefore be defined also for the general government (i.e., central and local governments) or the public sector (i.e., general government and public enterprises). It would, however, be incorrect to add the expenditure recorded by the central government, local governments, and public enterprises to yield total public expenditure. Part of central government expenditure typically reflects transfers to local governments and public enterprises which are in turn spent by the recipients. Transfers between different levels of government have to be eliminated to avoid double counting. In the case of public enterprises, current spending on wages and salaries, purchases of goods and services, etc., is not included in public expenditure, the argument being that it is only to the extent that this expenditure is not covered by internally generated income that public enterprise activities impinge upon the economy and society.

In defining public expenditure, the preference should always be for properly consolidated data (i.e., with intergovernmental transfers eliminated) relating to the public sector as a whole. However, in many cases only more limited data are available and the resulting incompleteness of coverage, combined with the complexity of financial relationships that normally exist between the covered and omitted levels of government, will necessitate careful interpretation of these data. To the extent that expenditure and expenditure-type activities are not reflected in reported data, even greater care is needed. This problem arises especially in the context of measures of government expenditure derived from budget data.

Off-Budget Expenditure

Off-budget expenditure derives from the operations of a wide range of extrabudgetary accounts, special funds and decentralized agencies. To the extent possible, all expenditure of the government should be reflected in measured expenditure even if some of it is not included in the expenditure budget. Common omissions include expenditure by social security schemes, government lending, and noncommercial expenditure by public enterprises.

Social security

Social security expenditure and the corresponding taxes are sometimes included in the budget. However, in many cases there is a separate financial agency, often a social insurance fund, through which social security revenue and expenditure flows. There is some ambiguity as to whether funded social insurance payments should be included in public expenditure only to the extent that they are not covered by revenues, as would be the case with the expenditure of other public financial institutions, or in total, as with social security expenditure in the budget. The compulsory nature of social insurance tends to point to the latter treatment.

Government lending

It is not uncommon for government lending operations to be outside the formal budget, except insofar as the lending institution or program receives funds directly from the budget. However, in many cases the government is on-lending foreign loans and this has a direct budgetary impact only if borrowers are delinquent, if the government lends on more concessional terms than it receives, or if the government is required to cover foreign exchange losses. Ideally, these lending operations should be fully reflected in expenditure data for the central government, as part of net lending. Inasmuch as the central government lends to other levels of government—especially public enterprises—on-lending is netted out upon consolidation. But if the borrower is the private sector, and in many countries the government has been forced to inject capital into failing nonfinancial enterprises and financial institutions, such lending should be included in public expenditure.

Noncommercial activities of public enterprises

The above-mentioned treatment of current spending by public enterprises assumes that the activities concerned are of a commercial nature, as is the case in the private sector. Yet public enterprises are charged with a wide range of social objectives—employment generation, supplying goods and services to remote areas, charging low prices—and are required to concede profit in the process. Sometimes enterprises will be paid a subsidy to cover the cost of a specific noncommercial activity; other times an operating subsidy will be paid to loss-making enterprises; and profitable enterprises will simply make reduced profit transfers to government. Generally, the cost of the public policy objectives pursued by public enterprises is not included in expenditure data. The note on *Fiscal Activities of Public Institutions* discusses how these and similar activities of public financial institutions can be better reflected in such data.

Other Off-Budget Activities

In addition to off-budget expenditure, the government also undertakes activities which affect the economy in ways that are underestimated by their contemporaneous expenditure requirements. Regulation and government loan guarantees are examples.

Regulation

Only the direct—mainly administrative—costs of government regulatory activity are reflected in the fiscal accounts. This is clearly a highly imperfect measure of the scope and influence of such activity. While there have been many attempts to measure the impact of regulatory policy, these are contentious at best. Efforts to measure private expenditure mandated by regulatory policy (e.g., the cost of fitting catalytic convertors to motor cars) come closest to what might be considered reasonable. There are, however, obvious difficulties in attempting to measure the private costs associated with many other regulations, such as those regarding environmental health, urban planning, and consumer product safety. Moreover, it would be inconsistent to aggregate a measure of the cost impact of regulatory policy on the private sector with public expenditure, the consequences of which for private spending are not taken into account. When regulation takes the form of wage and price controls (the latter also including fixed exchange rates and administered interest rates), this will also distort measures of public expenditure. Corrected measures should reflect the use of appropriate **shadow prices**, which are discussed in more detail in the note on *Public Investment*. However, given measurement difficulties, the best one can usually hope for is some appreciation of the significance of regulatory activities when discussing the impact of the government on the economy.

Government loan guarantees

In addition to its direct lending activities, the government also guarantees loans to other levels of government, and in particular public enterprises, and to the private sector. At the time a guarantee is given no expenditure is involved; it is a **contingent liability** which will only give rise to a payment in the event of default. Such guarantees nevertheless have an economic impact, and to ignore them is to understate the influence of government on the economy. However, like regulation, it is difficult to reflect the importance of loan guarantees (as distinct from payments to which such guarantees give rise) in measured public expenditure; while loan guarantees can be valued on a probability basis, this is not the same as expenditure. But there is nevertheless a strong case for making provision for the likely expenditure implications of guarantees. Contingent liabilities are discussed further in the note on *Fiscal Activities of Public Institutions*.

Tax Expenditures

Expenditure figures are also misleading when the same objective is met through the expenditure budget in some countries and through the tax system in others. For example, financial assistance to families with children can be provided either by paying a cash benefit or by granting additional tax-free income in the form of an allowance or a tax credit. While these alternative methods of provision can have the same impact on the family concerned and on public finances, one is treated as an expenditure item while the other is an offset against tax revenue. There is a general consensus that these offsets are to all intents and purposes expenditure—hence the term tax expenditures. By the same token, items of recorded expenditure in some countries, such as tax refunds, should properly be treated as offsets against revenue.

Measuring tax expenditures is not straightforward. First, a question arises as to what is the "normal" tax structure from which a tax expenditure represents a departure. There may be many features of the current tax structure that reflect the existence of tax expenditures, and if the latter were eliminated the former would also be removed. Second, there is disagreement as to whether the impact of tax expenditures should be quantified on a revenue forgone basis (calculated on *ceteris paribus* assumptions), a revenue gain from removal basis (which incorporates behavioral responses) or an outlay-equivalent basis (by estimating the expenditure necessary to achieve the same objectives). From the point of view of measuring and comparing expenditure, it is probably the latter that is most appropriate. Estimates of tax expenditures are available for only a few industrial countries; these do reveal, however, that such expenditures can be quantitatively significant.

Cost Recovery

While off-budget expenditure and tax expenditures lead to an underestimation of expenditure, cost recovery could constitute an at least partially offsetting influence. Public expenditure can be defined on a net or gross basis. Many goods and services provided by public agencies are subject to fees and charges, and a case can be made for adjusting expenditure to reflect the extent of cost recovery. The imposition of fees and charges makes public sector activities largely indistinguishable from those undertaken in the private sector, and as such they could justifiably be excluded from public spending. Nevertheless, the standard procedure is to define government expenditure on a gross basis, and as indicated above, only the current outlays of public enterprises on a net basis.

Full adjustment of expenditure data to reflect off-budget spending and tax expenditures may not be possible, but a minimum requirement is reasonably consistent treatment both over time and between countries. Similarly, there should also be consistency in reflecting the activities of other levels of government in public expenditure aggregates. However, in interpreting the resulting expenditure data, due account needs to be taken of off-budget activities, such as regulation and the provision of loan guarantees, that have an influence on the economy far greater than associated expenditure figures suggest. In addition, it is necessary to look at the composition of expenditure, and in particular the role of transfers.

The Impact of Transfers

Public expenditure can be separated into **exhaustive spending** and **transfer payments**. Exhaustive spending reflects purchases of goods and services while transfer payments redistribute purchasing power between different members of society. For a given level of total expenditure, the split between exhaustive spending and transfer payments affects the extent to which the public sector absorbs real resources, and to many people it is the latter that provides the most meaningful indicator of the economic impact of public expenditure. But the way public expenditure is paid for is also of economic significance, and a definition of public expenditure which attempts to capture the influence of taxation and borrowing associated with a particular level of expenditure on the economy should include transfers. Clearly, the appropriate definition depends upon the purpose to which the resulting measure is put. The choice of definition and measure also implies that expenditure to national income ratios have to be interpreted with special care. Since exhaustive expenditure is reflected in national income but transfers are not, similar levels of total expenditure can correspond to widely different expenditure to national income ratios at the same level of private sector activity.

Consider, for example, the following possibilities:

	A	B	C	D
Exhaustive spending	100	50	—	100
Transfers	—	50	100	200
Public expenditure	100	100	100	300
Private expenditure	200	200	200	200
National income	300	250	200	300
Public expenditure/national income	33%	40%	50%	100%

In case A public expenditure is half the size of private expenditure, and all public spending is on consumption and investment. Public expenditure is therefore 33 percent of national income. However, if public expenditure is split equally between exhaustive spending and transfers, as in case B, the public expenditure ratio rises to 40 percent, reflecting the exclusion of transfers from national income. When the government does nothing but redistribute income through transfers, as in case C, the public expenditure ratio climbs further to 50 percent. With a particularly redistributive government—that is, one that imposes heavy taxes to finance large transfers—the public expenditure ratio can rise to 100 percent, as in case D, and higher. The implications of different mixes of exhaustive spending and transfer payments in any expenditure aggregate are therefore that: (i) high public expenditure, in particular a high public expenditure ratio, need not correspond to a large share of public spending in aggregate demand; and (ii) similar expenditure ratios can have quite different impacts on the economy and society. It is therefore important to know the broad composition of the aggregate, even for macroeconomic analysis.

Public Expenditure and Public Sector Output

Ideally, changes in public sector output should be judged by measuring public goods and services valued at appropriate prices. Public expenditure is only the **cost** of providing these goods and services. Thus, a 10 percent increase in nominal expenditure does not translate into a similar increase in the volume of goods and services provided by the public sector. Expenditure has to be deflated by the relevant price index, which should in turn reflect the price indices for the various components of expenditure. In general, these will differ from indices corresponding to private sector output, the usual argument being that the price of public sector output rises faster than that of private sector output. While wage costs are similar, productivity growth is slower in the public sector, reflecting the low level of competition, the inefficiency of complex bureaucracies etc. There is therefore a built-in tendency for public expenditure to grow relative to national income without any increase in output, because of this **relative price effect**. To assess properly the underlying output growth associated with a particular rate of expenditure growth, it is necessary to construct an appropriate output price deflator, or shadow price. But because public output is largely unmarketed, an input price deflator is often all that is available. Comparison based upon changes in the relative prices of public sector inputs and private sector outputs (or inputs)—which define away productivity improvements in the public sector (and, in the care of input price comparisons, also in the private sector)—are therefore not uncommon.

Bibliography

International Monetary Fund, *A Manual on Government Finance Statistics* (Washington, 1986).

Saunders, P., and F. Klau, *The Role of the Public Sector*, OECD Economic Studies, No. 4 (Paris: Organization for Economic Cooperation and Development, 1985).

Analysis of Major Expenditure Categories

VI. Public Sector Employment

G.A. Mackenzie

What determines the number of public sector employees?

What is the relationship between the public and private sector labor markets?

Is public sector employment excessive? What implications does this have?

What measures can be taken to reduce employment in the short run and the long run?

The wage bill of government employees represents a sizable share of government expenditure in both industrial and developing countries (Table 1). Wage and employment policy in the public sector therefore has a significant impact on total expenditure. A proper grasp of this important area of expenditure policy has to start from the premise that employment policy is intimately linked with pay policy. For convenience, employment issues are dealt with in this note and issues relating to the level and structure of pay in the note on *Public Sector Pay*. The strong interconnections between these two subjects is reflected in the country illustrations included in the latter note.

Table 1. Government Wage Bill in Selected Countries, 1988
(As a percentage of total government expenditure)

General government		Central government	
United Kingdom	25.4	Ghana	33.0
United States	24.6	Malaysia	36.4
Malawi	33.1	Bahrain	63.4
Indonesia	20.6	Argentina	23.1
Bolivia	39.0		

Source: *IMF Government Finance Statistics Yearbook.*

In relation to total population, employment at the general government level is much higher in most industrial countries than it is in most developing countries. In several Northern European countries, there were more than 10 general government employees per 100 inhabitants in 1978-80, and the OECD average was about 7 employees per 100 inhabitants. Regional and local governments account for more than half of the total in most industrial countries, and much of this employment is attributable to the health and education sectors. The government is often a direct provider of educational and health services, and the coverage of health insurance schemes and school enrollment levels are in both instances high. These statistics are in stark contrast to those of developing countries, particularly Africa: in most of the African countries for which data are available, there were fewer than 2 general government employees per 100 inhabitants. Nonetheless, general government employment in developing countries can represent a very large share of employment in the formal sector, particularly in sub-Saharan Africa. Thus, in a sample of five countries in this area, employment at the general government level accounted for between 15 and 45 percent of total formal sector employment; the share rises to 75 percent in Zambia if parastatal employees are included.

Employment Demand in the Public Sector

Labor market analysis starts from the premise that the private sector employs labor solely for the purpose of the value of its productive services, and the demand for labor services will depend on the cost of labor relative to the value of the output it produces and the cost of the other inputs into the productive process. With the exception of health and education sector personnel, however, labor employed in the public sector produces goods and services that generally cannot be profitably produced by the private sector. A government seeking to minimize the cost of a given volume of production of public goods would do so by making a choice between available techniques of delivering a public service based upon their technical characteristics and relative input prices.

It is very difficult to measure the volume of output and to estimate a production function for the public sector. Nonetheless, if the relative cost of labor and other inputs does not change, and the demand for publicly provided goods tends to increase with income, then public sector employment would tend to grow with GDP. Broadly speaking, this is what is observed; international cross-section data reveal that there is a strong relationship between employment per capita and real income per capita at the general government level.

There is a wealth of casual evidence that public sector employment decisions are influenced by far more than cost minimization, and that public employment has a dynamic of its own. If public sector managers are not subject to pressures to minimize costs, and they gain status and enhanced responsibilities from a larger staff, pressures to increase employment will emerge that are quite independent of any increase in demand derived from an increase in the demand for public services (see the notes on *Public Expenditure and Resource Allocation* and *Public Expenditure Productivity* for additional discussion of this point). Moreover, increasing employment in the public sector is also often seen as an integral part of national employment policy.

Impact on the Private Sector

The economic impact of additional employment in the public sector depends partially on how private sector labor markets function and the extent and nature of unemployment. In a fully employed economy with **competitive labor markets**, an increase in public sector employment will reduce both output and employment in the private sector. It does so by bidding up the price of labor, thus reducing the quantity of labor the private sector will demand. In effect, the increase in public sector employment crowds out private sector employment through its impact on private sector wage rates.

If the extra output of the public sector is deemed to be at least as valuable as the private sector production it displaces, there is nothing inherently undesirable about an expansion of public sector employment, although it does affect the functional distribution of income and may also affect the personal distribution of income and the rate of return to private sector investment. It should also be noted that the displacement of some private sector labor by additional public sector labor does not imply that public sector salaries are too high. The story is different in the presence of labor market rigidities or unemployment, because an expansion in public sector employment need not entail a reduction in private sector employment; instead, it results in an increase in total employment. As an employment policy, however, increases in public sector employment are clearly inferior to measures that improve the functioning of labor markets.

It has been argued that there may be some critical level of public sector employment in relation to private sector employment, above which public sector wage settlements begin to affect private sector negotiations. The importance of this phenomenon will depend on the mechanism of wage determination in the private sector. Private sector markets will be affected to the extent that higher wage settlements in the public sector lead either to an increase in the reservation wage of private sector workers or to an increase in search unemployment, as private sector employees remain or become unemployed to better their chances of employment in the public sector. The strength of the link between public and private sector pay awards may also vary with the degree of unionization in the private sector.

Excess Public Sector Employment

It was noted at the outset that it was inherently difficult to quantify the extent of excess employment in the public sector, because it is hard to measure output and hence the productivity of labor. Yet in many developing countries it is generally conceded that the level of employment exceeds any reasonable estimate of requirements by a substantial margin, and often public offices are filled with personnel with little to do. Such **overemployment** is often associated with inadequate levels of expenditure on other current goods and services. The available evidence for public employment in Africa also shows very substantial rates of growth: for example, in Ghana the average annual rate of growth of the civil service, excluding the educational service, police, and military, was 15 percent over the period 1975–82 (Table 2).

Table 2. Public Employment Growth in Selected African Countries, 1975–83[1]
(Average annual percentage increase)

Country	Sector	Increase
Ghana	- Civil service	15.0
Malawi	- Civil service established posts	7.9
Mali	- Civil service	5.6
Nigeria	- Federal civil service	8.6
	- Total public sector	15.8
Senegal	- Civil service and public enterprises	5.4
Zambia	- Central and local government	0.7
	- Parastatals	3.3

Source: Lindauer, Astra, and Suebsaeng (1988)
[1] Data refer to various sub-periods.

The **rapid growth of employment** is usually associated with an increase in the wage bill as a percentage of government expenditure, in spite of the fact that average real public sector wages have generally declined. Employment growth has been most rapid for less-skilled groups of public labor; for some highly skilled groups such as doctors, employment levels have actually declined. This development has been attributed to the compression of the wage and salary structure that has come about as a result of attempts to favor the less well paid in periods of relative austerity.

Reducing Public Sector Employment

The realization that resources have been wasted on excess public employment has prompted experiments in many countries, particularly in Africa, with hiring freezes as well as wholesale reductions in the size of the civil service. Public sector employment has been restrained by the application of the following measures, more or less in increasing order of implementation difficulty:

(i) Eliminating ghost workers: this measure has been implemented in several African countries, where it has been found that the payroll included the names of nonexistent or departed public employees. This particular problem is typically found only in countries whose administrative capacity is especially weak.

(ii) Firing temporary workers: this has been an element in programs of public sector reform pursued in The Gambia and Jamaica, presumably because it is easier to dismiss temporary staff than full-time staff.

(iii) Hiring freezes: these have been used in many countries, although usually only as a temporary measure. A variant of this approach is the policy of only partially replacing departing employees; in order to prevent upward pressure on the wage bill, the policy may take the form of restraining the remuneration of new employees to some fraction of the remuneration of the old. Its intent has been thwarted by replacing former regular employees with day laborers, as is the case in at least one African country.

(iv) Abandonment or suspension of the policy of employer-of-last-resort for university graduates: this policy is easiest to apply when steps have already been taken to reduce excessive intake by universities and technical or professional schools, although the latter policy has a long lag before its effects are felt. Forward-looking educational planning can prevent the emergence of the problem in the first place (see the note on *Education* for discussion of imbalances in educational programs at the tertiary level).

(v) Voluntary retirement or resignation: several African countries have tried to implement a policy of voluntary retirement or resignation, under which generous severance arrangements are used to induce public sector employees to quit their jobs; this type of policy requires considerable administrative expertise, may be quite costly, and is open to abuse. The more "voluntary" the retirement the more costly it has to be. This approach was tried in Guinea in 1987–88, but it met with little success.

(vi) Early retirement: this policy has been promoted in some countries, including Nigeria, where it proved to be costly. If the main aim of the policy is a permanent reduction in the public sector's labor costs it is necessary to ensure that the terms of retirement are not excessively generous. If there is an important lump-sum component to the early retirement or voluntary retirement bonus, the immediate effect of the policy will be to increase the size of the budget deficit, although if most of the bonus is saved the impact on aggregate demand would be comparable to an annuity. These sorts of policies would appear to have a greater chance of success the greater the opportunity for employment in the private sector.

(vii) Dismissal: few countries have adopted a policy of outright dismissal. Those that have done so have tried to soften the blow by offering generous severance pay. Ghana has had some success in reducing excess employment at its cocoa marketing agency in this way.

(viii) Privatization: public sector employment will fall as a result of the sale of public enterprises and the devolution of activities to the private sector; however, overmanning is more likely to be reduced if the market in which the privatized enterprise operates or the privatized activity takes place is relatively competitive (see the note on *Privatization*).

The experience with policies to reduce public sector employment points to a number of conclusions. Massive employment reductions are generally not feasible, although measures affecting selected groups of the public sector work force—for example, temporary employees or employees in a particular sector—have been successfully employed in some countries. It is easier to avoid hiring new employees than to dismiss existing employees, and the lower status of part-time or temporary workers makes their dismissal less unpalatable. Freezes on hiring have also worked, at least for a time. The reduction in public sector employment, although often a more durable means of lowering the public sector wage bill than wage restraint, has not been without short-run or medium-term costs. Many governments have had to design compensatory schemes for redundant public employees.

By way of a more general conclusion, employment policy is an area where the dictum that an ounce of prevention is worth a pound of cure is of particular validity. To avoid the creation of excessive employment or the aggravation of an already existing problem, it is necessary that there be centralized control of new appointments, by which requests for new positions can be subjected to some sort of check. Only budgeted positions should be authorized. To avoid the diversion of wages and salaries to unauthorized persons, a strict correspondence between public service records and payroll lists needs to be maintained.

Bibliography

Heller, Peter S. and Alan A. Tait, *Government Employment and Pay: Some International Comparisons*, IMF Occasional Paper No. 24 (Washington: International Monetary Fund, 1984).

Lindauer, David L., "Government Wage and Employment Policy: an Analytical Treatment with Special Reference to Africa," Discussion Paper No. 1987-3 (Washington: World Bank, March 1987).

Lindauer, David L., Meesook Oey Astra, and Parita Suebsaeng, "Government Wage Policy in Africa—Some Findings and Policy Issues," *World Bank Research Observer* (Washington, January 1988).

Nunberg, Barbara, "Public Sector Pay and Employment Reform," County Economic Department Working Paper Series 113 (Washington: World Bank, October 1988).

VII. Public Sector Pay

G.A. Mackenzie and Jerald Schiff

What determines wages and salaries in the public sector?

Is public sector pay out of line with that in comparable private sector jobs? Is this desirable?

How important are fringe benefits? Are they necessary?

What measures can be taken to control the growth of the wage and salary bill? Do these measures have unintended consequences?

Public Sector Wage and Salary Determination

Public sector wages are subject to different forces than private sector wages. If the salary paid to certain occupational groups in the civil service is substantially lower than it is in the private sector, it would be expected that the civil service would have difficulty hiring labor, but the government would not be subject to the same kinds of financial pressures to fill vacancies as private sector managers. Similarly, if civil service salaries were higher than they needed to be to hire suitably qualified candidates, the government would not suffer the same kind of financial consequences as a private sector enterprise functioning in a competitive environment. Public sector pay awards in many countries are also undoubtedly affected by the relatively high degree of unionization in the public sector. As a result, civil service pay may diverge from private sector pay for long periods of time unless pay-setting mechanisms are adopted to ensure comparability.

The differences in the manner in which public and private sector wages are set should not, however, be exaggerated. A position of market dominance can partially insulate some private sector enterprises from market forces, and give them a degree of monopsony power in hiring labor. At the same time, some occupational groups are clearly able to exploit a position of monopoly power in the sale of their services, thereby extracting a rent over and above the wages they would need to be paid for the same supply of services in a competitive market.

Pay Disequilibria in the Public Sector

Pay levels

There are obvious costs to society in setting public sector wages at unreasonably high levels, unless paying civil service employees at levels above their reservation wage is a means of achieving a desired redistribution of income. In addition to their budgetary costs, high wage settlements in the public sector can influence settlements throughout the economy. Although disentangling the causal link between wage settlements can be difficult—does one high nominal wage settlement lead to another, or are they both a reflection of high inflationary expectations?—the presence of **parallelism in wage settlements** implies that public sector pay policy can have a macroeconomic impact that reflects more than its direct expenditure consequences.

Are wages and salaries in the public sector too high, in the sense that they could be significantly less but still be high enough to attract and retain a suitably qualified work force? This is not a question that can be satisfactorily answered by reference to aggregate indicators of compensation or income in the public and private sectors, although these kinds of indicators allow some interesting international comparisons. In particular, public sector salaries in developing countries are typically much higher in relation to per capita income than are public sector salaries in the industrialized countries. Many different influences could contribute to these differences. Even these aggregate statistics, however, are plagued by problems of data comparability, and in any case a satisfactory answer to the question posed above would require a wealth of information for each distinct occupational group and each country under study.

Low pay

There is some evidence in a number of African countries, and rather anecdotal evidence in other developing countries, that average public wages and salaries may be too low. In Uganda, for example, in the period 1975-83, real salaries fell by between 1/5 to 1/3 every year, and by the early 1980s it was recognized that most civil servants could not survive on even a full-time salary, so that it was imperative for them to supplement their income by one means or another. As one often-quoted government report put it: "The civil servant had either to survive by lowering his standards of ethics, or remain upright and perish. He chose to survive." Real per capita salaries declined significantly during this period in other African countries as well, in particular in Ghana, Nigeria, and Zambia. The fall in total compensation, particularly among higher-ranking civil servants, was probably mitigated by the importance in total compensation of fringe benefits (see below).

The response to declining real salaries seems to have been a combination of increasing corruption, moonlighting, absenteeism, declining performance standards, and reductions in the supply of public services, often in critical areas such as education and health. Ironically, while the wage bill was accounting for an excessive share of public expenditure because of the swollen ranks of the civil service, per capita salaries in some of these countries were simply too low to compensate adequately a well-trained and well-motivated civil service. The appropriate policy response to this situation is to reduce employment and increase average levels of compensation. Inevitably, this policy would encounter strong resistance from those civil servants who would be dropped from the payrolls.

Pay differentials

In addition to reducing civil-service-wide real salaries, efforts at restraining the growth of the wage bill in the civil service in many developing countries have contributed to a substantial compression of the pay structure. Although part of the decline that has been observed in the relative pay rate of the more highly skilled and the professional occupational groupings in such countries as Jamaica, Peru, and some of the African countries noted above could be justified on the ground that investment in education has reduced the relative scarcity of the better educated, this phenomenon has also been associated with shortages in the highly skilled occupations. Because pay scales in public enterprises are generally not subject to the same pressures as civil service pay scales, senior executives are lost to both the private sector and to public enterprises. It is also alleged that pay compression leads to an increase in other forms of compensation, which, being less visible, may not be as politically sensitive or as controllable as wages and salaries.

While pay differentials cannot in general be fixed by the market, it would not be efficient to let them be determined by line managers, because the result would be different levels of compensation within the civil service for the same jobs and levels of experience and expertise. A policy is necessary for the civil service as a whole and, to the extent possible, public sector wages and salaries should be linked to their nearest equivalents in the private sector. This principle of **comparable worth** is applied in a number of industrialized countries and involves an elaborate compilation of data on private sector wage and salary settlements for jobs deemed to be equivalent to the various occupations and grades found in the public sector. However, such a comparison can pose a problem for professions, such as tax collectors, where it can be difficult to determine the private sector equivalent. Although it may be hard to gauge when salaries for such a profession are out of line, excessively low salaries will be reflected in growing numbers of vacancies and in recruitment difficulties, while high salaries can result in a superabundance of well-qualified candidates.

Fringe Benefits

Characteristics

Fringe benefits in the public sector come in all shapes and sizes. They include spouse and dependents' allowances, pensions, health and disability insurance, free or subsidized housing, free or subsidized lunches, transportation allowances, and leave with pay. To this list can be added travel allowances to the extent that they exceed normal travel costs. In addition to fringe benefits proper, in many countries the base salary is supplemented by bonuses of various kinds, supplements for dangerous or unpleasant work, and the like.

The great variety of fringe benefits and the terms on which they are offered means that hard data on their importance is typically lacking, but they are obviously important in the upper echelons of the civil service in many countries, and they can be important at lower levels as well. To refer again to the African experience, nonsalary compensation in Senegal, which mainly took the form of allowances (cash payments), represented about 45 percent of base salary in December 1984. Total fringe benefits in Nigeria have been estimated to represent from 35 percent to 100 percent of base salary.

Impact and policies

Fringe benefits may be classified according to four criteria: (i) eligibility (across-the-board or restricted in some way), (ii) form (in cash or in kind), (iii) timing (deferred or contemporaneous with employment), and (iv) relation with base pay (related or unrelated). Thus, a pension is a deferred cash benefit, to which eligibility restrictions may or may not apply and which may or may not be related to base pay. To take another example, free housing for senior civil servants is a restricted benefit in kind that is contemporaneous with employment but which may bear little relation to base pay.

Fringe benefits obviously have a role to play in a well-designed compensation policy, but certain kinds of fringe benefits are also highly inefficient means of compensation that can create perverse incentive effects. For example, the value of free housing provided to one civil servant may be substantially different from the value of the housing provided another, and in each case the amount of housing supplied may be unrelated to their needs. If housing is in short supply, then a substantial real income gap is created between those lucky enough to enjoy this benefit and their less fortunate colleagues, and this gap may be unrelated to differences in their rank within the civil service. Moreover, the provision of subsidized or free housing creates a substantial disincentive to regional and occupational mobility. Excessive travel allowances obviously also stimulate excessive travel, and so forth.

As a general rule of policy, benefits in kind or subsidies tied to the consumption of one particular good are undesirable on efficiency grounds, because they restrict the freedom to substitute consumption of one good or service for another. In the case of free provision of housing or transportation, moreover, what may be an important part of the compensation package is not included in the budgetary estimate of civil service compensation or under any other budgetary heading, so that the budgetary presentation suffers from a lack of transparency. An exception to this rule is justifiable for subsidized meals, because these can provide a strong incentive for a more productive work day as well as a boost to productivity in low-income countries by improving nutrition. But in the case of most benefits in kind, it is more efficient to replace them with a compensating adjustment in pay and allow civil servants to pay for the quantity of the goods or services they consume. Policy reforms along these lines were adopted in Indonesia, Liberia and other countries, where official automobiles previously given to civil servants were sold to them, and in Botswana, where civil servants were encouraged to buy or rent the government-owned housing.

Although fringe benefits do not necessarily have to be related to pay—i.e., they can be a flat rate, for example in the form of a flat rate dependency or transportation allowance—if a substantial share of the total compensation package is unrelated to base salary, then the motivational role of merit awards and promotions is reduced. A proliferation of flat rate benefits also makes the calculation and comparison of pay relativities within the civil service more difficult, as well as complicating indexation policy.

From the point of view of expenditure policy, the most important characteristics of fringe benefits are their relative importance in the overall compensation package, their relationship with base pay, and the degree to which they can be subjected to the same controls as base salary. Benefits in kind or benefits tied to the consumption of particular goods are in general undesirable and should, where possible, be replaced by cash substitutes.

Wage and Salary Restraint

A basic consideration of any program to restrain the real wages of the civil service relative to the private sector must be the impact of such a policy on morale and productivity within the civil service. Are there strong grounds for thinking that public sector salaries are too high, and that they could be reduced substantially without prompting an exodus to the private sector, increased absenteeism, or reduced productivity and permanent damage to civil service morale? If this is not the case, a policy of wage restraint may achieve the short-run goal of reducing public expenditure but lead to an undesirable reduction in the quality and quantity of public services. If public salaries are already low, further reductions can threaten the provision of basic public services.

As noted above, per capita real compensation had declined substantially in some African countries, and there was impressionistic evidence that these declines caused reductions in work effort if not in employment. Nonetheless, reductions in real wages by means of a wage freeze or a policy of less than full indexation to price changes will reduce real expenditure. Such policies may be less difficult politically than policies to reduce employment, even if the real problem with the public sector wage bill is not the level of real wages but the excessive size of the payroll. Nonetheless, such a policy can be vitiated if there is no control over the hiring process. The substitution of fringe benefits for wages and salaries can also undermine efforts to contain pay. Moreover, the indiscriminate application of across-the-board restraint will often result in serious sectoral manpower shortages.

Policies affecting advancement within and between ranges or grades also have important consequences for wage policy. In a number of countries, efforts to freeze wages were thwarted by increases in either the average rate of advancement within grades or in the frequency of promotions, indicating that there was a serious lack of control of the overall salary structure. Such **wage drift** may simply not be foreseen, and cannot be contained unless there is centralized control over the granting of merit or longevity increments and promotions, and a careful analysis of the cost of alternative policies. Although all the details of compensation policy cannot be dealt with adequately in a stabilization or structural adjustment program, it is important to estimate the share of average wage increases accounted for by wage drift and to have an idea of the scope that uncontrolled wage drift offers for offsetting the intended impact of wage restraint on the average salary of civil servants.

Country Illustrations

Public sector employment and pay in Argentina

The recent evolution of public sector employment and pay in Argentina illustrates the tendency for relatively rapid growth of employment in the public sector coupled with a decline in average real wages and salaries. However, data on public sector pay and employment in Argentina, although better than those of many countries, are nonetheless deficient: in particular, basic pay can exclude a substantial part of total compensation. As a consequence, any interpretation of the data has to be made with some caution.

Public sector employment in Argentina has accounted for about 18 percent of estimated total employment in recent years. Of some 1,960,000 public sector employees in 1988, regional- and local-government employees accounted for almost 50 percent, reflecting in part the important role the provinces play in the provision of social services. Employment at the National Administration (central government) level accounted for 34 percent, while employment in public enterprises accounted for 18 percent. The share of employment in the public sector in Argentina is high in comparison to other countries with a comparable per capita GDP and tax base.

The number of public sector employees in Argentina is estimated to have grown at an average annual rate of about 2.2 percent in the 1980–88 period, with the fastest-growing component being employment at the regional level. Employment in the private sector is estimated to have increased at about 1.2 percent annually over the same period. The relatively rapid growth of public employment at a time when the growth of GDP was essentially stagnant contributed to deteriorating public finances and led to pressure to restrain public sector pay. As a result of these pressures, the average real wage of public sector employees fell relative to that in the private sector. While private sector real manufacturing wages rose by 12 percent between 1982 and 1988, the real basic wage of middle-ranking civil servants fell by 17 percent. Moreover, this relative decline continued when private sector wages were themselves subsequently depressed by rising unemployment. In 1989 private sector wages fell to slightly below their 1982 average, but public sector real wages fell even more sharply. In addition to the decline in average real wages of civil servants, there is evidence that the compression of the public sector salary scale increased during the 1980s. The decline in real wages also led to an increase in the number of civil servants holding a second job, and public sector productivity has suffered as a result.

A policy to reduce public sector employment in the National Administration and the public enterprises has now been adopted. In addition to the decline in public sector employment that will result from the privatization of a number of public enterprises, and the elimination or curtailment in the activities of a number of public financial institutions, employment reductions are being sought through the implementation of early retirement, a stricter interpretation of the statutory retirement provisions, and layoffs in branches of government departments deemed to be overstaffed. Once employment levels have been reduced sufficiently, it will be possible to increase real public sector pay, and to widen relativities through discretionary increases for those higher occupational groups whose remuneration has fallen particularly sharply relative to comparable groups in the private sector.

Public sector employment and pay in Ghana

The 1970s and early 1980s were characterized by rapid growth in public employment in Ghana, and dramatic declines in productivity and real wages. By 1983, real monthly earnings per government employee were less than 11 percent of their 1975 level. The result was an overstaffed, poorly trained and unmotivated civil service. The ongoing civil service reform program, initiated in 1987, has three primary goals. First, the Government aims to reduce overstaffing, mostly at lower levels, while at the same time relieving shortages in high-skilled areas. Second, to bring this about, it has become necessary to improve the competitiveness of civil service pay, particularly at higher levels; this requires both a rise in overall public sector wages as well as increasing pay relativities between highest- and lowest-paid civil servants. Finally, the reform is attempting to increase productivity by providing incentives for performance, restructuring the job grading system, and enhancing training and management.

Government employment—including the civil service, the Ghana Education Service, and the prisons, fire and foreign services— totaled 305,000 in December 1986, of which 144,000 were in the civil service. By August 1990, total public employment had been reduced to 274,000, with 112,000 in the civil service. A "Special Efficiency" budget has been established to provide severance pay and retraining/relocating grants for retrenched public employees. A significant widening of pay relativities has also been achieved. The ratio of total compensation for highest- to lowest-paid civil servant was increased from 5.4:1 to 9.4:1 between 1987 and 1990. The goal, in the context of the World Bank Structural Adjustment Program, is a ratio of 13.4:1. The authorities plan to introduce performance-related pay in 1992. In addition, the possibility of privatizing some low-skilled civil service activities, such as cleaning and maintenance, is being considered.

Bibliography

Lindauer, David L., "Government Wage and Employment Policy: an Analytical Treatment with Special Reference to Africa," Discussion Paper No. 1987–3 (Washington: World Bank, March 1987).

Lindauer, David L., Meesook Oey Astra, and Parita Suebsaeng, "Government Wage Policy in Africa—Some Findings and Policy Issues," *World Bank Research Observer* (Washington: World Bank, January 1988).

Nunberg, Barbara, "Public Sector Pay and Employment Reform," Country Economic Department Working Paper Series 113 (Washington: World Bank, October 1988).

Schiller, Christian, "Government Pay Policies and Structural Adjustment," Working Paper 88/73 (Washington: International Monetary Fund, 1988).

VIII. Operations and Maintenance

Peter S. Heller

Why is provision for operations and maintenance often inadequate? Why have donors failed to make provision for the recurrent cost implications of aid-financed projects?
Can the flow of resources for operations and maintenance be increased? What are the constraints? How can these be overcome?
What factors have to be considered in formulating an operations and maintenance strategy?

Operations and maintenance (O&M) expenditures are recurrent outlays necessary to sustain a project or program at the intended level. **Operations** usually refer to the procedures and activities involved in the actual delivery of services to the public, while **maintenance** refers to the wide range of activities aimed at keeping the infrastructure in a serviceable condition. Operations expenditures are generally recurrent in nature while maintenance expenditures can be both recurrent (as in the case of routine and periodic maintenance) and capital (as in the case of rehabilitation). For some public services like roads, drainage and sewage systems, etc., the physical condition of the capital infrastructure effectively determines the quality of service. These services tend, therefore, to be relatively maintenance-intensive. The provision of other services, such as health and education, requires the use of labor and other intermediate inputs, and hence the role of the associated capital infrastructure is more variable in its significance. These services are naturally relatively operations-intensive. Others, such as irrigation facilities, require the intensive application of both operations and maintenance.

Over the last decade, problems have emerged in the provision of O&M, with governments tending to concentrate their efforts on new investments and failing to provide adequately for the recurrent costs of operating and maintaining previous projects. Sectors in which there have been the largest shortfalls in O&M expenditure are, typically, road networks, public and government buildings, agricultural equipment, and communications equipment. Failure to provide adequate O&M has economic consequences for the level of public output, for the capital endowment of the economy, and the implied rate of return associated with public investments. In the past, the O&M problem in developing countries had been viewed as a problem of planning and budgeting, that is, a failure to ensure that the O&M implications of a new investment are considered when a project or program is evaluated. In recent years, the problem has also become one of providing for adequate expenditure on the O&M of existing programs and infrastructure, and to redress the effects of past failures to provide O&M.

Causes of the Problem

A number of factors contribute to inadequate provision for O&M expenditure. A shortage of funds for existing O&M and for newly completed projects may arise from overall budgetary pressures owing to limited resources, and/or excessive levels of expenditure on other programs. Also, O&M expenditures often have a low priority in government budgets as they are politically less appealing and visible than new investment projects. In addition, since poor maintenance and inadequate operations have delayed consequences or less obvious effects, expenditure on these items tends to get postponed. Moreover, external donors have facilitated the efforts of countries to mount ambitious investment projects while providing little support for recurrent costs, thus creating the basis for subsequent O&M problems. Inadequate understanding of the costly downstream consequences of neglecting maintenance, lack of local expertise, and unclearly delegated responsibilities and accountability also contribute to the problem of inadequate O&M expenditure and inefficient use of O&M funds.

Overall budgetary constraints

Inadequate expenditure on O&M may arise both from insufficient overall revenues and from inadequate revenue generation by the project itself. Budgetary inflexibilities with respect to the reallocation of funds to offset deficiencies in specific sectors would compound this problem. An O&M problem may also arise from excessive expenditures on non-O&M items such as the military, interest payments, and subsidy and transfer payments, which are often subject to significant political and social pressures and may therefore be difficult to control. Another factor that may give rise to inadequate expenditures, particularly on maintenance, is lack of foreign exchange. Balance of payments difficulties may impose limits on the availability of imported inputs for projects, thereby skewing the mix of O&M inputs towards labor and nontradable goods. A dramatic and permanent change in the economic environment that a country faces may require a re-ordering of budgetary priorities which may or may not be feasible. Finally, ongoing pressures to invest may also adversely affect outlays on O&M. In many cases, however, the importance given to curtailing current expenditure in favor of investment expenditure reflects a failure to recognize that the rate of return to some types of O&M expenditures may be considerably higher than that on new investment.

Misallocation of resources

Problems of inadequate O&M expenditure in certain sectors can arise from deficiencies in the process by which projects are evaluated, expenditure programs are budgeted, and overall budget decisions are made. These deficiencies arise from insufficient consideration of the future stream of O&M requirements, the traditional dichotomy between the capital and the current budget, undue political intervention, and the lack of a well-articulated overall development strategy.

The role of donors

For many years, donors did not apply pressures on governments to ensure the adequacy of recurrent funding for aid-financed projects. In recent years, however, donors have been more willing to examine this issue and to provide O&M financing, particularly when formulated as a project to rehabilitate deteriorated infrastructure. Another problem that arises from external funding of investment projects is that aid agreements often require that equipment be obtained from the donor country—so-called tied aid. Such procurement conditions have disadvantaged O&M in three ways: spare part availability is limited; the lack of standardization in the capital stock raises the unit cost of purchasing spare parts; and the lack of standardization also requires a higher level of technical manpower. In addition, the deterioration of imported equipment, due to inadequate O&M, may give rise to the need to import new equipment in the future, thus further straining an already fragile foreign exchange budget.

Institutional deficiencies

The technical and management capacity to implement O&M is often lacking, leading to O&M outlays that do not result in any effective change in output. In addition, the lack of data on the extent and the condition of existing assets may preclude the formulation of a sectoral O&M strategy. Weaknesses in the monitoring, supervision, and auditing functions are such that failures in O&M implementation never surface and are not acted upon. Examples of such weaknesses are noncompliance with procurement procedures, poor inventory control, and misappropriation of funds. Routine maintenance suffers the most from this deficiency, since it requires the greatest degree of monitoring and supervision because of its highly labor-intensive character.

Consequences of Inadequate O&M Outlays

While the initial impact of inadequate O&M is felt at the microeconomic level in the form of deteriorated infrastructure, it has serious macroeconomic consequences as well. The payoff to increased O&M expenditure is likely to include favorable effects on growth, employment, and the balance of payments. Increasingly, it is being realized that higher growth depends as much on efforts to reduce the inefficient utilization of the existing capital stock as on the creation of new capacity. This is because poorly maintained and unreliable infrastructure and service delivery systems hamper both public and private sector activity. Also, as the maintenance of infrastructure tends to be relatively labor-intensive, increasing O&M expenditures can have positive consequences for the level of employment in the economy. Failure to operate and maintain public assets adequately also has direct and sizable consequences for the balance of payments. This is particularly important in developing countries with foreign debt problems and scarcity of foreign exchange. In many cases, proper maintenance and more efficient operations could provide additional output from existing facilities and therefore limit or eliminate the need for new facilities which typically have a high foreign exchange component. It also may facilitate the marketing of export products. Thus, efforts to improve operations and maintenance of the existing infrastructure can be seen as both an import substitution and an export promoting activity.

In addition to its macroeconomic consequences, adequate O&M expenditure has a beneficial impact on social welfare. In many developing countries, the delivery of essential social services—such as education, health, water and sanitation—is adversely affected by inadequate O&M. Therefore, devoting additional resources to improving service delivery will not only have desirable distributional consequences in general, but will also help protect the poor during periods of adjustment.

Issues in the Formulation of an O&M Strategy

While the underlying basis for the choice of an O&M strategy is technical, it will ultimately reflect economic considerations. In principle, given a thorough understanding of the underlying production relationships, the guiding economic framework is the cost-benefit analysis of the various policy options. The present cost of providing operations and maintenance must be compared with the benefits derived at present and in the future (both in terms of deferring the time when expensive rehabilitation is necessary and of realizing economic and social objectives). A number of issues arise in making such cost-benefit calculations.

Operations outlays

Outlays on operations reflect the purchase of goods and services (labor, materials, and supplies) to facilitate the contemporaneous production of public output. The physical relationship between the inputs and current output with a given capital stock effectively defines a significant part of the payoff to increasing or decreasing the funding for operations. However, since decision-makers often have very limited information, they are not always able to apply cost-benefit analysis on the basis of underlying technical relationships. As a result, they may establish operational norms for certain services that have been known to yield acceptable results. While such norms are usually a reasonable compromise, they may make it very difficult, particularly in periods of fiscal retrenchment, to assess the benefits of shifting resources for operations within and between sectors. All that they allow is a reasonable sense of the likely outcome for a specific level of spending.

Maintenance outlays

Proper maintenance brings immediate and future benefits by enhancing current productivity and retarding the depreciation of assets. **Routine maintenance** is meant to protect the usefulness of infrastructure and assets; **periodic maintenance** addresses actual breakdowns and **rehabilitation** corrects major problems and wear-and-tear so as to restore a facility to good working condition. These different forms of maintenance are complementary and each by itself has limited benefits. Current failure to maintain infrastructure will render future maintenance less productive and of lower value. The two halves of operations and maintenance are obviously interdependent: the greater the use of the infrastructure, the more rapid its deterioration and the greater the need for maintenance. While operations can be relatively independent for a short period of time—that is, the lack of maintenance may not reduce productivity immediately—a balanced approach will be more cost effective over the medium term.

New investment versus rehabilitation

While both have the same nominal effect of increasing the public sector's aggregate capital stock, new investment adds to the stock of infrastructure that would need maintenance, while rehabilitation strengthens the quality of existing facilities, without necessarily increasing the overall need for maintenance. As with other aspects of the O&M question, the choice between the two will depend on the net present value of new assets compared with the costs associated with the failure to prevent the deterioration of existing capital assets.

Financing O&M expenditures

The main sources of funding for O&M expenditure are: direct cost recovery through user charges; earmarked levies on specific beneficiaries; allocations from general revenues; counterpart funds from external assistance; and foreign borrowing.

Measuring the size of the O&M problem

Five measures of O&M need can be distinguished. These measures are not necessarily alternatives and may need to be used jointly. It is, however, difficult to have one single measure of the need of a given stock of public infrastructure and services for O&M. Which measure is used depends on the particular objectives of the government.

(i) The amount of additional O&M outlays that could be spent productively, given the physical condition of the existing capital stock. This measure presumes that infrastructure which is in need of rehabilitation is not brought up to the requisite standards and that maintenance on such deteriorated infrastructure would be done only to the extent that some minimal functioning of the infrastructure is required. In operational terms, this measure would depend on the demand for public goods and services and the desire of the government to respond to this demand.

(ii) The amount of maintenance or rehabilitation expenditure required to rehabilitate infrastructure that has prematurely deteriorated.

(iii) The additional amount of operations and maintenance expenditure that would be required if the rehabilitation described in (ii) was undertaken (for example, including the maintenance of the rehabilitated network of infrastructure).

(iv) The additional O&M outlays required if significant improvements were made in the efficiency of O&M spending. While O&M spending is clearly needed, the marginal outlays required would be substantially reduced if existing amounts were spent more efficiently.

(v) The increase in O&M outlays required to meet the O&M implications of the present investment program. This abstracts from the underfinancing of O&M on existing infrastructure and programs. A useful concept in this context is the *r* coefficient, or the ratio of net recurrent expenditure requirements to the total investment cost of a project. Given these coefficients for each project, an examination of the long-term fiscal consistency of a country's public sector investment program can be made using data available to the Fund and the World Bank. Simulations of the fiscal impact of shifts in the level and sectoral composition of the program could then be made. Table 1 reports some typical *r* coefficients.

Table 1. Selected *r* Coefficients for Developing Countries

Sector	*r* Coefficient
Fisheries	0.08
Agriculture	0.10
Rural development	0.08-0.43
Primary schools	0.06-0.70
Secondary schools	0.08-0.72
Rural health centers	0.27-0.71
Urban health centers	0.17
District hospitals	0.11-0.30
Buildings	0.01
Feeder roads	0.06-0.14
Paved roads	0.03-0.07

Source: Heller (1979).

These coefficients are drawn from a very restricted sample of developing countries and are meant to illustrate the observed variability across sectors and projects. On the basis of these coefficients, one may, for example, estimate that a building that cost $1 million to construct would entail $10,000 in O&M expenditures each year to operate the facilities and maintain the building.

One caveat in interpreting these quantitative dimensions of the O&M problem is that one is often forced to rely on data on the average cost of maintenance of particular types of infrastructure or operations of particular program or projects. However, the marginal cost of maintenance per unit of infrastructure does not remain constant. Given that there may be diminishing returns to O&M expenditures with a given amount of technical and managerial ability, the marginal cost of O&M will increase. Also, it is important to point out that increased spending on O&M by itself does not guarantee significantly improved operations and maintenance of public infrastructure, without concomitant improvement in the efficiency of O&M.

A Strategy for Action on O&M Expenditure

First, governments should develop a national policy on O&M expenditure, stressing the importance of maintaining the quality of public infrastructure and of realizing the maximum productivity in its use. This necessitates reforms of the planning and budgeting process. In this context, a number of initiatives should be considered. There should be a single locus of responsibility to assess the adequacy of resources devoted to O&M, to evaluate the use of these resources, and to advise decision makers on policies to increase the flow of resources to O&M. Efforts should be made to ensure that the government accounting system facilitates the identification of the magnitude and composition of sectoral outlays for O&M. Project evaluation procedures should include projections of O&M requirements. Some effort should be made to assess the medium-term O&M implications of the investment program. Lastly, sectoral data bases describing the nature of assets, and their age, condition, and maintenance history, should be developed.

At the sectoral level, O&M objectives need to be defined, with detailed estimates of O&M costs and staffing requirements, together with indicators of operating effectiveness. Over the medium term, the institutional infrastructure will need to be strengthened, ensuring that biases against O&M are eliminated. Also, the monitoring and supervision of O&M will need to be strengthened. Finally, external financing agencies should place increased emphasis on estimating the recurrent cost implications of projects. Donors should also play a more active role in post-project performance audits, with particular reference to O&M issues.

Country Illustration

O&M needs in Indonesia

Overall, O&M needs can be divided into three categories: (i) immediate needs; (ii) rehabilitation; and (iii) O&M needs for rehabilitated infrastructure. Reflecting the judgement of sectoral specialists, Table 2 provides a quantitative indication of these various needs in five sectors in 1986/87.

Immediate needs

With the exception of building maintenance, these estimates embody the assumption that such outlays could in fact be spent without a significant increase in the average cost of O&M. The estimates in respect of building maintenance come from official sources. The estimate for roads relates to what would be necessary to maintain the current condition of roads. The estimated deficiency in operational outlays in the curative health sector relates to existing norms for salary and nonsalary outlays for particular institutions. Estimates for preventive health primarily relate to the deficiency from the levels spent in the preceding year. For higher education, estimates reflect the amount of funds that would have been necessary to restore real outlays per student to the levels of 1980/81. These estimates suggest that an additional Rp 1.2 trillion could have been productively spent on O&M in 1986/87, or approximately 1.5 percent of GDP and about 5 percent of government expenditure.

Table 2. Indonesia: O&M Needs, 1986/87
(In billions of rupiah)

Immediate needs	1,187
Roads	432
Irrigation	6
Nondefense buildings	410
Health	301
Higher education	38
Rehabilitation	5,782
Roads	3,400
Irrigation	2,382
O&M needs for rehabilitated infrastructure	976
Roads	880
Irrigation	96

Source: World Bank.

Rehabilitation

Much of the existing infrastructure in irrigation and roads would require special maintenance, upgrading or rehabilitation to raise it to a level adequate for productive O&M. Approximately Rp 5.8 trillion would have been required to achieve such rehabilitation, an amount equal to approximately 7 percent of GDP in 1986/87.

O&M needs for rehabilitated infrastructure

If the road and irrigation networks were to be rehabilitated, a further Rp 1.0 trillion of O&M outlays would have been required, over and above the Rp 1.2 trillion indicated above. The total additional requirement is equivalent to 2.6 percent of GDP; this compares with actual O&M outlays in 1986/87 of Rp 900 billion, or 1.1 percent of GDP.

Bibliography

Heller, Peter S., "The Underfinancing of Recurrent Development Costs," *Finance and Development*, 16 (Washington: International Monetary Fund, 1979).

Heller, Peter S., "The Operations and Maintenance Problem: Sources, Issues, and Strategies," unpublished (Washington: International Monetary Fund, 1988).

Loritzen, Jens, "Overview of Issues and Strategic Options in Operations and Maintenance of Urban Infrastructure in Developing Countries," unpublished (Washington: World Bank, 1987).

IX. Price Subsidies

G.A. Mackenzie

Under what circumstances are subsidies justified? How is their impact on resource allocation, distribution, the budget, and the balance of payments assessed?

What alternative forms can food subsidies take? Which form is most effective in helping the poor while containing budgetary cost?

Is there a case for a general subsidy on energy products in developing countries, or should it be restricted to products such as kerosene, which are used more by the poor?

What are the arguments for fertilizer subsidies? Why is there resistance to reducing such subsidies?

A commodity subsidy is created when, as a result of public policy, the price paid by the consumer of a good is lowered below or the price received by a producer is increased above what it would otherwise be in the absence of the policy. Subsidies may be either explicit, taking the form of payments by the government to producers or consumers showing up in the budget, or they may be implicit, and entail no apparent budgetary cost. In centrally planned and many developing economies, in addition to budgetary subsidies, subsidies take the form of sizable positive gaps between the world market price and the domestic price of a product. In developing countries, the most common type of explicit budgetary subsidy is arguably that paid by the government on basic foods such as rice and wheat or flour, or energy products such as kerosene. Often, the subsidy will be paid to a marketing agency owned or controlled by the government that is required to sell its commodities at a price less than that at which the goods were procured. In industrial countries, producer subsidies for various agricultural commodities are common.

Subsidies can take many forms. Most of the goods and services directly provided by the government are subsidized either by providing them free of charge, as with primary and secondary education, or at prices that are substantially below costs. Tax expenditures are another form of subsidy common in industrial countries. In particular, owner-occupied housing is often indirectly subsidized through the income tax system by deducting mortgage interest payments and excluding capital gains on the sale of a taxpayer's principal residence from taxable income.

Arguments for Subsidies

Broadly speaking, there are two basic rationales for commodity subsidies: first, they are a means of **redistributing income**, and secondly, they can be used to offset **market failures** of one kind or another. As regards their redistributive aspect, commodity subsidies are second-best instruments of redistribution in countries where the tax and transfer system is not a practical means of redistribution. Subsidies can be viewed as negative taxes, and rates (some of which may be negative) should be set to equalize the marginal social cost of revenue across commodities. If society values extra income for the poor more highly than for the affluent, then commodities that account for a relatively large share of the budget of the poor, or commodities on which the poor spend more than the rich, are appropriate candidates for a low rate of tax or subsidization. The ideal good for a redistributive subsidy should satisfy both these conditions, but finding such a commodity may be difficult.

Market failure describes situations where the level of production or consumption of a good or service would be inappropriate without the government's intervention. For example, it has been argued that subsidies on fertilizers that reduce their price below the free market level are justified because farmers in many countries lack the information necessary to make a fully informed appraisal of the potential impact of fertilizer on crop yields. The absence of well-functioning rural credit markets is cited to justify the provision of subsidized agricultural credit. Public transportation is implicitly subsidized when user charges are set at levels below the cost of provision, and this practice is justified by the argument that it reduces the costs of road congestion entailed by excessive use of private transportation. As a final example, a subsidy on basic foods has been justified on the grounds that it enhances the productivity of the work force through its beneficial impact on nutrition.

The Impact of Subsidies

Allocative effects

An understanding of the allocative impact of a subsidy scheme is critical to any appraisal of its impact on the economy. The analysis of the allocative impact of a subsidy becomes a complicated matter, however, when the subsidy is large enough that its effects spill over into other markets. Consider the case of a subsidy on a consumer good, where a marketing agency processes that good and sells it for less than the cost of production and distribution. The subsidy lowers the price of the good, which will normally increase the quantity demanded. If the domestic producer price is controlled and not allowed to increase, the additional quantity demanded must be supplied by imports, because there will be no incentive to increase domestic production. Reliance on imports will be even greater if the government tries to finance the subsidy to consumers by lowering the producer price.

This strategy has been adopted for agricultural commodities by governments who have assumed that the domestic supply response to producer price changes is negligible. While the short-run price elasticity of supply of some goods may not be large, often it is likely to increase over time as resources are reallocated from the production of other goods, so that governments resorting to this strategy find their reliance on imports growing or exports declining.

The allocative effect also depends on the impact of the subsidy on demand for the subsidized commodity and other commodities. A **general subsidy**—one where there is no limit to the quantity of purchases that is subsidized—will have both an income and a substitution effect. By lowering the relative price of the subsidized good, it encourages the substitution of that good for other goods. The income effect will also boost the consumption of the subsidized good and other goods, unless the good is inferior.

By contrast, when a subsidy applies to only a limited quantity of purchases—as in the case of a **rationed commodity**—no substitution effect exists when a household is already consuming more of the good than the amount to which it is entitled under the rationing scheme. These inframarginal subsidies are equivalent to an income transfer equal to the amount of the subsidy per unit times the quantity of rationed purchases. In these cases, the subsidy will not lead to a substantial increase in demand for the good unless the subsidy represents a substantial share of the average consumer's income and the subsidized good has a high income elasticity of demand.

The allocative effects of a subsidy will also depend on the way it is financed. When a government has many different tax instruments at its disposal, the introduction of a subsidy can in principle lead to changes in tax rates. The allocative effect of all these changes would have to be taken into account, and it would be hazardous to consider in isolation the impact of the subsidy. If, however, the subsidy is financed by an increase in the rate of a broad-based tax such as a general sales tax, the allocative effects on markets other than the market for subsidized good are likely to be diffused, and can probably be ignored.

Redistributive effects

There is an obvious difficulty with the use of consumer subsidies as an instrument of income redistribution, in that it is not easy to limit them to goods that are consumed primarily or exclusively by the poor. This does not mean that generalized subsidies cannot be an effective means of redistributing income, but it does imply that to have an effect on the poor a subsidy program must be relatively large, implying significant transfers to the nonpoor. Marketed goods with a negative income elasticity (i.e., inferior goods) are ideal candidates for a redistributive subsidy. One such good found in a number of West African countries is cassava. In other countries, however, it may not be possible to identify an inferior good that makes up a significant part of the budgets of poor households. Alternative means of targeting subsidies at the poor are explored in the note on *Poverty and Social Security.*

Fiscal and trade effects

There is no reason in principle why a subsidy program should entail a budgetary problem, but generalized subsidies for staple products have sometimes caused difficulties. One reason for this is that subsidies are created by the operations of state marketing agencies that sell the subsidized commodities at prices that are not adjusted regularly for increases in the cost of production. In this case, when there is no mechanism in place to put a cap on the subsidy per unit of product, the subsidy is said to be **open-ended**. Such subsidies have explosive potential, and there are many instances where they have risen sharply and then become entrenched. Failure to adjust the regulated price can also reduce domestic supply, and lead to an increase in imports. These imports will often be more expensive than local production, and thus lead to an increase in the subsidy. Under these conditions, food subsidy programs will be vulnerable to a bad harvest if domestic stocks are low. The failure to adjust prices increases the temptation to move the subsidy off budget or to finance it through an implicit tax on producers in the form of producer price controls. The cost of imported food can be disguised by adopting a special exchange rate for food imports. The subsidy then shows up as a loss of the central bank (see the note on *Fiscal Activities of Public Institutions*).

A subsidy that takes the form of a fixed payment per unit of the subsidized good is not affected by rising costs. However, this type of subsidy is not common. If producers are instead subsidized through direct payments, the effect on the market price is uncertain and depends on the elasticities of supply and demand for the subsidized commodity. If supply is relatively inelastic, most of the subsidy is a transfer to the producer. Direct payments to consumers lower the price effectively paid for the product, but these are both difficult and potentially costly to administer, because the consumer's purchase of the subsidized commodity must be validated. These real or apparent drawbacks with direct payments may explain why state marketing boards are heavily involved in the administration of commodity subsidies. Governments often want to exercise direct control over the prices of certain staples, and this control generally is not achievable through direct payments.

Food Subsidies

Food subsidies of one kind or another are common in developing countries, and in a number of cases have accounted for a substantial share of government expenditure. Perhaps the best known case is that of Egypt, where food subsidies represented between 7 to 15 percent of total public expenditure between 1973 and 1981. The subsidy for the rice ration scheme in Sri Lanka, which up to 1977 was available to the whole population, accounted for 11 percent of total expenditure in that year. Other examples include the general subsidy for wheat in Morocco—a producer subsidy which was in effect during much of the 1980s—and the subsidy for maize in Zambia.

Subsidy mechanisms

Food subsidies may be either general or restricted in some way. In addition to the often substantial direct cost of the subsidy, a general subsidy may entail additional expenditures by the public sector for storage and distribution. These expenditures arise because the government, to ensure that the price is less than the unregulated market price, will have to intervene in the procurement and distribution network. Its intervention is usually carried out through a state-owned marketing agency, which is responsible for procuring the subsidized crop or food from local producers and reselling it to wholesalers or retailers. Where support prices for agricultural products are maintained above world prices, a **producer subsidy** results, which may be compounded by a budgetary subsidy to ensure prices lower than world prices for consumers.

Public ownership is not essential, however, if it is possible to subsidize the private distribution network. Payment of the subsidy near the stage of first sale is usually the most feasible way of implementing it, because this stage of the distributive chain is likely to comprise relatively few establishments. It will, however, be necessary to ensure that the subsidy is ultimately passed on to the final consumer. The increase in the quantity of food demanded requires that local producers be paid a price higher than would prevail in an unregulated market, unless the increase in the quantity demanded is to be met through an increase in the volume of imports. If the increase in demand is to be met at least in part by an increase in domestic production, a general subsidy, if explicit, would normally entail a subsidy to both producers and consumers, and the price received by the producer could exceed the price paid by the consumers. The resulting two-tier market would create substantial opportunities for fraud, which may explain why countries come to rely on increased imports to satisfy the increase in demand entailed by the subsidized final price.

Food subsidies and malnutrition

Over and above their impact on income distribution, food subsidies can be used to increase the intake of nutrients among the malnourished, and to lessen the incidence of malnutrition, and thereby enhance labor productivity. Viewed from this perspective, generalized subsidies have been supported as a sound food policy tool on the ground that they increase the probability that the malnourished receive adequate food. In part, this maximization of coverage may result from the absence of stigma attached to purchases of foods that are subject to a generalized subsidy. In addition, with generalized subsidies both income and substitution effects act to increase the quantity of food demanded. Because both income and price elasticities of demand for staple food tend to be high among the poor, their food consumption will increase. However, there may be substitution of subsidized for nonsubsidized food, so that the increase in consumption of the subsidized food will overstate the increase in caloric intake.

The clear disadvantage of a generalized subsidy is its lack of precision—many or most of those who benefit from it are not malnourished, and its broad coverage constrains the average subsidy per unit of food. Nonetheless, a general subsidy can increase the overall progressivity of a country's tax and transfer system, depending on the changes in tax and other subsidy rates associated with its implementation. When viewed in isolation from the impact of such changes, several subsidy programs in developing countries have been found to entail an increase in the real income of the poor by 15–25 percent.

From the perspective of nutrition policy, a general subsidy may not be the most cost-effective policy because a low intake of food may not be the principal cause of malnutrition. The Egyptian food subsidy contributes to a relatively high level of consumption of food among the poor, but the incidence of malnutrition is significant because of diseases caused by inadequate sanitation. There is little direct evidence as to whether subsidies improve nutritional status significantly, although there is some evidence that they lead to an increase in children's weight. An additional drawback to such subsidies is that, despite their name, general subsidies can have an urban bias because distribution outlets will tend to be located in larger towns and cities. If the subsidy covers only transport and distribution costs, however, the final price to the consumer will differ little from the rural price. Providing grains at below-market prices in the producing areas is undesirable because it distorts incentives and creates opportunities for profiteering.

Subsidies on Energy Products

Subsidies on energy products are often found in developing countries, especially in oil exporting countries. These subsidies are often implicit—for example, they may take the form of below-world-market prices for the products of the national petroleum company, in which case they need not figure in budgetary subsidies, and their effect is to lower profits of the petroleum company below what they otherwise would be.

Cross-subsidization is also a common phenomenon, and in many countries the petroleum companies will administer a fund that compensates producers of subsidized products from special levies on other products. Often kerosene and heating oil are subsidized by levies on regular or high-octane gasoline. Rarely are all subsidies in the energy sector included in the budget. Subsidization of energy products is by no means the universal rule, however; in countries that are net importers of energy products, these products may bear very high rates of tax. Subsidies on energy products can result from efforts to insulate domestic prices from temporary fluctuations in world market prices. Such price stabilization programs will result at a minimum in periodic subsidies, which can become permanent if domestic price adjustments tend to lag increases in world market prices.

Arguments for energy subsidies

Subsidies for energy products are usually justified on either distributive grounds or because they promote industrial development. The sharp increases in petroleum prices in 1973–74 and again in 1979–80 led to an increased degree of subsidization in many countries for these reasons and from a more general concern that adjustment to a drastic change in the price of a major commodity should be gradual. In many oil exporting countries, the existence of subsidies is probably explained by the political impossibility of not subsidizing a product that the country appears to have in great abundance. The notion that an exhaustible resource may be really more expensive than the costs of extraction and distribution alone is one that carries little weight with the public at large.

As noted earlier, the use of subsidies as a redistributive tool is more easily justified in developing than industrial countries. The argument for general subsidization of energy products on distributive grounds in developing countries, however, is not as strong as it might appear. The poor are not necessarily heavy direct or indirect consumers of such products as high-octane gasoline. The subsidization of public transport may be a more efficient way of increasing the real incomes of the poor than a subsidy on high-octane gasoline, because only the very affluent tend to own automobiles. Certain products, such as kerosene, may be more suitable for a redistributive subsidy if used for heating and cooking in relatively poor households.

The argument for subsidization of energy products to promote industrial development is really quite weak. Even if industrial promotion is considered desirable, the subsidization of energy products is a highly indirect and inefficient means to this end: it subsidizes energy-intensive industries more than other industries and promotes the use of energy-intensive production techniques. This is inappropriate in countries which are net importers of energy products. There are additional and more urgent reasons for avoiding the subsidization of energy products. Their use generally entails costs to society in the form of environmental degradation and congestion of public transport facilities, and extra taxes on these products may be the most efficient way of internalizing these costs (see also the notes on *Public Expenditure and the Environment* and *Pricing and Cost Recovery*).

Fertilizer Subsidies

Fertilizer subsidies are also found in many developing countries. They are relatively easy to administer when fertilizer is either imported or produced by a small number of domestic enterprises. In many countries, fertilizer subsidies have been used to encourage use of high-yield varieties of rice and wheat.

There are several possible rationales for such a subsidy. First, purchases of fertilizer are typically concentrated in a relatively short period of the crop cycle, and capital market imperfections may mean that farmers are unable to finance the necessary outlay. As an instrument to compensate for capital market imperfections, this subsidy is clearly second-best. Second, subsidies may be justified if farmers are unaware of the technical properties of fertilizer or more recent varieties of fertilizer: the demonstration effect means that the costs of promoting fertilizer use exceed its value to the farmers who first benefit, but fertilizer use by other farmers is encouraged. The argument based on imperfect knowledge and the demonstration effect implies that over time the subsidy on given varieties of fertilizer should be reduced and eventually eliminated. Any assessment of the benefits of a subsidy should bear in mind the risks of overfertilization, when fertilizer is applied to the point where its cost at the margin exceeds the value of the additional output it produces.

Fertilizer subsidies have also been used to offset the impact of price controls on farm output on the supply of agricultural products and the incomes of farmers—China is a prominent example—and as a redistributive device. As a means of reducing the disincentive effects of price controls on agricultural supply, the subsidy is inefficient, because it affects only one element of costs and encourages overfertilization. They are also ineffective as a redistributive tool, because they tend to subsidize farmers with larger holdings of land, but have little impact on the subsistence farmer. Hence, there is considerable resistance to their removal from better-off beneficiaries. Moreover, it may not be possible to eliminate or even significantly reduce a subsidy on fertilizer as long as agricultural product prices are controlled.

Country Illustration

The Indian fertilizer subsidy

Subsidies are an important item in the budget of the central government of India; in recent years their share of total expenditure and net lending has approached 10 percent. The largest single commodity subsidy is that for fertilizer. In 1988/89, it accounted for 4 percent of total expenditure and net lending and represented 0.8 percent of GDP. The justification for the fertilizer subsidy is that insufficient use is made of "non-traditional" factors of production, and the subsidy encourages the use of a productive input whose marginal cost remains below its marginal return.

Expenditure on the fertilizer subsidy has grown rapidly during the 1980s, mainly because of a failure to adjust the farmgate price of fertilizer to reflect increases in the cost of production. Until 1974, the Government set a single country-wide factory price and then established the farmgate price by adding margins to cover the costs of freight and distribution. As a result, changes in the cost of manufacturing were reflected in changes in the farmgate price. The enormous increase in the price of feedstock in 1973/74 led to a change in this policy, and the link between factory and farmgate prices was broken. One farmgate price is still set for the entire country—it differs somewhat from the price actually paid by farmers, which includes an additional margin to reflect local costs—but this is no higher in nominal terms than it was in 1981, and has therefore fallen substantially relative to costs.

In 1977, a substantial change was also made to the way in which factory prices are determined. This price—called the retention price—is now set for each factory individually, on the basis of an estimate of average unit costs at a specified capacity utilization rate, which currently ranges from 80 to 90 percent. This estimate is premised on the assumption that the given capacity utilization rate for each factory is achieved at minimum cost in terms of the employment of labor and use of feedstock and other productive inputs. The retention price is set so that the return on net worth is 12 percent.

Two separate issues raised by the Indian fertilizer subsidy need to be considered: (i) Is the amount of the subsidy justifiable as a correction for market failure or some other distortion?; and (ii) Is the subsidy mechanism efficient? With regard to the first issue, it is noteworthy that the increase in the per unit subsidy for fertilizer that has taken place since 1980 has been associated with an increase in fertilizer consumption of over 50 percent. It may be that the subsidy results in additional use of fertilizer on land where its marginal productivity is still high enough to cover its real cost, but with the passage of time this becomes increasingly less likely. This would suggest that the subsidy should be declining over time. As regards the second issue, there can be little dispute that the mechanism of the subsidy is inefficient. If each fertilizer plant expands its production to the point at which its marginal cost equals its (unique) reference price, then marginal costs will differ from one factory to the next, and a basic condition of efficiency in production is violated. This would not be the case if one reference price were set for all producers. The reference price mechanism also destroys the incentive for new entrants to the market to adopt the best-practice technology.

Bibliography

Gittinger, J. Price, Joanne Leslie, and Caroline Hoisington, *Food Policy-Integrating Supply, Distribution, and Consumption* (Baltimore: Johns Hopkins University, 1987).

Pinstrup-Andersen, Per, ed., *Food Subsidies in Developing Countries—Costs, Benefits, and Policy Options,* (Baltimore: Johns Hopkins University, 1988).

Schneider, Robert R., "Food Subsidies—a Multiple Price Model," *IMF Staff Papers,* 32 (Washington: International Monetary Fund, 1985).

X. Interest Payments

Richard Hemming and Kenneth Miranda

What is the impact of inflation on interest payments and the fiscal deficit?

Which concept of the fiscal deficit best reflects shifts in fiscal stance in an inflationary environment?

How is the growth of public debt determined? Under what conditions does an economy fall into a debt trap?

What determines a sustainable level of public debt? What does this imply for the fiscal deficit?

Expenditure on interest payments has been the focus of much recent attention. Since interest payments are usually linked to market interest rates, the level of such expenditures can be dramatically affected by the rate of inflation. Through its impact on the level of nominal interest expenditures, inflation complicates the interpretation of the fiscal deficit and of the sustainability of the government's fiscal stance. The purpose of this note is to trace through the link between interest payments, inflation, fiscal deficits, and public debt, and to discuss some issues related to assessing the sustainable level of public debt.

Interest Payments, Inflation, and the Fiscal Deficit: An Example

Consider a country whose outstanding stock of public debt is $100 million, held by the private sector in the form of short-term floating-interest domestic bonds. The government pays 7.1 percent interest on this debt, reflecting an expected rate of inflation of 4 percent and a 3 percent real return to bondholders. For simplicity it is assumed that real GDP is constant, the budget is initially in balance—with both revenue and expenditure also equal to $100 million—and revenue and noninterest expenditure grow in line with inflation, thus maintaining their ratio to nominal GDP. If the expected rate of inflation were to rise to 7 percent, the government would then have to pay bondholders 10.2 percent, equivalent to $10.2 million, resulting in a deficit, in the conventional sense, of $2.9 million. This reflects an increase in interest expenditure of 10.2 - 7.1 = 3.1 less 0.2 which represents the excess of increased revenue over increased noninterest expenditure owing to higher inflation. The increase in interest expenditure, however, merely compensates bondholders for a drop in the real value of the bonds they hold. In other words, part of the return to the bondholder—the inflationary component of the yield—is a **return of** capital (as opposed to a **return on** capital). This return of capital represents an implicit amortization of the outstanding stock of debt, although in an accounting sense it is a payment of interest.

From the government's point of view, any return of capital during the year is exactly counterbalanced by a reduction in the real value of the stock of public debt at the end of the year. Thus, although the conventional deficit has increased as a result of higher interest payments, the real stock of public debt by the end of the year is the same as when inflation was assumed to be 4 percent and the budget was in balance. Table 1 illustrates a number of scenarios that are identical in real terms (the preceding paragraph describes the transition between scenarios B and C), but which, because of alternative inflation assumptions and levels of nominal interest payments, yield markedly different conventionally measured fiscal deficits. This raises questions about the usefulness of the conventional measure of the deficit as an indicator of fiscal policy stance.

Table 1. Inflation, Interest Payments, and the Fiscal Deficit

	A	B	C	D	E
Assumptions					
Inflation rate (in percent)	0.0	4.0	7.0	20.0	100.0
Nominal interest rate (in percent)	3.0	7.1	10.2	23.6	106.0
Fiscal balance					
Revenue	96.2	100.0	102.9	115.4	192.3
Expenditure	92.3	100.0	105.8	130.8	284.6
Noninterest	89.3	92.9	95.6	107.2	178.6
Interest	3.0	7.1	10.2	23.6	106.0
Of which: Real interest	3.0	3.0	3.0	3.0	3.0
Deficit measures (- deficit)					
Conventional	3.9	0.0	-2.9	-15.4	-92.3
Primary	6.9	7.1	7.3	8.2	13.7
Operational	3.9	4.1	4.3	5.2	10.7
Debt					
Nominal debt, beginning of year	100.0	100.0	100.0	100.0	100.0
Flow (- conventional deficit)	-3.9	0.0	2.9	15.4	92.3
Nominal debt, end of year	96.1	100.0	102.9	115.4	192.3
Real debt, end of year	96.1	96.1	96.1	96.1	96.1

Three Concepts of the Fiscal Deficit

Given that interest payments and the fiscal deficit are affected by the rate of inflation, alternative approaches to measuring the real impact of budgetary policy are needed. Three alternative concepts of the fiscal deficit, each of which treats the interest expenditure component of public expenditures in a different manner, have been proposed in recent years. The choice between these alternatives, however, depends on the purpose at hand.

To measure the net claim on financial resources by the public sector, the **conventional deficit** should be used. The conventional deficit, or the **public sector borrowing requirement** (PSBR), is the standard measure of the fiscal deficit used by the Fund. Defined on a cash basis, it measures the difference between total government cash outlays, including interest outlays but excluding amortization payments on the outstanding stock of public debt, and total cash receipts, including tax revenue, nontax revenue, and grants. Since interest paid on the stock of debt in a particular year is chiefly the result of past deficits rather than current behavior, a measure of the current fiscal policy stance might exclude all interest payments. The **primary deficit**, that is, the noninterest component of the conventional fiscal deficit, measures how the current fiscal policy stance improves or worsens the net indebtedness of the public sector, thus providing important information on the sustainability of the fiscal policy stance. The link between the primary deficit, interest payments, and public debt is further discussed below.

The third concept of the deficit is a hybrid of the conventional and primary deficit concepts. The **operational deficit**—or the **inflation-corrected deficit**—is defined as the conventional deficit less the inflationary component of current interest payments or, alternatively, as the sum of the primary deficit and the real component of interest payments. This indicates whether fiscal policy affects the real public debt. In an inflationary environment, the time path of real debt can provide a different perspective on the sustainability of fiscal policy than the prospective evolution of nominal debt (this is also discussed below).

Table 1 shows how these different concepts of the fiscal deficit behave under the various hypothetical scenarios. While the conventional deficit widens (from an initial surplus) by $96.2 million as the inflation rate increases from 0 to 100 percent, both the primary and the operational surpluses increase by only $6.8 million.

Debt and Interest Rates

When public debt is held in the form of floating-interest domestic bonds, as is assumed above, the growth rate of nominal interest payments will exceed the inflation rate with a positive real interest rate if real GDP is constant. This will in turn push up the conventional deficit relative to GDP. In the case where the stock of public debt is either denominated in foreign currency or is index-linked, however, interest payments will tend to rise at the same rate as prices. The intuition behind this result is as follows. Assuming that the exchange rate is adjusted to reflect the evolution of domestic prices, the domestic value of external debt will rise in proportion to the increase in the price level. Since interest rates on external debt will not be affected by domestic inflation, interest payments will rise in proportion to the increase in the domestic value of external debt. When both GDP and noninterest expenditure are assumed to increase in line with inflation, the conventional deficit as a proportion of GDP will be unaffected. The behavior of interest payments with domestic indexed debt is similar, provided that the adjustment of principal is treated as amortization. Interest payments are affected because a nominal fixed interest rate is applied to the principal after adjustment for inflation. Thus, nominal interest payments on such debt grow in line with the price level, and under earlier assumptions, the conventional deficit as a proportion of GDP is unaffected by domestic inflation. In cases where the adjustment of principal is not treated as amortization, but rather as a **monetary correction** classified as an interest expenditure, the evolution of interest payments is exactly the same as with floating-rate domestic debt. The conventional deficit can, however, fall relative to GDP if nominal interest payments do not adjust in line with inflation. If the government has issued significant quantities of long-term debt, this could happen up to the point where inflation leaves creditors willing to hold only short-term bonds. It would also be the case where the government manipulates the interest rate on its debt instruments to artificially lower its debt service costs. However, it is argued in the note on *Public Expenditure and Sustainable Fiscal Policy* that such a practice is likely to be self-defeating.

Interest Payments and Public Debt Dynamics

The preceding sections illustrate how interest payments and fiscal deficits are influenced by inflation. To determine how the sustainability of the government's fiscal stance is affected, the implications for public debt have to be determined. The following framework describes the link between the overall fiscal balance, the primary balance, and debt accumulation.

Public debt at the end of period t can be written as

$$D_t = D_{t-1} + d_t, \tag{1}$$

where D_{t-1} is the debt outstanding at the end of period $t-1$ and d_t is the overall deficit in period t. The overall deficit can be expressed as

$$d_t = p_t + i_t = p_t + [(1+r)(1+\pi) -1]\, D_{t-1}, \tag{2}$$

where p_t is the primary deficit, r is the real interest rate on government debt, π is the inflation rate, and $[(1+r)(1+\pi) -1]\, D_{t-1}$ are interest payments. Substituting (2) into (1) yields

$$D_t = D_{t-1}\, (1+ r)(1+\pi) + p_t, \tag{3}$$

As a proportion of GDP, (3) can be expressed as

$$\hat{D}_t = \hat{D}_{t-1}\, [(1 + r)/(1 + g)] + \hat{p}_t, \tag{4}$$

where ^ denotes a ratio to nominal GDP, and g is the growth rate of real GDP. Subtracting D_{t-1} from both sides of (4) yields

$$\Delta\hat{D}_t = \hat{D}_{t-1}\, [(r - g)/(1 + g)] + \hat{p}_t, \tag{5}$$

from which it follows that for $\hat{p}_t = 0$:

$$\Delta\hat{D}_t \geq 0 \text{ as } g \leq r. \tag{6}$$

Since nominal GDP can be written $Y_t = (1 + g)(1+\pi)\, Y_{t-1}$, (5) can be expressed as

$$\Delta\hat{D}_t = (D_{t-1}/Y_t)[(r - g)(1+\pi) + p_t/D_{t-1}], \tag{7}$$

from which it follows that for $\hat{p}_t \neq 0$:

$$\Delta\hat{D}_t \geq 0 \text{ as } g(1+\pi) + \pi \leq r(1+\pi) + \pi + p_t/D_{t-1}, \tag{8}$$

Conditions (6) and (8) have a straightforward interpretation. The nominal interest rate, $r(1+\pi) + \pi$, is the growth rate of the debt resulting from expenditure on interest payments while p_t/D_{t-1} is the growth rate of debt attributable to the noninterest component of the deficit. These combine to give the overall growth rate of the debt. The debt-to-GDP ratio will increase indefinitely if the growth rate of nominal GDP, $g(1+\pi) + \pi$, is smaller than the growth rate of the debt. If the primary deficit is zero, then this outcome requires only that the real (or nominal) rate of interest exceed the real (or nominal) growth rate of the economy. This is often referred to as a **domestic debt trap**. However, the built-in tendency for the debt-to-GDP ratio to increase can be offset if there is a primary surplus. By the same token, while the interest rate may be less than the growth rate, a sufficiently large primary deficit will lead to an increase in the debt-to-GDP ratio.

Sustainability

The sustainability of public debt can be assessed according to a variety of criteria. However, by analogy with the way such judgements are made in the private sector, the prospect of insolvency and debt default probably provides the clearest indication of unsustainability. But how is the solvency of the government or the public sector judged? The private sector analogy points to the need to reflect all current and future assets and liabilities in a comprehensive balance sheet and then ensure that assets are sufficient to cover liabilities, in which case public spending plans are sustainable. It has been argued that this should be the government's guiding principle in assessing its fiscal policy stance. But while assessing sustainability in terms of government or public sector solvency has considerable intuitive appeal, its information requirements are enormous. Indeed, in the few industrial countries where there has been an attempt to construct a public sector balance sheet, only limited success has been achieved. The prospects of much progress in developing countries are slight. An informationally less demanding approach is required.

One alternative is to judge sustainability using simple rules that describe the time path of the debt. For example, condition (8) can yield a rule to ensure that the debt-to-GDP ratio does not increase. For projected paths of the real interest rate and output growth, this rule specifies a benchmark primary balance consistent with an unchanged debt ratio. Fiscal policy is sustainable if the primary balance exceeds the benchmark. A problem with this rule is that it is not sufficiently forward looking, in that it takes no account of the impact of future changes in fiscal policy, and in particular known expenditure demands. A number of rules have been proposed that assess sustainability in the light of projected noninterest expenditure. Such rules gauge sustainability relative to the tax ratio consistent with unchanged debt ratio. However, their ease of interpretation and implementation notwithstanding, the attraction of these simple rules is deceptive. Major limitations remain. The absence of any feedback effects from the fiscal deficit to the real interest rate and output growth deprives the rules of an important policy dimension. Moreover, targeting an unchanged debt ratio is arbitrary. Just as there are good reasons why governments should under certain circumstances run deficits, so it is also reasonable to expect an often prolonged increase in government debt relative to GDP. The question is what the upper limit to the debt-to-GDP ratio should be. This question, however, does not lend itself to a clear-cut answer without reference to the issue of solvency.

Lastly, it should be noted that these rules focus on nominal debt, which in an inflationary environment can be misleading, at least in the short term. While nominal debt is increasing, the government can effectively amortize unindexed debt through an unanticipated increase in inflation, thus reducing real debt. But such a response to a high or rising level of debt does not offer a permanent solution to a sustainability problem. First, the burden of the debt is shifted from future taxpayers to current bondholders and other holders of money. Bondholders are likely to respond by requiring higher rates of return to reflect the inflation risk associated with nominal assets and will demand shorter maturity bonds. Ultimately, the pressure for indexation will be irresistible, in which case the distinction between nominal and real debt will disappear. Second, high rates of inflation themselves have implications that may be harder to tolerate than the action required to bring debt under control.

Country Illustration

Fiscal adjustment in Brazil

Inflation rates in Brazil during the mid-1980s were high and variable, which had implications for the design of fiscal policy in the context of broad stabilization objectives. As Table 2 indicates, the conventional fiscal deficit more than doubled to nearly 50 percent of GDP between 1984 and 1988. However, virtually the entire deficit reflected a monetary correction to compensate bondholders for the impact of inflation. The operational deficit was only modest, and there was a primary surplus in all but one year. In the adjustment program followed during 1988/89 (which was supported by the Fund), both the conventional and operational deficits were thus targeted. The primary deficit, however, was not targeted, because accurate data on interest payments were not available on a timely basis given Brazil's federal structure. Data on debt were more reliable, making it easier to compute the operational deficit, although lags in the availability of price data presented some problems in making a quick assessment of the monetary correction.

Table 2. Brazil: Conventional, Operational, and Primary Balances

	1984	1985	1986	1987	1988
			(In percent of GDP)		
Conventional fiscal balance	-23.6	-28.0	-11.1	-31.4	-48.5
Of which: Monetary correction	-21.1	-23.7	-7.5	-25.9	-44.3
Operational fiscal balance	-2.5	-4.3	-3.6	-5.5	-4.3
Of which: Interest payments (noninflationary component)	-6.9	-6.4	-4.5	-4.8	-5.6
Primary balance	4.4	2.1	0.9	-0.7	1.3
			(In percent)		
Inflation rate (annual)	195.8	220.0	136.0	224.8	638.7

Source: International Monetary Fund.

Bibliography

Buiter, Willem, "Government Deficits Reinterpreted," *Economic Policy*, 1, 1985.

Heller, Peter S., Richard D. Haas, and Ahsan S. Mansur, *A Review of the Fiscal Impulse Measure*, IMF Occasional Paper No. 44 (Washington: International Monetary Fund, 1986).

Mackenzie, George A., "Conventionally Measured and Inflation-Adjusted Deficits as Indicators of the Stance of Fiscal Policy in Inflationary Periods," *Finanzarchiv*, 45, 1987.

Tanzi, Vito, Mario Blejer, and Mario Tejeiro, "Inflation and Measurement of Fiscal Deficits," *IMF Staff Papers*, 34 (Washington: International Monetary Fund, 1987).

XI. Transfers to Public Enterprises

Richard Hemming

What forms of financial assistance do governments provide to public enterprises through the budget? In what other ways is support given to public enterprises?

Why do public enterprises rely so heavily on subsidies and other forms of government support?

How can the financial burden of public enterprises on the government be reduced?

What is an appropriate pricing policy for public enterprises? How should noncommercial objectives be taken into account?

In the majority of developing countries, nonfinancial public enterprises play an important role in the economy through their responsibility for a significant proportion of investment, employment and output. Their activities also have implications for the government budget, which in part reflects the inefficiency with which they undertake their assigned responsibilities. In particular, financial support to unprofitable public enterprises often accounts for a sizable share of government expenditure. As a consequence, the scope for reducing public expenditure, or for accommodating new expenditure demands within the constraint of fixed resource availability, is inextricably linked with the prospects for successful public enterprise reform.

The Budgetary Impact of Public Enterprise Operations

Financial transactions between the government and public enterprises affect both the expenditure and revenue sides of the budget. Government expenditure comprises subsidies, equity and loans. **Subsidies** can be related to specific activities or general operating subsidies. Thus if an enterprise is charged with the responsibility of noncommercial activities, such as selling goods at below cost, a subsidy can be directly related to the cost-price differential and either a prespecified or unlimited quantity sold. Alternately, an enterprise can receive a subsidy to cover its operating losses. In principle, if there is compelling justification for a subsidy it should be related to the cost of the subsidized activity. The problem with the general subsidy is that it does not distinguish between the losses resulting from commercial as distinct from noncommercial activities.

To the extent that an enterprise does not generate sufficient profit to finance its investment, the government usually puts up some of the necessary capital. **Equity** injections do not give rise to any repayment obligations, although they often entitle the government to receive dividends based upon profitability. **Loans** imply both amortization and interest payments by the enterprise to the government. Unlike the private sector, where the debt-equity ratio is managed with a view to optimizing capital structure in light of corporate objectives and capital market constraints, the choice between debt and equity in the case of public enterprises does not reflect the fine-tuning of financial policy. Enterprises generally prefer equity to loans, for obvious reasons. The government preference should be for loans, which provide a means of imposing financial discipline on enterprises that usually is missing in the case of equity.

In practice, the distinction between equity and loans is blurred. Moreover, to all intents and purposes, both equity and loans are often indistinguishable from subsidies. While the government may prefer to make loans, the provision of additional equity often reflects the realistic assessment that enterprises may not be able to service the resulting debt. It is also common for the government to convert outstanding loans into equity, and not only in the event of default. The government also writes off enterprise debt, which is equivalent to providing a capital grant. And insofar as equity carries with it little prospect of ever receiving dividends, this too is the same as a capital grant. In other words, the government heavily subsidizes public enterprise investment.

Government subsidies, however, extend even further. For example, government loans often involve on-lending of foreign borrowing contracted by the government. Interest rate differentials favoring enterprises and the costs arising from exchange rate risk borne by the government imply a subsidy. Moreover, even where public enterprises have to fill any financing gap by borrowing abroad or on the domestic market, the government usually guarantees the loans and is called upon to meet its contingent liability in the event of default. Preferential interest rates on nongovernment borrowing by public enterprises—including loans from public sector banks—also constitute an implicit subsidy. Less obviously, it can be argued that to the extent that the government receives a rate of return on its investment in public enterprises (including both outstanding loans and equity) lower than that which is typically obtained in the private sector, this should be reflected in any subsidy measure. However, insofar as a lower yield can be justified by noncommercial objectives, resource misallocation is not implied—indeed if these objectives are achieved, resources are more efficiently allocated—and an unwarranted subsidy does not result.

Offsetting government payments to public enterprises are enterprise contributions to government revenue. These include direct and indirect taxes, dividends, profits, and amortization and interest payments. Taking all these into account, and in particular large indirect tax payments on imported equipment and inputs, it is sometimes argued that public enterprises make a significant **net** contribution to the budget. However, any belief that this in a sense weakens the case for improving public enterprise performance and reducing government payments to public enterprises is entirely mistaken. Many activities undertaken by public enterprises would be attractive to the private sector if they were not precluded from them, either by statute or because private enterprises cannot compete on equal terms with public enterprises. The government would likely receive higher revenues from such activities if private enterprises undertook them. And even if private production is not a viable alternative, available revenue should not be diverted to supporting inefficient enterprises. It can be better used elsewhere.

Where the public enterprise sector is large and there are significant financial transactions between the government and public enterprises, consolidated public sector accounts are essential if a proper assessment of the role of government in the economy is to be made. While the necessary data are often not available for the whole public enterprise sector, it should be possible to reflect the activities of the largest enterprises in partially consolidated accounts. This would appear to be especially important where one enterprise rivals the government in size and influence, as is the case with the copper companies in Zambia and Zaire.

Public Enterprise Performance and Problems

While the general perception is that, by commercial standards, the financial performance of public enterprises is poor, this is quite difficult to establish. Direct comparisons between public and private enterprises are rare, since there are few activities together undertaken by both. Where such comparisons are possible they are inconclusive, but this is hardly surprising. In competitive markets, markedly dissimilar performance should be the exception. Moreover, to the extent that there are differences, if public enterprises are charged with a wider range of objectives than private enterprises, profitability will be conceded in the process. The complicated issue is assessing how much profit should be forgone to achieve these objectives.

Rather than attempting an answer in this question, there is instead a tendency to point out how the environment in which public enterprises currently operate would be expected to result in inefficiency and lower profitability than justified by reference to multiple objectives, and to base a case for reform on these observations.

Control and management

As originally conceived, governments were to adopt an **arm's length approach** to the public enterprise sector—managers were to be given clear objectives and left free to pursue them. The relationship between governments and public enterprises has, however, turned out to be one characterized by extensive political and ministerial involvement in management decisions affecting pricing, investment, and employment. As a result, management often finds itself charged with wide-ranging, and often conflicting objectives, with little guidance as to which it should be most actively pursuing. Indeed, ineffective monitoring by government gives rise to **principal-agent problems**, which allow managers to include their own self- interest among the list of objectives.

Employment policy

A commitment to providing and protecting employment has often led to a significant enlargement of public enterprise sectors for this purpose alone. The takeover of enterprises that could not survive in the private sector has been primarily for this reason. Because of the priority attached to the employment objective, and the importance to the economy of the sectors dominated by public enterprises, **trade unions** are especially influential. As a result, public enterprises tend to be overstaffed and wages are often considerably higher than can be justified by reference to productivity levels.

Price control

High labor costs, together with excessive capital costs—mainly a consequence of inadequate monitoring of key investment decisions and poor project implementation—lead to **productive inefficiency** in that enterprises could generate the same output at considerably lower cost. However, administered prices that are set on a cost-plus basis shield the profits of public enterprises from their cost structures. While cost-plus pricing should ensure that enterprises make a profit, administered pricing is still often associated with losses, either because inefficiency is excessive or, more usually, because prices are held at a low level to meet social or other noncommercial objectives.

The competitive environment

Inefficiency is compounded in the uncompetitive environment in which most public enterprises operate. In monopolistic markets, or with only a few suppliers at best, consumers are forced to bear the higher prices that result from inefficiency. Also, consumers have little influence over the range and quality of public enterprise output. The resulting **allocative inefficiency** adds to the productive inefficiency of public enterprise activities. Moreover, in those instances when public enterprises do compete, they most times have an advantage over private firms, for example in purchasing inputs from other public enterprises. Nevertheless, many enterprises in competitive markets still fail to make a profit.

Budget support

When administrative prices are held below costs or enterprises are unable to compete in contested markets, the ready availability of budgetary resources prevents them from going bankrupt. While budget support can be justified by reference to those compelling noncommercial objectives that prevent otherwise efficient enterprises from making a profit, it often compensates for inefficiency.

To varying degrees, the problems identified above characterize public enterprise sectors in most industrial and developing countries, and, except in a few cases, it is difficult to argue that the current low profits and high levels of budget support are justified. Equally, the fact that public enterprise profits are high, and budget support modest, does not indicate that these problems are not present. Administered prices can generate profits from extremely inefficient activities. Moreover, an environment that encourages and sustains inefficiency is not one in which such inefficiency is likely to be reversed. Consequently, the key to improving efficiency, raising profit, and reducing unproductive government expenditure is to provide an appropriate environment in which public enterprises should operate.

Public Enterprise Reform

The note on *Public Expenditure and Resource Allocation* describes how a significant proportion of welfare economics is devoted to establishing the case for government intervention to compensate for market failure and to meet social needs. Clearly, some of the efficiency and distributional objectives of intervention have been achieved through the ownership of public enterprises. At the same time, the problems that currently afflict public enterprises provide a rationale for reform aimed at the efficient pursuit of clearly specified and appropriately costed objectives. However, current objectives reflect a wide range of economic, social, political, and strategic concerns which may prove resilient to charges of unreasonableness, and therefore difficult to dispense with. Moreover, many of these objectives may be hard to articulate in any precise way, especially insofar as they relate to the "national interest". Consequently, the pursuit of public enterprise efficiency cannot in practice be conducted as a constrained optimization exercise. Rather, the only achievable goals may be the elimination of the least compelling objectives and the gradual implementation of measures to encourage efficiency.

Promoting competition

The market mechanism must inevitably play a central role in promoting efficiency. In a competitive economy, the product market guides prices and output while the capital market (including the market for corporate control) constrains costs. A firm that cannot sell its products will not make profits; unprofitable firms will go bankrupt or be taken over. The market therefore regulates firms, providing the incentive for them to achieve both productive and allocative efficiency. Certainly, some of the worst excesses of public ownership would be diminished by a shift to private ownership. Simply taking public enterprise decision making out of the political arena and withdrawing government financial backing will eliminate some inefficiency. But many of the problems associated with public enterprises arise not from the fact that they are publicly owned; rather, they reflect an absence of market discipline. Therefore, by exposing public monopolies to competition—for which privatization may or may not be necessary—significant efficiency gains are likely to result (for further discussion see the note on *Privatization*).

To the extent that public ownership reflects circumstances in which markets do not work well or produce outcomes that are considered socially or politically undesirable, removing barriers to competition would be insufficient or inappropriate. Natural monopoly, for example, is a market outcome; to introduce competition in a natural monopoly setting, the market has to be redefined. One solution is to make the right to run a natural monopoly the object of competition by auctioning franchises to the private sector. Also, some activities associated with natural monopoly, such as maintenance, are likely to be contestable, and these can be contracted out to the private sector. But insofar as the core activities of natural monopolies are inherently noncontestable, public ownership is likely to remain the most efficient way of regulating such activities. Also, priority social objectives will inevitably continue to be primarily a responsibility of the public sector, including public enterprises.

Administrative controls

The design of mechanisms to improve the efficiency of enterprises that must remain under government control constitutes a major challenge for public policy. Attention should be focused on the following: limiting the influence politicians can have over public enterprises; specifying clear goals for enterprises; providing managers with autonomy over business decisions, giving them incentives to pursue efficiency (such as profit shares) and making them accountable to the government; establishing appropriate reporting requirements and monitoring mechanisms; and putting in place incentive mechanisms (such as pay linked to productivity) to limit the impact of restrictive labor practices. A number of countries are making significant progress in this regard.

Pricing and subsidy policies

Exposing activities to the full implications of market forces presumes competitive prices and an absence of subsidies. Moreover, even where the market outcomes are tempered by noncommercial objectives and a subsidy is justified, insofar as market prices can continue to play an allocative role, this is preferable from an efficiency standpoint. As far as noncompetitive enterprises are concerned, pricing is a more complex issue. Efficiency considerations suggest that prices be set equal to marginal cost; but where public enterprises are required to contribute to government revenue—because the tax base is narrow or administrative capability is weak—prices can be set above marginal cost. **Ramsey pricing** implies larger deviations from marginal cost for goods in inelastic demand (see the note on *Pricing and Cost Recovery* for further discussion).

In the case of natural monopolies, continuously decreasing average costs imply that marginal cost pricing, and in some cases Ramsey pricing, will result in losses and a compensating subsidy will be needed. Otherwise, subsidies to competitive and noncompetitive enterprises should be matched to the specific objectives they support. They should reflect an assessment of benefits and costs of intervention, and be well targeted towards intended beneficiaries. Similarly, government support of public enterprise investment through equity and loans should reflect a careful appraisal of the returns to the projects involved.

Country Illustration

Government payments to public enterprises in Nepal

The public enterprise sector in Nepal is not large by developing country standards, but is does dominate key areas of the economy. Standard financial indicators also suggest that it performs rather badly; for example, in 1988/89 the major enterprises averaged an after-tax rate of return of -5 percent and financed less than 15 percent of capital spending out of their own resources. This implied significant explicit and implicit payments from the budget to public enterprises. In particular, the government provides equity and loans to the investment-intensive electricity, telecommunications, and water utilities and subsidies to agricultural trading companies to bridge the gap between the import cost and domestic price of fertilizer and to meet the cost of transporting food and fertilizer to remote regions. However, food and fertilizer subsidies are not sufficient to cover operating losses, and the Nepal Food Corporation, together with a number of other enterprises, has been forced to borrow from commercial banks but has defaulted on its loans; the government is in the process of paying off the resulting arrears. The Agricultural Inputs Corporation has resorted mainly to withholding the proceeds from the sale of fertilizer received as aid rather than depositing them in government counterpart funds. In addition, the government undertakes large capital projects on behalf of the major utilities, and then transfers them off-budget to the enterprises concerned, usually but not always upon completion. Taking all these transactions into account, total government payments to public enterprises were equivalent to 2.4 percent of GDP in 1988/89; the budget formally reflects only about two thirds of this amount.

Table 1. Nepal: Government Payments to Major Public Enterprises, 1988/89
(In millions of Nepalese rupees)

Equity	273
Net lending	602
Subsidies	295
Sub-total	1,170
(In percent of GDP)	(1.6)
Payment of commercial bank arrears	80
Shortfall in counterpart fund deposits	58
Off-budget	499
Total	1,807
(In percent of GDP)	(2.4)

Source: International Monetary Fund.

Bibliography

Floyd, R.H., C.S. Gray, and R.P. Short, *Public Enterprise in Mixed Economies: Some Macroeconomic Aspects* (Washington: International Monetary Fund, 1984).

"Strengthening Public Finance Through Reform of State-Owned Enterprises" in *World Development Report* (Washington: The World Bank, 1988).

XII. Transfers to Local Governments

Daniel P. Hewitt

What are the advantages and disadvantages of decentralizing government expenditure?

What criteria are commonly used in assessing the efficiency of decentralization?

Should revenue collection also be decentralized?

What is the intended purpose of revenue sharing (block) grants, matching grants, and special purpose grants?

In many countries, grants from the central government to local governments are the primary means through which the central government provides local services. A typical allocation of responsibilities is for the central government to focus on primarily national concerns, such as defense and social insurance; regional governments to handle transportation and higher education; and the local governments to have responsibility for primary and secondary education, police and fire protection, local parks, and sanitation services. Although this degree of decentralization is more often observed in industrial countries, some developing countries have significant levels of decentralization. In India, for example, local governments account for over two fifths of consolidated government expenditures. Intergovernmental transfers account for nearly one fifth of central government spending in India and constitute 37 percent of total local government resources. There is also a significant degree of decentralization in other developing countries—see Table 1.

Table 1. Intergovernmental Grants in Developing Countries, 1986

	Local and Regional Govt. Expenditure	Central Govt. Expenditure	Of which: Inter-governmental Grants	Central Govt. Transfers to Local Govts.	Grant Receipts by Local and Regional Govts.
		(In percent of GDP)		*(In percent of expenditure)*	*(In percent of receipts)*
India	14.6	22.5	4.4	19.5	36.9
Brazil	13.7	35.5	3.4	9.6	32.8
Zimbabwe	11.6	40.5	3.5	8.6	30.3
Uruguay	2.1	24.1	0.3	1.4	15.7
Thailand	1.6	20.8	0.4	2.0	25.5

Source: *IMF Government Finance Statistics Yearbook.*

In any country with decentralized functions, grants are the principal means through which the central government can influence local government decisions. However, the existence of intergovernmental grants raises questions regarding the costs and benefits of decentralization of government responsibilities. Why should the central government resort to indirect controls of local government decisions (i.e., grants), instead of assuming direct responsibility for local services or simply issuing guidelines to the local governments? Furthermore, if the central government needs to control local decisions in this manner, why decentralize?

There are some well-established advantages of decentralization of expenditure, both in terms of the decisions regarding the mix of local services to provide and the actual production of the services. However, in most cases, revenue is more efficiently collected in a centralized fashion. Therefore, a tension exists between efficient revenue collection and efficient service delivery, and grants serve the purpose of bridging the gap. Grants allow a country to rely on normally more efficient centralized tax collection agencies while still availing itself of the advantages of decentralized expenditure decisions. Additionally, grants afford the centralized authority the opportunity to influence local expenditure decisions to ensure that, when appropriate, such decisions take account of national interests.

Decentralization of Government Expenditure

Although there is little controversy as to the need for government within a market-oriented economy, there is strong disagreement over the proper scope of government. Considerable difficulty is involved in choosing both the right level of government expenditure (and taxation) and the mix of government services that maximizes social welfare, as determined by the needs and preferences of society. One means of improving the decision-making process is through the decentralization of certain government functions. Government functions that lend themselves to decentralization are referred to as **local public goods (LPGs)**. The efficiency advantages of decentralization of LPGs are varied and quite significant. The first advantage of decentralization is the possibility of having regional variety in the mix and level of LPGs, which can greatly enhance social welfare. For instance, in a high-crime area where most of the housing is constructed of stone, the local population will desire high police expenditures and minimal spending on fire prevention. Alternatively, in one locality the road network might be in particular need of repair while in another region an upgrade of the water and sanitary services might be preferable. Once it is accepted that regional variety is desirable, the second advantage of decentralization is in the area of preference revelation. Regionally based governments are in a better position to determine the preferences of the local population. Research has indicated that preference revelation problems encountered in public finance are greatly diminished as the size and heterogeneity of the population decreases.

The third advantage of decentralization is that competition, proximity, and transparency provide a strong motivation for local governments to be more responsive to the desires of the public. In a democracy, there is competition among political parties at the national level which engenders responsiveness to the public. However, at the regional level, competition for residents and businesses provides an additional incentive for the local authorities to be responsive to the public. Furthermore, the smaller size of the operation makes it much easier for the public to monitor local governments and to influence local policies. The fourth advantage stems from scale advantages—smaller bureaucracies are easier to administer efficiently. In general, there is an absence of economies of scale in centralizing the supply of LPGs.

The advantages to decentralization are offset somewhat by three factors. The potential gains from decentralization are likely to be lower in a geographically small country—there is normally less regional diversification of needs. Second, decentralization can increase the scope for corruption within government since the number of officials in a position to benefit from corruption increases. Furthermore, large, centralized bureaucracies are easier to monitor than a series of decentralized offices. Finally, decentralization tends to increase the demand for skilled administrators by the government sector. Since each autonomous regional and local authority requires its own administrative staff, in a country where capable public management is scarce, a greater degree of centralization might enable the conservation of scarce management resources.

National Public Goods and Inter-Regional Externalities

While it is often preferable to decentralize the functions of government that are local in nature, there are strong reasons to advise against decentralizing all government activities. There are no advantages to local supply of national public goods, that is, government services which provide nonrival benefits to all regions. In fact, technically speaking, the same kind of **free-rider problems** that exist with the private provision of public goods will emerge. Local control of national public goods will almost certainly lead to inadequate provision, given the needs and desires of society. For instance, a local government is not likely to be willing to fund expenditures on a highway used substantially by nonresidents to travel through its locality. A similar, nearly identical, issue arises when essentially local public goods have strong interregional externalities which require national coordination. There are a number of possible solutions, depending on the severity of the externality. When the externality is quite substantial compared to the local component of the program, centralized provision is often a sensible solution. In other cases, the externality may be insignificant enough to warrant no action on the part of the central government. However, in many cases, the advantages of decentralization need not be forgone, but the externality is significant enough to warrant centralized action. In these circumstances, the use of **grants** (see below)—and occasional sanctions when negative externalities exist—is the prescribed solution.

Centralized Tax Collection and Deficit Financing

As is the case with expenditure activities, there are revenue devices that are national in nature and others that are local. However, in general, it is more efficient to centralize collection of income taxes, trade taxes, and taxes on goods and services. The reasons for the greater efficiency with centralized revenue collection relate to both administration and economic efficiency.

Centralized tax collection is often less costly to administer for informational reasons. A centralized system requires only one file on each economic entity, while a decentralized system could lead to multiple agencies collecting essentially the same information. It is also more difficult to assess taxable income with decentralized tax collection. Many residents and companies normally acquire income in multiple regions outside the jurisdiction of the tax authority. A locality is always at a disadvantage in collecting data on events that occur outside its jurisdiction.

The economic efficiency reasons for centralized tax collection revolve around the issue of locational distortions. A high tax in one region can lead to relocation of economic activity to another region. Tax-induced relocation can either lead to a lower output—for instance, when a firm locates farther away from a port than is economical because of high taxes in the port district, or cause a direct decrease in economic well-being—such as when a family lives in a less desirable location to avoid high taxes elsewhere. High local taxes have been found to have a severe impact on the economic health of a region. Distortions of this sort can be avoided with a national tax.

At least one local tax does not have these problems—**land-value property taxation.** A property tax that is based purely on the value of land is an efficient local tax for two reasons. Such a tax has to be administered at the local level since property values vary from district to district and region to region. Furthermore, because land is immobile, the tax causes no relocation or economic inefficiency. In a competitive market setting, the tax is capitalized into the value of the property (the sale price of the property falls), and thus the tax does not affect relative prices. In contrast, a traditional property tax on both the value of land and the value of buildings does distort economic decisions by discouraging building. Local user fees are another nondistorting potential source of local revenue. When local governments provide goods that are partially private in nature, there is often a valid reason to impose a fee on the users—see the note on *Pricing and Cost Recovery* for further discussion.

With respect to deficit financing, this too is generally the prerogative of the centralized authority. In many countries, localities are prohibited from incurring a budget deficit. In other countries, bond financing is restricted to the funding of capital projects. For several reasons, the scope for localities and regional governments to use deficit financing is more limited than for the central government. First, a locality's ability to repay a loan is constrained by the limitations on tax instruments. Second, unlike most central governments, localities cannot print money. Finally, localities operate in a more open economic environment. Thus, a large overhanging debt can be a serious deterrent to the economic vitality of a region because businesses and households will avoid communities where the prospect of raising taxes in the future is high. Therefore, local borrowing should be closely linked to the ability to repay and to the timing of benefits (such as for capital projects). For these reasons, market forces normally limit the ability of local and regional governments to use deficit financing. If market forces do not impose constraints on the ability of localities to borrow, the central government often steps in to limit budget deficits.

Intergovernmental Grants

Block grants

A block grant or a general purpose grant is the principal means of increasing the level of funds available to local governments. Block grants are usually disbursed through a formula based on the goals of the central government. For instance, the grants are normally inversely proportional to per capita community income and positively correlated with community population. Therefore, they are a means of providing both general revenues to localities to fund LPGs and of redistributing funds in favor of more needy localities, which enables the locality to increase its level of services or to lower local taxes.

Matching grants

A matching grant is normally related to a specific functional category of expenditure, such as primary education or health clinics. The size of the grant is variable and depends upon the level of local expenditure on the given program. The purpose of these grants is to encourage localities to spend more on a targeted service both by providing funds and by providing the locality with an incentive to use more of its own resources for this purpose.

Special purpose grants

Special purpose grants are restricted-use funds offered to local governments. The locality must use the funds for the specifically designated purpose prescribed by the central government in order to qualify for the grant. Economists do not generally favor special purpose grants because they are either ineffective or inefficient. When a special purpose grant pays for a program that the locality intended to provide anyway, they are simply equivalent to block grants. If the specific purpose grant is for a program the locality intended to fund, but the amount exceeds the locality's intended budgetary allocation, the locality will often use all the available funds for this purpose. In this case, the special purpose grant is equivalent in part to a block grant and has the effect of forcing an increase in local expenditures on the program in question. However, unlike a matching grant, the locality will normally spend less of its own funds on the program. Finally, when a specific purpose grant is provided for a program that the locality did not intend to fund and does not consider to be very desirable, the locality will sometimes simply not apply for the funds (this is common in the United States). In conclusion, economic theory suggests that both block grants and matching grants, are preferable to special purpose grants.

The impact of grants

The impact of grants on local expenditure patterns has been found to be extremely large in a wide variety of settings and over a long period of time. Block grants have been found to be used by localities to increase the level of local government services; they do not seem to induce localities to lower local taxes. Likewise, matching grants have proven to be extremely effective in increasing local expenditures. While most of the empirical studies of the impact of grants used data from Europe, the United States, and Canada, the same effect has been observed elsewhere. An example, a matching grant program to help fund local infrastructure in Ghana yielded a local response far in excess of expectations. Numerous theoretical explanations have been offered for the unexpected potency of grants, however, there is as yet no consensus as to the explanation of this so-called **flypaper effect.**

Country Illustration

Fiscal federalism in Brazil

Brazil has 24 state governments and nearly 4,000 municipalities, in addition to the central government. The distribution of revenue and expenditure among the various levels of government is shown in Table 2. State and local governments collect a little under one third of total tax revenue, most of which is accounted for by a state-level value-added tax and local property taxes. Revenue collections are, however, insufficient to cover local expenditure, which necessitates intergovernmental grants. Some of these grants reflect revenue-sharing arrangements: for example, both state and local governments receive a mandated (and steadily rising) share of central government income tax and excise duty revenue while local governments receive a fixed share of VAT revenue from the states. Block grants are also fairly common; some use is made of special purpose grants; but matching grants are unusual.

On the expenditure side, the central government is primarily responsible for debt service, subsidies, and net lending. Both state and local governments are an integral part of public administration, and account for the bulk of expenditure on wages and salaries. They also undertake major capital projects, partly financed through loans from the central government. As regards the functional breakdown of expenditure, the central government is responsible for military spending, national transportation and communications, support for industry and commerce, and social security. State governments provide police services, local transportation, energy and education and health services. Localities are primarily responsible for housing. This pattern of expenditure is similar to that found in other countries with decentralized government. The indications are that the decentralization of both revenue collection and expenditure is likely to be increased, after a period of centralization since the mid-1970s.

Table 2. Brazil: Government Revenue and Expenditure, 1986
(In percent of GDP)

	Level of Government			
	General	Central	State	Local
Total revenue	30.4	22.4	9.1	3.4
Tax revenue	23.9	16.8	6.6	0.5
Income taxes	12.0	11.8	0.3	—
VAT and excises	10.8	4.5	6.0	0.3
Nontax revenue	6.6	5.3	0.7	0.5
Intergovernmental grants	4.5	0.3	1.7	2.4
Expenditure and net lending	44.8	35.5	10.1	3.6
Current expenditure	33.0	27.0	3.2	2.7
Of which: Wages and salaries	6.6	2.0	3.5	1.2
Interest payments	12.6	12.0	0.6	0.1
Subsidies	10.4	8.0	1.8	0.5
Intergovernmental grants	4.8	3.4	1.4	—
Capital expenditure	4.1	1.9	1.4	0.8
Net lending	8.6	8.0	0.5	0.1

Source: *IMF Government Finance Statistics Yearbook.*

Bibliography

Mieszkowski, Peter M., and William H. Oakland, *Fiscal Federalism and Grants-in-Aid* (Washington: The Urban Institute, 1979).

Mueller, Dennis C., *Public Choice II* (New York: Cambridge University Press, 1989).

Tiebout, Charles M., "The Pure Theory of Local Expenditures," *Journal of Political Economy*, 64, 1956.

Winer, Stanley L., "Some Evidence on the Effects of the Separation of Spending and Tax Decisions," *Journal of Political Economy*, 91, 1983.

XIII. Military Expenditure

Richard Hemming and Daniel P. Hewitt

What information is available about military expenditure?

Can an appropriate level of military expenditure be defined?

Does military expenditure have a beneficial impact on the economy?

Is military spending undertaken at the expense of more socially desirable expenditure programs?

How can the efficiency of military expenditure be improved?

Military expenditure averages about 5 1/2 percent of GNP across industrial and developing countries, and has grown more or less in line with average income between the late 1970s and late 1980s. Military spending is of a similar order of magnitude to that on each of the two other major functional expenditure categories—health and education. Military expenditure is a subject of special concern because of the widespread perception that it is mostly unproductive, and the resources it consumes could be more productively used to expand other economic and social programs. The most severe critics of large military budgets advocate sharp reductions in military expenditure across the world, with little or no such spending by many developing countries. Others contend that while most countries have legitimate defense objectives, these and other less compelling military activities require lower levels of expenditure than at present.

The Pattern of Military Expenditure

Data

A prerequisite for any meaningful discussion of military expenditure is an appreciation of the current situation. However, the IMF's *Government Finance Statistics Yearbook (GFS)* reports a series which is incomplete in its country coverage and there is a tendency for high or rapidly rising levels of military expenditure to be understated. Perhaps the most widely quoted data are those compiled by the United States *Arms Control and Disarmament Agency (ACDA)*; these are derived from a variety of national sources and information collected by other US agencies, including USAID and the CIA. The principal shortcoming of the *ACDA* data is that they probably overstate military expenditure in Eastern Europe.

Expenditure levels and trends

ACDA data for the period 1977–87 are summarized in Table 1. These data reveal that over 80 percent of total military spending is undertaken by industrial countries (including Eastern Europe). Moreover, while expenditure in industrial countries has been growing, especially in the United States, expenditure in developing countries has been stable in real terms, and on average therefore fell relative to GDP. Among the main developing country regions, expenditure growth in Africa, East Asia and Latin America has been modest, and the share of military expenditure in GNP in the first two cases has fallen—especially in some of the more heavily indebted countries, including those in Latin America—while more rapid growth in South Asia has been swamped by a sharp decline in the heavy military spending undertaken by countries in the Middle East. Nevertheless, the list of heavy spenders (relative to income) is still dominated by countries in the Middle East (Oman, Israel, Jordan, Saudi Arabia, Egypt, Iraq, Syria, Yemen Arab Republic, and Libya are nine of the world's ten heaviest spenders). Other heavy spenders include Angola and Mozambique in Africa, and Nicaragua, Guyana and Chile in Latin America. Except for relatively high military expenditure by China, there is little disparity between countries in Asia.

Table 1. Military Expenditure, 1977–87

	In percent of GNP 1977	In percent of GNP 1987	In US dollars (billions) 1987	Annual real growth (in percent) 1977–87
Industrial countries	5.2	5.5	844	2.7
North America	4.8	6.2	305	4.7
Western Europe (NATO)	3.5	3.5	142	1.7
Eastern Europe (Warsaw Pact)	11.0	10.8	364	1.6
Developing countries	6.8	5.1	173	—
Africa	4.7	4.3	14	0.9
Latin America	2.0	2.0	15	1.9
Middle East	13.7	11.0	68	-2.0
East Asia	2.7	2.1	70	2.1
South Asia	3.6	4.1	13	5.1
World	5.5	5.4	1,016	2.2

Source: *World Military Expenditure and Arms Transfers* (*ACDA*, 1988).

Determinants of Military Spending

Defense spending

For analytical purposes it is useful to distinguish between military spending and defense spending. National defense—that is, the provision of protection against the threat of external attack—is a classic public good. If the public sentiment is that such a threat does or could potentially exist, then it is the role of government to make the necessary provision. However, the question is how much to spend on providing protection. The magnitude of the threat a nation faces and the appropriate defense services to provide in response is difficult for most people to gauge; in practice, the most influential judges are usually the suppliers of defense services who have a vested interest in large defense budgets. Consequently, ends and means get confused, and an assessment of military spending relative to defense needs is difficult to make.

Internal security

In many countries, military spending is not only for the purpose of national defense, but also to maintain internal security. This may be undertaken by defense forces or may entail an expansion of the military. It may substitute for expenditure that would otherwise be required on the police, which is a separate expenditure category in the *GFS* and not covered by the *ACDA* data. It may be for purposes that the rest of the world regards as legitimate or illegitimate. For these and other reasons it is certainly difficult and probably inappropriate to make a judgement on the need for internal security.

Military intervention

It is one thing to be militarily prepared, but quite another to engage in military conflicts. Preparations depend upon judgements about risks and appropriate responses. A prospective aggressor is usually aware of these preparations, and instigating a conflict will often require some military build-up. Fearing attack, potential victims generally increase their defense capabilities. Actual conflict then leads to a further escalation of military spending on both sides. With an end to conflict, a reassessment of risk and response will almost certainly leave military expenditure at a permanently higher level. For these reasons, it is hardly surprising that a principal determinant of military spending is current or past involvement in civil or international conflict. This is the case with a number of the heavier spenders identified above.

Other influences on military spending

A number of empirical studies have used *ACDA* and other data to identify the range of factors that determine both international differences in military spending and changes over time. In addition to civil or international conflict, other political factors are also important. For example, a country's political regime also has a bearing on military expenditure; not only do nondemocratic governments tend to place a higher priority on military preparedness but they also often require military support to retain their power. In this latter connection, it has been suggested that part of the justification for a large military establishment is that a smaller, more cohesive military force is potentially more destabilizing. In general, however, the link between the military spending and political stability is not a strong one.

Political alliances

Clearly, some countries that have few political alliances, such as neutral Switzerland, give defense a low priority. At the same time, those with strong alliances can take advantage of international cooperation to reduce defense spending. For example, in return for allowing the US armed forces to locate in the Philippines, part of the burden of defense of the Philippines is shifted to the United States. As a result, military expenditure in the Philippines is less than in many other countries in East Asia, despite serious internal security difficulties. However, while a small country may be able to benefit from an alliance with a larger country, it is less clear that the major alliances between large countries (NATO, Warsaw Pact) have reaped the benefits of cooperation.

Indeed, it is widely believed that polarizing potential adversaries into two alliances has led to an escalation of military spending.

Economic factors

Population size and income levels are important factors. There is little evidence that the smallest and poorest countries are devoting an unusually large share of national income to military spending. However, while some of the heavy spenders, and in particular the oil exporting countries of the Middle East, have the resources to finance their expenditure, it is becoming increasingly clear that the burden of military spending is a strain even on these richer economies. The composition of expenditure is also relevant. In countries with modest budgets and limited foreign exchange, military costs can be held down by building up personnel rather than importing sophisticated military equipment. The evidence suggests that variations in expenditure both between countries and over time are closely linked to the size of military imports. The availability of military aid plays a central role in this regard.

The preceding discussion clearly suggests that explaining differences in military expenditure lies outside the purview of economics, being primarily a reflection of political decision making. However, there are three aspects of military expenditure that do lend themselves to economic analysis. These concern: (i) whether military expenditure has beneficial spillover effects on the economy, as is often claimed by its proponents; (ii) the efficiency of military spending; and (iii) the extent to which resources are diverted from more productive programs to pay for military spending, as is often claimed by its critics.

Economic Analysis of Military Expenditure

Military spending, investment, and growth

There can be little doubt that military expenditure has some beneficial consequences for the economy beyond any additional political, social, and economic stability associated with the provision of core military services. At the same time it is difficult to identify what these are, and this is reflected in the way military expenditure is treated in fiscal accounts. In particular, while capital spending on military hardware and construction for purely military use is viewed as unproductive and therefore classified as current expenditure, to the extent that the private sector benefits directly from the construction of roads and other infrastructure, and because provision of military accommodation relieves pressure on private alternatives, this is regarded as the creation of productive capital assets (see the *A Manual on Government Finance Statistics*, IMF, 1986, for further discussion), although it may not be very efficient.

However, it is argued that the beneficial impact of military expenditure extends beyond the direct provision of productive capital assets. In particular, reference is frequently made to the **spin-off benefits** from military research and technological developments, and the value of **military training**. Certainly the former is explicitly recognized by the European aircraft industry, which defends the subsidies it receives by reference to the implicit subsidy its US competitors receive through the military research and development budget. And military recruitment campaigns in many industrial countries emphasize the enhanced employment prospects that result from military training. It is also argued that military expenditure that results in some military-related orientation in the private sector can promote military exports, and that the formation of military alliances increases foreign assistance, both military and nonmilitary.

Clearly, arguments concerning research and development and the growth of the military-industrial complex relate primarily to industrial countries. However, a few developing countries—Brazil and India, for example—produce significant quantities of military equipment. The arguments about military training and foreign assistance are more relevant to developing countries. But, even if military expenditure has beneficial consequences, the issue is whether these could have been achieved more effectively through other programs. It is difficult to believe that military spending is necessarily the best way to educate the work force in developing countries or to persuade donors that they are deserving of assistance. Moreover, even in industrial countries, the argument that improving the design of commercial aircraft and the promotion of exports are best served by military expenditure is not particularly convincing.

A considerable amount of research has been devoted to the identification of the impact of military expenditure on growth. However, the evidence is contradictory, some studies finding that higher military spending is positively correlated with the growth of nonmilitary output, while others find that higher military expenditure is negatively correlated with growth. On closer inspection, it appears that the link may be negative for resource-constrained countries and positive for resource-abundant countries. The evidence therefore points to a negative impact of large military budgets on growth in developing countries. This contrasts with the so-called **Benoit hypothesis**, which argued that high military expenditure had been associated with more rapid developing-country growth during the 1950s and 1960s. These two opposing findings can, however, be reconciled by noting that developing countries utilized more underemployed domestic resources in this period; but more recently, the tendency to import military equipment appears to have had adverse consequences for growth.

Expenditure efficiency

Efficiency in general requires that objectives are met at least cost. Evidence from the industrial countries suggests that traditional economic analysis has rather limited applicability in the area of military expenditure. Cost-benefit analysis can in principle be applied where measurable objectives are involved, for example when choosing between alternative missile systems or deciding how many missiles to deploy. And cost-effectiveness analysis can be applied to specific defense objectives such as achieving second-strike capability in the event of a well-specified attack. But because military objectives cannot in general be defined with much precision, efficient resource allocation in the military sector is difficult to characterize.

It is clear, however, that military costs are a concern. For example, the lack of competition in US defense procurement policy has led to calls for increased public scrutiny and accountability. Insofar as most developing countries rely on imported military equipment, they may face less of a problem. The international arms market is highly competitive, and within the constraints implied by political alliances there are savings from shopping around. Perhaps the principal way in which developing countries can contain military costs is through the appropriate choice of equipment. Given the power of the military establishment, there is an inevitable tendency to confuse ends and means. This is especially true where high-technology equipment is concerned. While military prestige may well be served by having the latest weapons, this may be inappropriate given military objectives, manpower skills and available resources. A powerful military establishment may also be able to secure pay and benefits for military personnel that are substantially better than those of other public sector and private sector employees, which adds to excess costs.

Trade-off against other programs

While it is obvious that military spending is undertaken at the expense of some other programs (or lower taxes and borrowing), it is less clear that displaced expenditures are more productive. Military objectives may be perfectly legitimate, there may be beneficial spillover effects, and spending may be efficient. An optimal public expenditure program could then feature a fairly large military budget. It is, however, fanciful to believe that military budgets around the world can be justified by reference to such considerations. Critics who claim that defense expenditure ought to be reduced are probably on safe ground. But evidence is hard to come by. Attention has focused mainly on changes in the pattern of expenditure in the context of fiscal adjustment. The evidence reveals that, in the short term, military expenditure is more resilient to budgetary cutbacks than most other expenditure categories. In the long term, however, the often-heard claim that expenditure on social programs is the worst affected category is in general misplaced. The brunt of adjustment is borne primarily by public investment and other economically productive programs. Indeed, in some cases social expenditure appears to be more resilient than military spending; but both bear some of the costs of adjustment.

Policy Aspects of Military Expenditure

A sovereign country's military objectives cannot be questioned, nor can the way in which it decides to respond to them. However, the following issues can legitimately be the subject of policy discussion: (i) the extent to which military spending is used to promote nonmilitary objectives that can be more efficiently met in other ways; (ii) the trade-offs that are implied for the size and composition of other expenditure programs given the size of the military budget; and to a limited extent (iii) the efficiency of military spending given military objectives. Issue (ii) in particular would appear to be directly relevant in many adjusting countries. Reductions in economically productive expenditure and inadequate protection of the poor during periods of adjustment imply that military spending could have a large opportunity cost in terms of lower growth and welfare. This may not be widely appreciated. There is then a strong case for arguing that military expenditure should bear at least its fair share of the costs of adjustment.

Bibliography

Benoit, Emile, *Defense and Economic Growth in Developing Countries* (Lexington: Lexington Books, 1983).

De Masi, Paula, and Henri Lorie, "How Resilient Are Military Expenditures?," *IMF Staff Papers*, 36 (Washington: International Monetary Fund, 1989).

Hewitt, Daniel P., "Military Expenditure: International Comparison of Trends," Working Paper 91/54 (Washington: International Monetary Fund, 1991).

Porter, R.C., "Recent Trends in LDC Military Expenditures," *World Development*, 17, 1989.

XIV. Public Investment

Kenneth Miranda

How should public investment projects be appraised?

Are overall public investment programs consistent with macroeconomic and institutional constraints?

How is the public investment programming problem solved in practice?

In many developing countries, public investment accounts for the bulk of total fixed investment, reflecting for the most part the central role played by governments in providing adequate infrastructure. While the rationale for extensive public sector investment activity at the theoretical level is generally linked to market failure and social objectives, at the operational level many governments are also involved in more commercially oriented investment activities. As a consequence, capital expenditure, together with associated operations and maintenance and debt servicing costs, often account for a large proportion of total public expenditure. This note reviews some key issues in public investment decision making from both the microeconomic and macroeconomic perspectives.

Project Appraisal

Irrespective of the type of investment activity undertaken, governments should use a systematic set of procedures to appraise alternative investments. For public investments that are essentially commercial in nature and for whose output the market is competitive, governments should follow the principles of private cost-benefit analysis. Otherwise, the appropriate decision rule should reflect social costs and benefits.

Social cost-benefit analysis

While there are a number of other decision rules (benefit/cost ratio, internal rate of return, and payback period) that can be used in applying social cost-benefit analysis, the **net present value rule** is the most reliable. According to this rule, a government should undertake all projects that generate a positive net present value (NPV). Within the limits of a fixed budget, however, governments should choose a subset of available projects in such a way that the NPV generated by available resources is maximized. The appropriate discount rate is the social opportunity cost of capital. Determining this is, however, controversial, given the usual divergence between the social rate of time preference and the rate of return on investment owing to capital market distortions. In practice, the tendency is to choose this key parameter to reflect market interest rates. There are also a number of other issues that arise in imparting a "social" (as distinct from private) dimension to the computation of net present value.

Valuation of nonmarketed commodities

Markets and hence prices may not exist for the output generated by many public sector investment activities, thus complicating the economic evaluation of such undertakings. In these cases, appropriate imputation of the value of output is necessary, as for example with clean air, lives saved, penetration roads, or natural beauty. Indirect methods of valuation, including the use of information gathered in related markets or from **willingness-to-pay** studies, can be used to estimate the gain in **consumer surplus,** and hence to approximate the value of additional output associated with a project.

Shadow prices

The rationale behind the use of shadow prices is that market prices may reflect significant distortions, such as those related to taxes and subsidies, externalities, or regulation (of prices, wages, interest rates, and the exchange rate, for example). When this is the case, market prices do not reflect scarcity values of inputs and outputs. Appropriate adjustments should therefore be made. In practice, however, the computation of shadow prices can be a complex and time-consuming process. One approach involves the calculation of **opportunity costs.** For example, the shadow price of an input to a particular project depends on the extent to which supply and demand elsewhere is affected. In essence, this approach attempts to ensure that a project is undertaken only if resources are transferred from lower-value to higher-value uses. While by nature a highly detailed process, the opportunity cost approach is most practicable when only a few markets are significantly affected by a project. More sophisticated approaches—which attempt to take into account a much wider range of market interactions—have information requirements that are often difficult to meet in practice.

Risk

Private cost benefit analysis takes into account the risk and uncertainties associated with projects. It is often argued that this is less important with social cost-benefit analyses, since the government undertakes a wide array of projects which provides effective pooling of risks. An unexpectedly bad project will likely be compensated for by a surprisingly good one. To the extent that public projects are divisible and separable, there is an element of truth in this argument. However, in reality the public sector invests in some lumpy projects, often with close links between them and with other smaller projects—for example, building a dam to generate electricity may be closely related to the provision of irrigation. Moreover, projects share many of the same risks—for example, an exchange rate depreciation or an increase in world interest rates raises project costs across the board.

Like the private sector, the government should choose an efficient portfolio of projects: that is, one for which the overall return cannot be raised without entailing unacceptably high risk. A number of options are available to aid judgment in this area. **Sensitivity analysis** shows how the NPV of a project changes with the value of a given variable in the analysis. While sensitivity analysis is useful in determining the degree of risk to which a project is exposed, it does not provide a basis for choosing among risky alternatives. **Risk analysis** is a more complicated form of sensitivity analysis, in which variables that are regarded as the principal sources of risk are assigned probability distributions defined over the range of possible outcomes for each. Risk analysis suggests comparing the **expected** NPVs of alternative projects. **Discount rate adjustments** are another popular technique used to deal with the problem of risk. Riskier projects, it is argued, should be discounted at a higher rate. A **risk premium** can be derived using information on the relationship between market rates of return and risk (based upon the capital asset pricing model, for example). However, this assumes a large private investment sector and well-organized capital markets in which risk is constantly being priced. While this is a good assumption for a financially developed economy, it is less applicable for most developing countries.

Distributional implications

Public investment projects often have distributional implications, and an issue arises as to the extent to which these should be reflected in investment decisions. One view is that distributional concerns are most efficiently addressed through taxes and transfers, and that such concerns should not impact upon cost-benefit analysis. However, if the government's ability to redistribute is limited by the range of available instruments or their potentially adverse efficiency consequences, a second-best case can be made for taking the distributional consequences of projects into account—either by explicitly attaching distributional weights to costs and benefits in computing NPV or by making less precise judgements about the impact of projects on inequality—and for deliberately pursuing distributional objectives explicitly through project choice. There are, however, limits to the concessions that can be made in terms of project choice and forgone efficiency to accommodate distributional objectives.

Public Investment Programming

In most developing countries, the aggregate cost of projects having a positive net present value far exceeds resource availability. A choice must therefore be made among alternative projects. The project appraisal techniques described above suggest that projects should be chosen to maximize their combined NPV. However, the size and composition of the public investment program (PIP) must also reflect macroeconomic and institutional constraints. It is the aim of public investment programming to maximize the NPV of the chosen projects subject to resource availability **and** these additional constraints.

Macroeconomic constraints

A PIP must be consistent with medium-term growth, balance of payments and inflation objectives. The note on ***Public Expenditure, Stabilization, and Structural Adjustment*** discusses the macroeconomic impact of expenditure in general terms. The principal conclusions are that growth is more a function of the composition of public expenditure than its level—with public investment being one of the main positive influences—and that the implications of public spending for stabilization policy are largely a policy choice, which reflects the stance of fiscal and monetary policies. In the context of a PIP, these general conclusions can be expanded upon.

Growth and stabilization

While most public investment probably makes a positive contribution to growth, some is clearly not very productive; as a consequence, the relationship between public investment and growth is generally much weaker than might be expected. For this reason, a high quality PIP should focus on those projects and sectors where investment is likely to be most productive. Structural adjustment programs often specify priority projects (such as infrastructure) and sectors (like export activities). To emphasize the importance attached to some investments, it is becoming increasingly common to define a **core investment program**. This also serves to protect such investments when public expenditure has to be scaled back as part of an adjustment effort.

Ideally, a PIP should be built up from the bottom, beginning with the most productive projects. However, in practice, an overall investment program tends to be purged of the least productive projects, and interest groups are typically more successful in preventing their pet projects from being excluded from the core than in arguing for their inclusion. The quality of the PIP suffers as a result. Moreover, to the extent that the core is identified only once a scaling bank of spending has begun, the cutting of both core and noncore projects before prioritization takes on any urgency is clearly harmful.

Project financing can have important balance of payments implications. Where the PIP has large external financing needs, the impact on external debt service costs should be taken into account. The nature of the financing is clearly important; the more concessional the borrowing terms, the less binding will be the foreign exchange constraint. Moreover, to the extent that the PIP is geared toward efficient import substitution and export activities, debt service capacity will be increased. Project financing can also have inflationary consequences if excessive monetary expansion is involved, but again productive investments can ease inflationary pressures as long as private investment has not been crowded out in the process.

Fiscal and monetary policies

While active fiscal and monetary policies can be used to ensure stable growth, a PIP affects the scope for discretionary financial policy to a greater degree than implied by the direct impact of the investment involved. Capital projects usually give rise to additional budgetary costs in the form of operations and maintenance requirements—see the note on *Operations and Maintenance* for details. These requirements have to be taken into account, and it is for this reason that many developing countries formulate a **development budget** that explicitly captures all project costs. Offsetting these additional expenditures, however, there should be revenues generated by new economic activity. In addition to its domestic financing needs, a PIP can affect monetary policy in other ways. For example, projects are often financed by commodity aid, the domestic proceeds from the sale of which are placed in blocked counterpart funds to await donor authorization for their utilization. The resulting monetary contraction and the compensating expansion when these accounts are unblocked can complicate monetary management.

Institutional constraints

The size and structure of a PIP has to reflect the **responsiveness of the private sector**. Overall investment requirements of the economy should be apportioned between the private and the public sector on the basis of the comparative advantage of each and the interrelationships between the two. With a weak private sector, the public sector will inevitably have a larger role. But at the same time, the **administrative capacity of the public sector** may be weak. Projects vary in the amount of administrative resources required for their implementation and monitoring. Complexity of implementation, together with demanding physical and financial monitoring requirements, can represent binding constraints on project choice. **Distributional objectives** that cannot be described in sufficient detail to precisely weight benefits and costs as part of the microeconomic project exercise can instead be characterized more generally in terms of acceptable and unacceptable outcomes. In this regard, a PIP may build in sectoral priorities not only to redress structural bottlenecks within an economy, but also to meet broader distributional objectives (to redistribute from the urban to the agricultural sector, for example).

Practical considerations

Public investment programming is complex, since the three elements of the programming problem—the set of worthwhile investment projects, the macroeconomic and institutional constraints, and the available resources—are interdependent. For example, an initially affordable investment program may promote growth but threaten macroeconomic stability, in which case financial policies will have to be tightened; this in turn reduces resource availability, so that the investment program is no longer affordable. A less ambitious program may lead to stable growth, but because it elicits a poor private sector response the growth rate will be low and the scope for redistribution limited. A somewhat more ambitious program may adequately meet growth, stabilization, and distributional objectives, but necessary fiscal tightening (say through labor shedding) may undermine the capacity to administer the program. The problem is clearly an iterative one; moreover, it may not converge without conceding some objectives.

The type of public investment programming undertaken by the World Bank in the context of public expenditure reviews attempts to reflect the above linkages. In practice, however, this is often not feasible. Thus examples of best practice include detailed information on the major projects and sectors, an estimate of the resource envelope, an assessment of institutional limitations, and (sometimes) an outline of the macroeconomic framework. However, the macroeconomic framework is rarely specified in great detail, and focuses mainly on the growth-investment-savings linkage as an input into determining the resource envelope. Moreover, there is not much explicit "programming". Rather, country authorities are urged to draw up a PIP specifying core projects, and the Bank then reviews the outcome in light of the above considerations. The emphasis is very much on improving the capacity of countries to undertake such an exercise themselves. It may therefore be some time before public investment programming fully reflects available information and analytical techniques.

Country Illustrations

Capturing ecological and environmental benefits in project analysis in Nigeria

The quality of soil of the arid zones of northern Nigeria has been threatened by the lack of protection against natural forces. Consumption of fuelwood, land clearance, and pressures on the land from farm cattle grazing have resulted in a substantial depletion of the tree stocks that serve as an environmental equilibrating factor. The lack of windbreaks in the region results in multiple environmental problems. Chief among these are (i) loss of topsoil due to wind erosion, (ii) reduced soil moisture and greater surface evaporation, as a result of both the lack of shade increasing wind velocities, (iii) reduced natural soil nutrient recycling, (iv) decline in soil fertility as a result of the diversion of crop residues and animal dung for fuel, (v) greater and more frequent storm damage to crops, especially immediately following seed germination, and (vi) gully erosion. Afforestation efforts would reduce current rates of soil erosion, and hence improve agricultural productivity over the medium term. Shelterbelts, a linear planting of six to eight rows of trees, spaced 200 meters apart, could each protect approximately 40 square kilometers of farmland.

Traditionally, cost-benefit analysis of afforestation projects has concentrated on the direct benefits of the tree products themselves. When this traditional methodology is applied to the arid zones of northern Nigeria, the net present value is negative. Clearly, however, a proper project appraisal should value the indirect and external ecological benefits of such an afforestation project, especially since available evidence indicates that well-designed and properly oriented shelterbelts have significant impacts on crop yields. In addition to the direct benefits of the tree products themselves (including firewood, fruit, and poles), a thorough cost-benefit analysis should value (i) the benefits of preventing further declines in soil fertility and hence agricultural productivity, (ii) the benefits of improving current soil fertility, and (iii) the benefits of an increased availability of fodder. Under highly conservative assumptions about ecological benefits, allowance for the indirect and external benefits (together with the direct benefits) raises the net present value of such a project substantially. This reflects the fact that shelterbelts, through their effects on agricultural productivity and despite the fact that their impact is felt from seven to ten years after planting, can raise gross farm income by 15 to 25 percent. Even under alternative assumptions, the net present value of the project remains high (Table 1).

Table 1. Nigeria: Net Present Value of Shelterbelts
(In naira per hectare farmed, using a 10 percent discount rate)

	Net Present Value
Wood benefits only	-95
Base case—indirect benefits added	170
Low-yield, high-cost case	110
High-yield case	221

Source: Anderson (1989).

Public investment programming in Madagascar

A three-year public investment program was established in February 1989. The PIP called for a significant real expansion of public investment along with a reorientation of investment toward infrastructure and an improvement in project quality. The financing of the PIP is on highly concessional terms, with about two-thirds financed through foreign aid—of which 40 percent is in grants and 60 percent is concessional loans—while 16 percent is to be domestically financed by the National Economic Development Fund and the remainder by other loan sources. Because of the magnitude of the PIP and the desire to ensure that PIP implementation and allocation proceed according to schedule, the government established a task force to monitor public investment expenditure systematically and regularly. At the same time, in recognition of the potential administrative and implementation difficulties that might be encountered, the government established a trigger mechanism which would allow for a mid- (as well as medium-) term adjustment of public investment expenditures and hence the overall financial operations of the government. Under this mechanism, if public investment was less than FMG 209.0 billion for the first six months of 1989 (compared to an annual investment program of FMG 470.7 billion), or if the sectoral allocations diverged significantly from the planned allocations, the government would reduce its public investment program for the rest of 1989 and for the 1990–92 period accordingly. This mechanism was triggered, and a revised PIP put in place, after six months. While a core PIP was never a part of the strategy, the downscaling of the original PIP was consistent with such a concept.

Bibliography

Anderson, Dennis, "Economic Aspects of Afforestation and Soil Conservation Projects," in Gunter Schramm and Jeremy J. Warford, eds., *Environmental Management and Economic Development* (John Hopkins University Press for the World Bank, 1989).

Harberger, A. C., *Project Evaluation* (London: Macmillan, 1972).

United Nations Industrial Development Organization (UNIDO), *Guidelines for Project Evaluation* (New York: United Nations, 1972).

Social Expenditure, Income Distribution, and Poverty

XV. Health

Kalpana Kochhar

Which health needs should be met by the public sector?

Can the efficiency of public health care services be improved?

Is there scope for targeting primary health care more directly toward the poor?

To what extent can user charges be imposed for public health care services in developing countries?

Public expenditure on health care ranges from about US$6 per capita in low-income developing countries to about US$600 per capita in high-income industrial countries. Health expenditure is highly correlated both with income levels—the income elasticity is usually well in excess of unity—and health indicators, such as life expectancy. From an economic standpoint, adequate health care improves **human capital** by strengthening an individual's capacity to work productively. To improve health standards, developing countries will have to generate resources to support larger health sectors. At the same time, they have to ensure that existing programs are effectively tailored to health needs. In this connection, developing countries face quite different problems from those that raise so much concern in industrial countries. In particular, the sources and implications of the rapid growth of expenditure on health care, and the role of insurance arrangements (both for consumers and producers) in explaining this growth, are of little immediate relevance to developing countries. While developing countries should seek to avoid the problems faced by industrial countries as their health sectors expand, the overriding concern should be with the efficient and equitable delivery of basic health services.

The Market for Health Care

In a properly functioning private market, the demand for health care would reflect consumer needs, preferences and willingness to pay, with unpredictable and potentially life-threatening contingencies provided for through efficient insurance markets. Distributional concerns would be addressed by income transfers, guaranteeing an appropriate degree of equality of access to health care. Competition among suppliers would ensure that least-cost methods of responding to health demands are adopted.

The characteristics of health care may, however, prevent a private market from functioning properly. A number of health services have public good characteristics, and consumers cannot be directly charged because others benefit from them once provided. Disease control and health education are examples. The private sector will not provide such services. Other services confer external benefits on individuals other than the direct consumers, for example, immunization against infectious illness. The demand for such services will be too low in a private market. Medical ethics make competition in supply difficult, and while the medical profession is regulated, information about medical competence is often denied to consumers. The medical profession can take advantage of less well-informed consumers to supply services on the basis of the profit they generate, rather than medical need; or they may collude with better-informed consumers to provide high-cost, discretionary services, and increase profits at the expense of insurance companies and, ultimately, consumers at large. As medical costs escalate, the poor and the chronically sick are excluded from insurance markets (see below), with the result that their health needs are not met and quality health care becomes the preserve of well-off insured consumers.

The failure of private markets for health care justifies government intervention. But the form this intervention should take is less clear. A fully subsidized public health system could clearly compensate for all the market failures just described. But it would be costly, and dispensing with the market mechanism entirely makes it difficult to regulate demand and contain costs effectively. Moreover, attempts to contain costs manifest themselves not so much in improvements in efficiency but more in a lowering of quality. In designing an appropriate health care system, the challenge is to identify: those activities that should be provided by the public sector and ensure efficiency in their provision; those activities that can be provided by the private sector but with a government subsidy; and those that can be left to the private sector. The private sector should be regulated to compensate for informational asymmetry, and especially the lack of consumer knowledge about health care.

Public Health Care in Developing Countries

Public goods are normally provided directly by the public sector and financed from general revenue. To the extent that a significant part of the health care budget in developing countries is devoted to providing **primary health care** with public good characteristics, it is appropriate that this should be in the public domain. Moreover, given that the external benefits associated with the private components of primary health care—such as immunization, pre- and post-natal care, and family planning services—are large, it is probably appropriate that these too are provided by the public sector.

The main problem in developing countries is that not only are financial resources limited and basic needs not met, but health care delivery is also inefficient. While improving the efficiency in resource allocation is desirable, there are constraints. It is not easy to determine how resources should be allocated in the health sector, as the benefits are difficult to identify and measure and often only the most obvious expenditure imbalances will reveal themselves. But, even these may not be easily reversible. For example, the health care system may exhibit **middle-class capture**, whereby better-off consumers use their influence to ensure that their nonbasic needs are met. There may therefore be strong political opposition to reducing the services used by the middle class. Moreover, it may not even be desirable. Given that the overall quality of supply may be higher because the better-off take more interest in the performance of the health service and willingly pay the bulk of the taxes which finance it, an expenditure reallocation toward primary health care could also harm the poor, because the quality of basic health services suffers. While there is in most cases some scope to improve efficiency and simultaneously target health care benefits more effectively to the poor by diverting resources to primary health care, there may be limits to what can be achieved.

Many higher-level services are closer to private goods in character in that the benefits accrue principally to the consumer. However, to the extent that they give rise to external benefits—and a wide range of **secondary health care** services, mainly of a curative nature, can be associated with general improvements in productivity and living standards—there may be a case for a subsidy. But there is no reason in principle why these services should be provided by the public sector, and as the health system develops to encompass such services, the private sector can be encouraged to provide them. Where the public sector already has this responsibility, or where there are impediments to appropriate private sector development, the public sector should charge for these services with a view to imposing some market discipline on demand and costs. One reason why public provision of higher-level services may be preferred to private provision is that public ownership can be a relatively efficient form of regulation. This is an argument that opponents of privatization of public monopolies commonly voice, having observed the problems of regulated private markets (see the note on *Privatization*). Another obstacle to the development of a private health care market, especially in developing countries, is inadequate insurance markets.

Health Insurance

The private market for health insurance is subject to both **adverse selection** and **moral hazard** problems. Adverse selection describes a failure of the market because good risks (healthy people) will drop out of the market if charged an insurance premium that reflects average risk, thus raising the premium which in turn leads to further withdrawals. In the end, the market collapses because only bad risks want to purchase insurance but premia are prohibitive. Moral hazard describes a failure of the market because people take insufficient care to prevent health problems, and spend too much correcting those they do have knowing that they have insurance coverage. This causes costs and premia to escalate, compounding adverse selection and accelerating market collapse. These problems can emerge in the insurance markets of both industrial and developing countries. However, in most developing countries, the main problem is the limited availability of private insurance.

While private insurance markets may not be extensive in developing countries, there are alternative ways of pooling risk. Replicating developments in industrial countries, insurance could be employer based. However, this would limit insurance to the formal sector, which would be inequitable. Although community-based insurance could provide for some extension of coverage, the public sector may have to provide wider coverage to ensure equality of access to health care. To the extent that the public sector could be left with the relatively bad risks, it may instead make publicly provided insurance up to some minimum level compulsory. However, while there are examples of public insurance to secure access to private services—including health care—direct public provision is often judged a more manageable alternative.

User Charges

As indicated above, the public good characteristic of many public health services limits the application of user charges. However, where there is a less-compelling case for public intervention, user charges may promote efficiency in public production without conceding distributional objectives. In particular, to the extent that consumers can be distinguished by relevant characteristics (the poor, lactating mothers, the disabled, the elderly, etc.) **personalized prices** can be used to pursue both objectives (see the note on *Pricing and Cost Recovery* for further discussion).

Even where there is a strong case for charging, however, it may have to be implemented with caution. For example, efforts may be needed to educate consumers so that they appreciate the private benefits of health services thereby increasing their willingness to pay. For this reason, cost recovery may in the first instance focus on curative rather than preventive health care (see the discussion of rural health care in Benin below, for an illustration). Administrative considerations may also point to a more intensive cost recovery effort in urban areas than in rural areas. In both cases, cost recovery is likely to support distributional objectives. At the moment, user fees cover only a small part of health costs in developing countries. However, evidence from willingness-to-pay studies suggests that the scope for cost recovery is large in the case of many services.

Country Illustration

Rural health care in Benin

The design of a rural health project in the Pahou region of Benin provides for the cross-subsidization of preventive health services from the proceeds of curative health services. User charges are collected for curative services, including charges for visits and the sale of pharmaceuticals. The preventive health care program includes, *inter alia*, routine home visits for pre-natal and post-natal care, distribution of oral rehydration packets, and provision of malaria prophylaxis. Because the benefits of preventive health care accrue only gradually over time, the willingness of villagers to pay for such services was initially limited, although clearly present. However, it was decided to provide such services free of charge, given that the benefits of the program greatly exceeded its costs. At the same time, it was recognized that the success of the program would eventually increase willingness to pay for such services, and the subsidy element could and would be gradually reduced. Thus the project in Pahou was able to address a difficult financing problem through user charges for relatively inelastically demanded curative services, while simultaneously addressing difficulties related to inadequate awareness of preventive health care benefits.

Bibliography

de Ferranti, David, "Paying for Health Services in Developing Countries: An Overview," Working Paper 721 (Washington: World Bank, 1985).

Griffin, Charles C., "User Charges for Health Care in Principle and Practice," PHN Technical Note 87–16 (Washington: World Bank, 1987).

Jimenez, Emmanuel, *Pricing Policy in Social Sectors: Cost Recovery for Education and Health in Developing Countries* (Baltimore: Johns Hopkins University Press, 1987).

XVI. Education

G.A. Mackenzie

Why does the government have a dominant role in the provision of education?
How should education expenditure be financed? What is the scope for user fees?
Can the efficiency of public education provision be improved?

Education expenditure at the general government level typically represents from 4.5 percent to 7 percent of GDP in industrial countries. In developing countries, education expenditure ranges from 2.5 percent to 7.5 percent of GDP, and represents a smaller share of GDP on average than in industrial countries. As a share of total expenditure at the general government level, education expenditure often exceeds 10 percent.

Most governments are direct providers of educational services on a large scale, and at the primary and secondary levels, at least, their share of the total supply of such services typically exceeds 90 percent. In addition to this direct role in the market for education, governments influence the demand for educational services by their provision of scholarships, grants and living allowances for students, through decisions regarding fees and tuition charges, and by the regulatory framework they establish for private education. Because public schools and colleges are often administered at the regional or local level, and because the local revenue base may not be sufficient to finance expenditure requirements, the government's role in education raises important issues concerning intergovernmental financial relations and coordination (see the note on *Transfers to Local Government* for a general discussion of these issues).

Objectives of Education Expenditure

The dominant role governments tend to play in the market for education reflects not only the importance governments have attached to what is taught but also special economic aspects of education.

Education expenditure as an investment

Expenditure on education may have a large element of consumption, but its character as an investment in **human capital** is especially important. One special feature of an educational investment is its long gestation period: thus, the expansion of the primary school system does not yield its returns until after 6-8 years; a graduate of medicine represents an investment of perhaps 20 or more years of formal education. The long gestation period required for education to pay off and the limited opportunities to borrow against prospective human capital imply that education costs are usually entirely or substantially subsidized. This also explains why certain kinds of vocational and professional training are provided by employers through apprenticeship programs.

Externalities

Education also offers wide-ranging external benefits to society. By improving the quality of the work force, education increases the rate of return on other investments and promotes growth; education provides the scope for greater specialization of labor and can facilitate more outward-looking economic development; and education is viewed by many governments as a means of promoting national identity, loyalty, and generally more social patterns of behavior. Because these external benefits do not accrue entirely to the student, there is a further rationale for the government to subsidize at least part of education costs. However, governments tend to supply educational services directly, rather than subsidize the operations of private schools. It is also worth noting that many of the objectives of public policy in the educational field could be achieved indirectly through subsidies and grants to the private sector rather than through the direct provision of educational services. But the direct provision of educational services allows governments to exercise more control over curriculum content and educational standards, and may therefore be viewed as a relatively efficient form of regulation.

Evidence on the rate of return to education

One of the most important conclusions to be drawn from the substantial body of literature on the economic aspects of education is that the returns to investment in education are generally high, particularly in less developed countries where the supply of educated persons is relatively small. These studies typically take into account both the direct cost of education—that is, teachers' salaries, the cost of classroom aids and other educational materials, and capital costs—as well as the indirect costs—mainly the income forgone by the student during the period spent in school or college; they do not as a rule attempt to measure the benefits of education other than the higher income that is typically associated with an increase in the number of years of formal education. The private rates of return to education are always higher than the social rates of return, because the private calculation excludes that part of the cost of education financed by the government. Another common finding is that the social rate of return to primary education is greater than that to higher education, because costs per student of higher education are typically a large multiple of the costs per student of primary education. In anglophone Africa, for example, the unit cost of higher education has been estimated to be 50 times that of primary education—see Table 1.

Table 1. Public Expenditure per Student on Education and Enrollment Ratios, Major World Regions, around 1980

Region	Expenditure per Student as a Multiple of Primary Level Expenditure		Enrollment Ratio (In percent)			Number of Countries
	Secondary	Higher	Primary	Secondary	Higher	
Developing countries	2.9	26.4	75	23	7	74
Anglophone Africa	2.8	51.1	77	17	1	16
Francophone Africa	4.9	27.7	46	14	2	18
South Asia	2.3	14.9	71	19	4	4
East Asia and Pacific	1.8	10.7	87	43	9	6
Latin America	2.9	9.8	90	44	12	19
Middle East and North Africa	14.0	75.0	82	36	9	11
Industrial countries	1.1	2.2	100	80	21	20

Source: World Bank.

The incidence of education expenditure

The incidence of education expenditure—that is, the relationship between expenditure per family and family income—can vary quite substantially from one level of education to another. Thus, at the primary level, public expenditure may have a progressive incidence, because expenditure per pupil is constant regardless of the level of income of the pupil's family. This observation needs to be qualified, however, to the extent that the enrollment ratio rises with the level of family income, and to the extent that local governments spend more on students from affluent neighborhoods. Students at higher levels of education tend to come from wealthier families, particularly in developing countries, because in spite of the large share of direct costs paid by the government in such countries the private cost of higher education will typically be prohibitive for students from poor families. As a result, a relatively large part of the government's education budget benefits a small number of persons from wealthier families, which has a significant regressive impact.

Implications for public policy

Capital market imperfections and positive externalities that may be associated with education imply that public intervention in the market for education has the potential both to improve allocative efficiency and to achieve a more equitable distribution of the direct benefits of education. For example, if the direct provision of education by the government, either free of charge or at highly subsidized rates, keeps more students in school for longer periods, and the return to society from further education is sufficiently high, then allocative efficiency is improved. Similarly, the distribution of income can be made more equal if the government's involvement results in a substantial increase in the enrollment of students from poor families, especially at higher levels.

Financing Education Expenditure

The very substantial costs of universal or widespread public education, and the sizable benefits that education can bestow on the educated in the form of more highly paid and prestigious employment, imply that tuition fees and other charges have a role to play in education financing and in the allocation of resources in the educational sector. Thus, a basic issue that must be addressed is the role of user charges. A related issue is the role of student loan programs in compensating for capital market imperfections.

The role of user charges

Charging fees for public schooling is a highly contentious issue. At the primary level, where such charges might affect a large number of pupils from poor families, the use of fees could have a regressive impact on income distribution and lead to the premature end of schooling. Where practical, these adverse consequences can, however, be avoided through personalized prices (see the note on *Pricing and Cost Recovery* for further discussion). At the higher level, however, there is more scope for using fees to enhance allocative efficiency, increase the resources for education, and produce a more equitable distribution of the benefits of higher education. Whether tuition charges and other fees are an appropriate policy or not again depends on the feasibility of student loan programs and special assistance for students from relatively poor families.

In many developing countries, both equity and efficiency could be enhanced by increasing the share of costs borne by students and their families, provided that assistance were available for the poorer student. The available evidence suggests that there would be little effect on the demand for higher education. The private rate of return to higher education would remain high, and students from wealthier families would not encounter difficulties in financing the extra expenditure. Despite their possibly adverse impact on income distribution, user fees at the primary level have been used to provide pupils with textbooks and other necessary materials that they would not otherwise receive. In a number of countries, user fees are necessary to correct an imbalance between expenditure on teachers' salaries and other goods and services. In some countries, because government expenditures on tertiary education are a large share of the education budget, the introduction of user charges, and the reinvestment of the proceeds, could finance a substantial increase in enrollment at the primary level. The increase in the share of cost borne by the student would also tend to weed out the less well-motivated students, as well as inspire the others, because the cost of failure for the student is increased.

Student loan programs

The absence of a credit market for educational services helps explain why higher education in less developed countries is generally the preserve of the wealthier classes, and accounts for the creation of student loan programs in industrial countries and a number of middle-income developing countries. Such programs can take various forms: the government can confine its participation in the market to providing guarantees to private-sector lending institutions, or it can make loans directly. If loans to students have a grant element, the cost of the loan is typically either borne directly by the budget in the form of a subsidy to the lending institution or implicitly in the form of a below-market rate of interest on government loans.

Student loan programs have the potential to increase the participation in tertiary education of students from poor families and, by increasing the competition for places, may improve educational attainment. These programs can have a significant impact on the distribution of the benefits of education even without a grant element because of the imperfections that characterize the human capital market. Such programs either make very great demands on the administrative capacities of governments or require an efficient and well-functioning financial system or both. As a result, the widespread use of such programs has been confined to a small number of countries. Precisely because investments in education do not create physical collateral, loan delinquency rates in these programs are high.

Efficiency in Education

Allocative efficiency

The evidence of higher social rates of return for primary than for secondary education argues for a shift in expenditure away from the secondary and tertiary levels to the primary level. However, this does not imply that universal primary education should be achieved at the expense of other levels of education. The objective should be to equalize social rates return at the margin. Moreover, this is an objective that should be pursued both between and within programs. Thus, it could be the case that there was over-investment in tertiary programs in the humanities, as evidenced by the fact that their chief accomplishment was producing graduates for an already overstaffed civil service, and under-investment in the sciences and engineering; the appropriate policy would therefore be a shift in resources out of humanities at the tertiary level to science and engineering, and to primary education. Interactions between education and other public expenditure programs should also be taken into account. For example, the mix of programs at the higher level also has important consequences for public sector wage and employment policy when there are pressures on the government to be an **employer of last resort**—see the note on *Public Sector Employment*.

Productive efficiency

Another conclusion that emerges from the literature is the importance of the input mix in education. In particular, there is evidence in many countries whose budgets have been under strain that expenditure on classroom aids and textbooks at the primary level is well below what it should be. Thus, in some African countries, schools with only one textbook per class are far from uncommon. This situation may result from the fact that, with pressure to reduce funding for education, political pressures cushion teachers' salaries from the consequences of budgetary austerity. Another possible explanation is the overcentralization of the educational establishment's managerial process, so that budgetary decisions are not made by those most familiar with students' needs or by those with the incentive or desire to respond to these needs.

Productive efficiency has been enhanced in some countries by the application of modest user charges (textbook fees) at the primary level, and by the devolution of management to local government. Even at the primary level, user charges have apparently not had a large impact on demand for school places and, if spent on the right inputs, can have a significant impact on the rate of return to primary education. It may be required, however, that user charges be earmarked for expenditure on these particular inputs (see the note on *Pricing and Cost Recovery* for further discussion).

Country Illustration

Distribution of education benefits in Brazil

The incidence of public education expenditure in Brazil by income class varies remarkably from one level of schooling to another. At the primary level, where enrollment ratios are about 90 percent, children whose family income is in the lowest decile are estimated to have accounted for 15 percent of total enrollment in 1980, but only 1 percent of total income. Children from families in the top two deciles, with 59 percent of total income, accounted for only 5 percent of total enrollment. Unless the value of expenditure per pupil rises quite strongly with the pupil's family income, Brazil would be spending more on primary education for the poor than for the affluent, and the incidence of expenditure at this level would be highly progressive. At higher levels of education, however, the incidence of public education expenditure becomes less progressive. Thus, at the secondary level, the share of students from poor families falls to 3 percent, and that of students from the most affluent 20 percent increases to 16 percent. At the tertiary level, the degree of progressivity falls even further, because the share of students from the poorest families falls to 1 percent, and the share of the most affluent rises to 48 percent. Overall, however, the incidence of public education expenditure appears to be progressive: expenditure per student rises less rapidly than income. At the same time, there is obvious scope for increasing the degree of progressivity, because the budget for tertiary education absorbs about 45 percent of the total education budget, and its direct benefits accrue disproportionately to the better off.

The Brazilian educational system is also characterized by important regional and institutional disparities in expenditure per pupil at the same educational level. For example, primary-level state schools in the Northeast in 1983 spent, on average, over three times as much per student as municipal schools, and rural schools spent less than urban schools. These disparities reflect the fact that primary education is financed largely at the state and local government level, where the tax base per capita varies substantially across the country, and redistributive grants from the federal government play a relatively limited role.

Although primary school enrollment ratios are high in Brazil, the disparity in expenditures across the country and the high failure rates point to a problem of quality at that level. Moreover, enrollment ratios decline from about 90 percent at the primary level to 20 percent at the secondary level, although evidence suggests that the social rate of return to secondary education is high. Both equity and efficiency considerations suggest that the share of total education resources devoted to the lower education levels be increased. One component of a solution might be the imposition of user charges at higher levels; at the moment, the direct costs of public education are subsidized almost 100 percent.

Bibliography

Psacharopoulos, George, "Education and Development: A Review," *The World Bank Research Observer*, 3, 1988.

The Financing of Education in Developing Countries: An Exploration of Policy Options (Washington: World Bank, 1986).

XVII. Pensions

Robert Holzmann

What is the appropriate structure of public pensions?

Does pension provision have adverse effects on the labor market and national savings?

How should public pensions be financed?

What is the likely impact of population aging on pension costs?

The large and rising share of GDP devoted to public pension programs, amounting at present to some 10 percent in industrial countries and about 5 percent in a number of middle-income countries, renders the control of program outlays an important public expenditure policy objective in these countries. However, pension reform has proven to be difficult. Radical restructuring is rare, and reforms have for the most part been limited to modifying existing pension schemes. The reason for this difficulty is that current pension provisions tend to be structured in a way that confers rights which governments have been reluctant to deny. This note explains why programs have developed in this way, describes some of the problems with which they are associated, and discusses the issues that arise in designing new programs and reforming old ones.

Institutional Aspects of Public Pension Programs

Rationale for public provision

Three arguments are generally advanced to explain government intervention in the provision of pension benefits. The first argument emphasizes the absence of efficient private provisions due to **market failure.** In countries with rudimentary financial systems, this relates to the lack of saving instruments that offer a guaranteed real return. An adequate annuity market would help insure against the uncertainty of an individual's life expectancy; therefore, inefficient or limited annuity markets justify public intervention. The pooling of all risk groups in one mandatory public pension scheme overcomes problems associated with **adverse selection,** where a private market will inevitably collapse because only people who anticipate an above-average life span will want to purchase insurance. The second argument is based upon **paternalism**; even if actuarially fair annuities are offered by private insurance markets, individuals may be myopic about saving and therefore not save enough for retirement. This saving shortfall may be due to a short planning horizon or to a high individual intertemporal discount rate. The third argument contends that even in the absence of market failure and myopic behavior, a public pension program can be used as a welfare-enhancing instrument of **income redistribution** over individual life cycles, between individuals and across generations.

Public pension systems

The two main objectives of pension arrangements are **poverty alleviation** and **income replacement.** The former guarantees that retirees maintain a level of income that enables them to achieve at least a minimum standard of living; the latter ensures that, on and through retirement, there is a link between their pre-retirement and post-retirement standards of living. The first objective is addressed by flat-rate benefits; the second objective is met by earnings-related benefits. These two objectives correspond closely to two alternative models of pension provision: the universal model and the social insurance model.

In the **universal model**, flat-rate benefits are provided either to all residents or citizens above a certain age, irrespective of income and employment status, or else as flat-rate benefits at means-tested minimum levels. The benefits are typically financed by general government revenue. The universal model has been adopted in only a few high-income countries and is often supplemented by an earnings-related pension scheme. In the **social insurance model**, benefits are related to former earnings and contribution periods. This system is mandatory for some or all occupational groups and the benefits are usually financed by contributions from the earnings of the insured. Earnings-related schemes remain the prevailing system for providing retirement income in industrial countries. This system can also be found in some Latin American countries, with varying degrees of coverage, and in most developing countries for government employees, including military personnel. In a number of developing countries (in particular, the francophone countries in North Africa), salaried employees in the formal sector are often covered by a public pension scheme of the social insurance type. In the anglophone developing countries of Africa and Asia, pension provision is more likely to reflect a voluntary agreement between employers and employees, usually set up as a **provident fund arrangement**, whereby pensions reflect accumulated contributions that are invested by the provident fund administration, usually in government bonds, housing loans, or other loans to public sector agencies. However, the majority of employees in developing countries are not covered by a pension plan, and rely instead on their own savings, the extended family and community support during retirement (see the note on *Poverty and Social Security* for further discussion of safety nets in developing countries).

Economic Aspects of Public Pension Programs

Effects on labor markets

It has been suggested that the provision of public pensions has a significant impact on labor supply. However, for the younger age groups it is difficult to separate the effects of pensions from those of other taxes and transfers. If contributions are viewed as a tax (because workers are short-sighted and ignore accumulated entitlements) or if benefits are unrelated to current taxes (as in universal schemes), they should affect labor supply in exactly the same way as do taxes and transfers. But, if workers recognize the value of accumulated future entitlements, these effects are reduced. The **tax-benefit link** is often cited as an advantage of the insurance approach to pension provision, and is used as an argument for a closer relation between contributions and benefits. A close tax-benefit link should also lead to fairly orderly retirement decisions of elderly workers. However, actual programs differ as a result of varying eligibility rules, replacement rate formulas, and indexation provisions that yield diverse financial implications of working an extra year at close to retirement age. Empirical studies show that these financial implications have a significant impact on labor force participation of the elderly.

Effects on savings

Public pension programs operate essentially on a **pay-as-you-go (PAYG)** basis; that is, a working generation directly finances the benefits of the contemporaneous retired generation. This contrasts with the funded provision common in the private sector, under which each active generation builds up its own stock of assets that it then draws down after retirement. The establishment of a PAYG system could affect the saving and dissaving rates of active and retired generations respectively. The active generation could reduce its saving rate, because the presence of the system implies a reduced need to save for retirement, while the retired generation might reduce its dissaving to reflect the benefit received from the pension system. The net effect is likely to be negative because, as the pension system matures, it will transfer income from the working generation, with a high propensity to save, to the retired generation, with a lower propensity to save. However, the effect is also likely to be small, and only temporary during the growth phase of the program. In the long run, the national saving rate should return to close to its pre-pension level.

Selected Policy Issues

Pension financing

The financing of public pension programs raises three interrelated but distinct issues: (i) the choice between contributions and general revenue financing; (ii) the split in the contribution burden between employees and employers; and (iii) the role of reserve funds. The first issue relates to the type of benefits provided. Flat-rate benefits are not linked to previous income levels, and it is therefore argued that financing should be provided from general revenues. Earnings-related benefits, on the other hand, require earnings-related contributions, as in the case of private pensions. However, since the link between contributions and benefits in public pension programs is usually not very precise, it is often argued that the implied welfare component should be financed from general government revenue. Further arguments for partial budgetary financing take into account that the low level of earnings of many of those insured prevents a full contribution burden and that the costs of shifts in demographic structure, and in particular population aging, should not be borne only by the insured.

The second issue is more political than economic. There is in principle little difference whether employers or employees are formally responsible for paying pension contributions. Total labor costs are the same in either case. But if labor markets are inflexible, the distinction may matter, at least in the short run. The higher employers' contributions that are a common feature of pension programs result primarily from voter-oriented political behavior that anticipates less resistance to an increase in employers' contributions. However, the resulting misperception of the true costs of public pension provision may be partly responsible for unsustainable extensions of benefits and coverage that have been demanded in some countries (see below).

The third issue is linked with the choice between PAYG and funded systems. Almost all public pension programs started out as fully or at least partially funded systems, accumulating reserves during the start-up period. However, the reserve funds rapidly grew to levels that brought forth demands for additional benefit increases or delays in contribution rate increases. Most public pension programs now operate on a pure PAYG basis with a small liquidity reserve of one to three months' outlays that serves only to cover the time lag between outlays and revenue collection and short-term cyclical factors. However, in some cases there is still a build up of sizable financial reserves—such as those in the United States (accumulated to provide for the retirement of the baby-boom generation) or in some developing countries (accumulated during the start-up phase)—that are as a rule used to finance deficits on the nonpension operations of the government.

As indicated above, public pension funds are usually invested in government bonds. Pension contributions then become a source of captive financing for the government budget. Moreover, since these contributions are forced savings, the government can pay below-market interest rates. Such arrangements have a number of implications. They often encourage governments to spend more than can be justified by reference to the taxable and borrowing capacities of the economy. While this is a criticism more often leveled at PAYG programs, a pension fund invested in government bonds is indistinguishable from a PAYG program, since future pension payments will require higher contributions or taxes. The low interest rate is also distortionary and inhibits the progress of financial liberalization. Ideally, the government should use temporary reserves of pension plans either to create assets, reduce debt, or lower taxes, and thereby provide room to accommodate increased pension expenditure in future years.

Inflation and indexation

An inflationary environment has a substantial impact on public pension programs, and indexation policies can play an important role in sustaining or generating inflationary pressures. Inflation combined with collection lags reduces effective contribution rates and provides strong incentives for employers to delay contribution remittances in the absence of appropriate penalties. If pensions are not indexed to inflation, the living standards of the retired deteriorate. Moreover, adjusting benefits to reflect inflation can combine with collection lags to widen the deficit of the pension program, which in turn can fuel inflation. This phenomenon has been observed in a number of high-inflation countries. Indexation also implies that pensioners receive special protection from the adverse effects of inflation. While the elderly are one of the most vulnerable groups in the population, a more targeted approach to protecting their well being—for example, a flat-rate increase which compensates only the poorest segment fully for the price level change—may be preferable.

Pensions and labor market adjustment

Increasing labor market disequilibria, pressing youth unemployment problems, and employment adjustments in declining industries are issues that are frequently addressed by special early retirement provisions, relaxed rules on eligibility for disability pensions, and a selective lowering of retirement age. Although these measures may mitigate the unemployment problem and related political pressures, they also have a number of drawbacks. First, they are costly. The few available studies indicate that unemployment compensation and retraining schemes, and other specially tailored temporary programs targeted at displaced workers, are more cost effective. Second, these measures may have longer-term financial consequences; for example, early retirees with low initial pensions will have a high poverty risk, requiring further government protection. Third, the measures are difficult to reverse even if the unemployment situation improves.

Population Aging and Long-Term Pension Costs

The cost implications of existing pension programs have become an issue in many industrial countries. In particular, it is now evident that extensions to benefits made in the 1960s and 1970s, when the baby-boom generation was swelling the work force and could absorb the additional taxes and contributions needed to finance them, will be unsustainable when this unusually large age cohort is retired. In a number of countries, benefits have been cut back so as to limit projected tax/contribution increases. It remains to be seen whether more extensive retrenchment will be needed in the future. This experience points to the need for a careful assessment of the long-term cost implications of pension reform. With a PAYG system, these costs are often not evident, since they do not materialize until long after commitments are made. This feature of PAYG can be used to pursue short-term political goals, which in turn exacerbates long-term financing problems. One of the principal advantages of funding is that program costs reflect benefits that are being accrued even if they do not become payable until long into the future; funding therefore embodies financial discipline inherently lacking with PAYG. However, as indicated above, imposing this discipline is a different matter. But there can be no justification for introducing new pension programs—either PAYG or funded—and changing existing programs without taking into account the long-run cost implications of so doing.

Country Illustration

Pension reform in Uruguay

Uruguay's pension plan underwent significant reform in 1979. At the time, it was part of a larger social security system comprising 10 pension funds, 6 unemployment funds, and numerous maternity programs. Social security expenditure amounted to over 10 percent of GDP, one of the highest spending levels in Latin America. Expenditure had grown fairly rapidly over the preceding decade, as the coverage of the social security system in general was extended, and the pension scheme in particular was maturing in the sense that people were retiring with increasingly larger pension rights because of longer service. At the same time, the population was aging and the dependency ratio, as a consequence, increasing.

The principal objectives of the 1979 reforms were to unify the system with a view to rationalizing pension administration, to contain benefit growth, and to broaden the base of the system's finances. The reforms did not achieve full unification, although 75 percent of pension expenditure is now undertaken by three plans managed by the central government. Benefit changes were modest; despite increases in retirement age and the elimination of early retirement provisions, the benefit structure remains highly variable across plans, average pensions are high, and retirement age is still low (60 for men, 55 for women in general, but lower for certain professional groups).

Before 1979, the social security system was financed from a payroll tax levied on employees and employers. Reserves were accumulated only to smooth short-term fluctuations in income and expenditure. Reflecting the level and pattern of expenditure, payroll tax rates were, on average, high and in some cases reached levels (up to 65 percent) that promoted capital-intensive economic activity and generated unemployment. Both the level and dispersion of rates were reduced in 1979, with additional revenue from a broadening of the value-added tax base being transferred to the social security funds. However, during the early 1980s, continued expenditure growth—compounded by rising unemployment and extensive tax evasion, which reduced the payroll tax base—required increases in payroll tax rates that largely reversed the 1979 reductions but without reducing claims on general revenue.

Bibliography

Mackenzie, G.A., "Social Security Issues in Developing Countries: The Latin American Experience," *IMF Staff Papers*, 3 (Washington: International Monetary Fund, 1988).

OECD, *Reforming Pension Finance*, Social Policy Studies No. 5 (Paris: Organization for Economic Cooperation and Development, 1988).

Thompson, L., "The Social Security Reform Debate", *Journal of Economic Literature*, 21, 1983.

Social Security Programs throughout the World—1987, Research Report No. 61 (Washington: United States Department of Health and Human Services, 1988).

XVIII. The Distributional Impact of Public Expenditure

Richard Hemming and Daniel P. Hewitt

What data are needed to determine the incidence of fiscal policy? Are such data likely to be available in developing countries?

Who benefits most from the provision of cash benefits and other public expenditure programs? Who bears the burden of taxation?

How should income inequality be measured? How redistributive is fiscal policy? Which programs are most beneficial to the poor?

How efficient is redistribution? Is it possible to achieve the same amount of redistribution with lower taxes?

The government has at its disposal a wide range of instruments with which it can influence both the functional and size distribution of income. Nonfiscal policy instruments include employment, wage, and price controls; the main fiscal policy instruments are taxation and cash transfers, although in-kind transfers and benefits from public goods have an effect on individual welfare that has an income equivalent. The focus of attention in this note is the impact of public expenditure on the size distribution of income. However, the redistribution that results from public expenditure should not be analyzed independently of the redistribution associated with the taxes that pay for it. Because a wide range of efficiency and equity objectives are served by both taxation and expenditure, in attempting to gauge the success with which the government meets these objectives it is necessary to examine the tax and expenditure system as a whole. Moreover, a case can also be made for looking at both nonfiscal and fiscal policies together, and reaching a judgment about the overall redistributive impact of government. This, however, is generally beyond the capacity of available methodology and data. Indeed, assessing the redistributive impact of fiscal policy alone presents as yet unresolved methodological difficulties and is hampered by inadequate data.

Fiscal Incidence

The standard approach to measuring the redistributive impact of fiscal policy is based upon fiscal incidence analysis, which involves a comparison of the distribution of income after taking into account taxes, transfers, and benefits with the distribution assumed to hold in their absence. In an ideal world, the methodology of a fiscal incidence study might proceed as follows:

(i) Beginning with the **distribution of original income** (i.e., private income from all sources);

(ii) Allocate taxable cash transfers by income to yield **the distribution of total income**;

(iii) Allocate direct taxes by income to yield the **distribution of post-tax income**;

(iv) Allocate indirect taxes, nontaxable cash transfers and in-kind transfers by income to yield the **distribution of net income**; and

(v) Allocate benefits from public goods by income to yield the **distribution of final income**.

The terms used here to describe different income distributions are not applied universally, and should be regarded as no more than labels to distinguish between the various income concepts employed.

While this methodology might seem straightforward, the only distributions that are generally available are those described in (ii) and (iii) from tax records; however, in some cases information is available from expenditure surveys and other sources to construct the distribution described in (iv). Major problems arise in constructing the distributions described in (i) and (v). Much of the concern about the efficiency consequences of government activity (see below) derives from the belief that taxes and transfers affect economic behavior; to derive the distribution of original income these behavioral responses should in principle be taken into account. In most practical applications, however, the distribution of original income differs from the distribution of post-tax income only by the exclusion of direct taxes and cash transfers. The distribution of benefits from public goods, and therefore the distribution of final income, cannot be observed and is either inferred or ignored.

Fiscal incidence studies are generally available only on industrial countries, and even then data limitations often mean that their coverage is incomplete or strong assumptions are required to arrive at meaningful results. Rarely in developing countries are even rudimentary analyses feasible. The focus of attention in this note is mainly fiscal incidence and redistribution in industrial countries. However, if suitable data are available in developing countries, the industrial country studies can be replicated. Moreover, a number of the recurring and especially unintended redistributive implications of policies in industrial countries probably carry over to developing countries, and should influence policy design even in the absence of supporting data.

Tax incidence

The study of tax incidence is one of the most highly developed subfields of public finance, and there is a large measure of agreement as to the broad incidence of most major taxes. Assessment of tax incidence is carried out on a tax-by-tax basis, and sophisticated economic models are sometimes used to determine who actually ends up paying each tax. The final economic incidence often differs quite appreciably from statutory (or legal) incidence. The main conclusion from tax incidence studies undertaken in industrial countries is that income taxes are usually progressive—the proportion of total income paid in tax increases with total income—while consumption taxes are generally regressive—the share of taxation declines with total income. Most countries have a mix of taxes on income and consumption, and overall tax incidence turns out to be roughly proportional—the share of taxation in total income does not change over most of the income range. However, there is some regressivity at lower incomes where consumption taxes dominate, and some progressivity at higher incomes where income tax rates often climb quite steeply.

Transfer incidence

Transfer incidence reflects the distribution of cash and in-kind transfers to individuals. Cash transfers are simply negative taxes, which tend to be highly progressive—implying that they are a decreasing proportion of income—since they are either a flat amount or are targeted toward the poor. When data on transfer receipts are not available these can be assigned on the basis of **entitlements**. However, in many countries there are problems with **low take-up** of benefits—reflecting inadequate information, poor administration, and stigma problems—which often undermine their progressivity. An in-kind transfer refers to the receipt of a good that is available in the private market or could be supplied privately, such as food, housing, health care, and education. The usual procedure is to assign program costs equally to identifiable recipients. As a result, the redistributional impact is reflected in the relationship between income and the use of those benefits. The tendency is for food and housing benefits, together with basic health care and primary education, to be progressive, and in the case of food often highly progressive. However, expenditure on more lavish health care and higher levels of education are biased toward the better-off and are therefore regressive (see the notes on *Price Subsidies, Health Care*, and *Education* for further discussion).

The equivalent treatment of cash and in-kind transfers, while convenient, can be misleading. Because income is fungible, the receipt of a $1 cash transfer can reasonably be valued at the direct cost of providing it, namely $1. This procedure is less valid in the case of in-kind transfers. Recipients may value the receipt of $1 in food at less than $1; the appropriate valuation should reflect **willingness to pay**. The procedure of allocating costs is a response to the fact that willingness to pay is unobservable. However, in adopting this approach, the possibility of a significant divergence between the measured distribution of income and the associated distribution of welfare or utility is being introduced.

Benefit incidence

Public goods have the characteristic of being nonrival in consumption. It is therefore impossible to identify one individual's consumption of the services associated with a public good. It is, however, clear that individual valuations of the benefits derived from public goods will vary; for example, pacifists presumably place little value in the provision of defense services. Allocating these benefits across individuals is therefore difficult, and attempts to do so are very approximate. While some fairly sophisticated procedures have been developed to place individual valuations on public good provision, the most common approach is to assume that incidence is proportional to income and that total benefit equals total cost. Such an assumption is unlikely to be valid. Indirect evidence from voting behavior, survey results, and information on the demand for close substitutes and complements to public goods, suggests that public good provision is most highly valued by the rich. For example, defense services are worth more to property owners, and environmental protection is important to those who engage in outdoor leisure activities. Furthermore, as in the case of in-kind transfers, there is no direct link between total benefits and total cost; available evidence suggests that the former exceeds the latter across a wide range of programs. While these are serious problems, the proportionality assumption is in effect equivalent to treating benefit incidence as unmeasurable and therefore ignoring the impact of public good provision on income distribution.

Net fiscal incidence

Net fiscal incidence refers to the net outcome of tax incidence, transfer incidence, and benefit incidence. Numerous empirical studies suggest that the pattern of incidence is broadly as shown in Chart 1. Taxes are regressive at the lower end of the income scale, broadly proportional over a wide range of middle incomes, and progressive at higher incomes. Cash transfers are very progressive. In-kind transfers are probably fairly progressive at low income levels and possibly regressive at high income levels, but such a conclusion is sensitive to how benefits from such transfers are calculated. Few attempts are made to characterize the incidence of benefits derived from public goods. The combination of taxes and cash transfers is fairly progressive at low income levels, reflecting largely the impact of transfers, and is then more or less proportional—or mildly progressive—over the range of the income distribution where most individuals are located. Taking in-kind transfers into account probably increases progressivity at low incomes but could give rise to some regressivity at higher incomes.

Chart 1. Fiscal Incidence

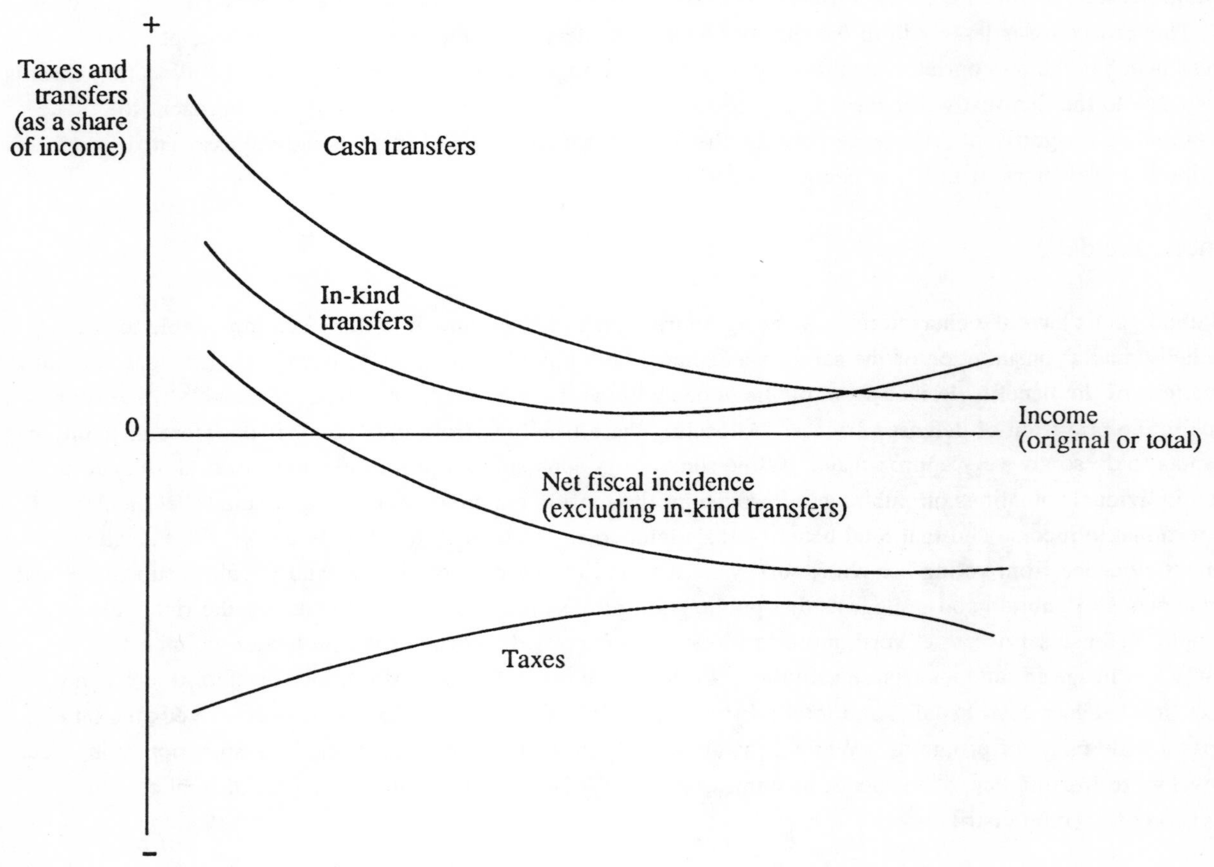

Measuring Inequality

In order to translate the pattern of fiscal incidence described above into a conclusion about the redistributive impact of fiscal policy, it is necessary to make some judgement about changes in distribution. It is common practice for such judgements to be based upon the **Lorenz curve** of the income distribution. The Lorenz curve maps the cumulative share of income received by the bottom X percent of income recipients against X (with X in the range 0-100 percent). An unequal distribution has the characteristic shape shown in Chart 2. The amount of redistribution associated with fiscal policy can be gauged from an examination of shifts in the Lorenz curve. Where Lorenz curves do not intersect, as is the case with Lorenz curves L(x) and L(y) in Chart 2, judgments about redistribution are straightforward. L(x) is unambiguously more equal than L(y). With a given total income, any equalizing (upward) shift of the Lorenz curve can be achieved by redistribution from the richer to poorer individuals. When some income is lost in the process of redistribution—due to administrative costs for example—an upward shift in the Lorenz curve is still equalizing. How the resulting reduction in average income should be reflected in inequality measures is discussed below.

Chart 2. The Lorenz Curve

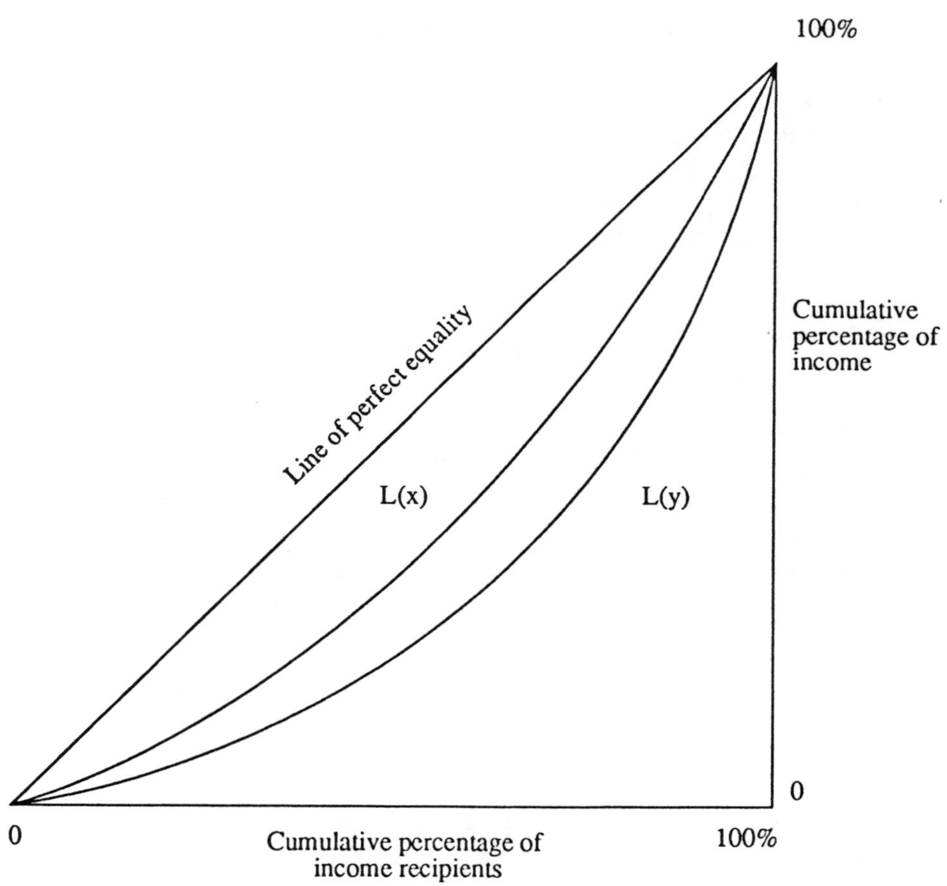

When Lorenz curves intersect—implying that one distribution cannot be arrived at from another purely by transfers from richer to poorer individuals (or vice versa)—it is necessary to attach a welfare weight to different incomes in order to yield a complete ranking of distributions. The problem with many measures of inequality is that they embody implicit weights that may not accord with widely held social values. For example, the popular **Gini coefficient**, which is closely related to the Lorenz curve, applies rank order weights to successively smaller incomes, independently of the size of these incomes. Rather than accepting such a weighting system, or any other implicit set of weights, it has been suggested that a measure based upon an explicit set of welfare weights be used. One such measure—the **Atkinson inequality index**—utilizes an **inequality aversion parameter** to reflect society's dislike of inequality. The Atkinson index measures the proportionate reduction in total income which, if the remaining income were equally distributed, would yield the same level of aggregate welfare as the existing unequal distribution—in a sense, it measures the welfare cost of inequality. While virtually all of the most widely used inequality indices would record an upward shift in the Lorenz curve as a reduction in inequality, different measures can yield conflicting results when Lorenz curves intersect. Moreover, the Atkinson index, and similar indices, need not yield the same ranking of distributions over different values of the inequality aversion parameter. Unfortunately, there is no fully scientific basis for placing values on this parameter, and the usual approach is to compute the index over a fairly wide range of values to test its robustness.

Poverty alleviation is an important aspect of redistribution policy, especially in developing countries. While there is some precedent for regarding concern about poverty as a limiting case of concern about inequality—for example, an extremely large value of the inequality aversion parameter of the Atkinson index implies a concern with the welfare of only the worst-off members of society (the Rawlsian approach to social justice)—it is more common to treat poverty as a quite separate concept from inequality. To integrate the two robs both concepts of part of their meaning, and to describe the bottom Y percent of the income distribution as the poor is generally inappropriate. That is not to say that the distribution of income is not relevant to defining poverty. But there has to be a possibility of eliminating poverty despite the persistence of inequality. Poverty measurement is discussed in the note on *Poverty and Social Security.*

Redistributive Impact

A tax and benefit system that is progressive over the entire income range is unambiguously equalizing. It implies that all redistribution is systematically from richer to poorer individuals. As a result, the Lorenz curve shifts upward, and most summary measures will reveal less inequality. When the tax and benefit system has a regressive range Lorenz curves need not intersect, in which case unambiguous conclusions about redistribution are still possible. But if Lorenz curves do intersect, unambiguous conclusions are not possible. Different people will usually be able to appeal to an inequality measure that supports their preferred position about redistributive impact. Clearly, references to the progressivity and regressivity of various taxes and benefits at different income levels are generally not a sufficient basis for distributional judgments, since there are both progressive and regressive influences. Rather, it is necessary to construct Lorenz curves or, where Lorenz curves intersect, to compute the preferred inequality index.

Both fiscal incidence and especially redistribution analysis are complex and highly subjective exercises. Indeed, even the most ambitious studies rarely explore the issues that arise out of the recent discussions of the appropriate way of measuring inequality. Lorenz curves and Gini coefficients remain the basis of most studies. Moreover, the preceding discussion has focused on the extent to which fiscal policy affects income distribution only in the very narrowest sense. To appreciate this, some of the limitations of the standard approach to redistribution analysis should be spelled out.

Limitations of Redistribution Analysis

Variations in average income

While it is clear that the more equal distribution with Lorenz curve L(x) in Chart 2 is preferred on distributive grounds when average income is the same or when associated with a higher average income, it is less obvious that for a given reduction in inequality there is no limit to the reduction in average income that is acceptable to achieve it. One solution to the trade-off is implied by the **generalized Lorenz curve**, which adjusts the standard Lorenz curve for changes to mean income. This is illustrated in Chart 3, where nonintersecting standard Lorenz curves yield ambiguous welfare comparisons when a more equal distribution is associated with a reduction in average income by a factor α, and generalized Lorenz curves GL(x) and GL(y) cross. It is easy to construct the case where standard Lorenz curves cross but generalized Lorenz curves do not. To generate complete rankings, it is necessary to specify a social welfare function that embodies an **inequality-efficiency trade-off**, inequality being reflected in an inequality index and efficiency being reflected in average income.

Chart 3. The Generalized Lorenz Curve

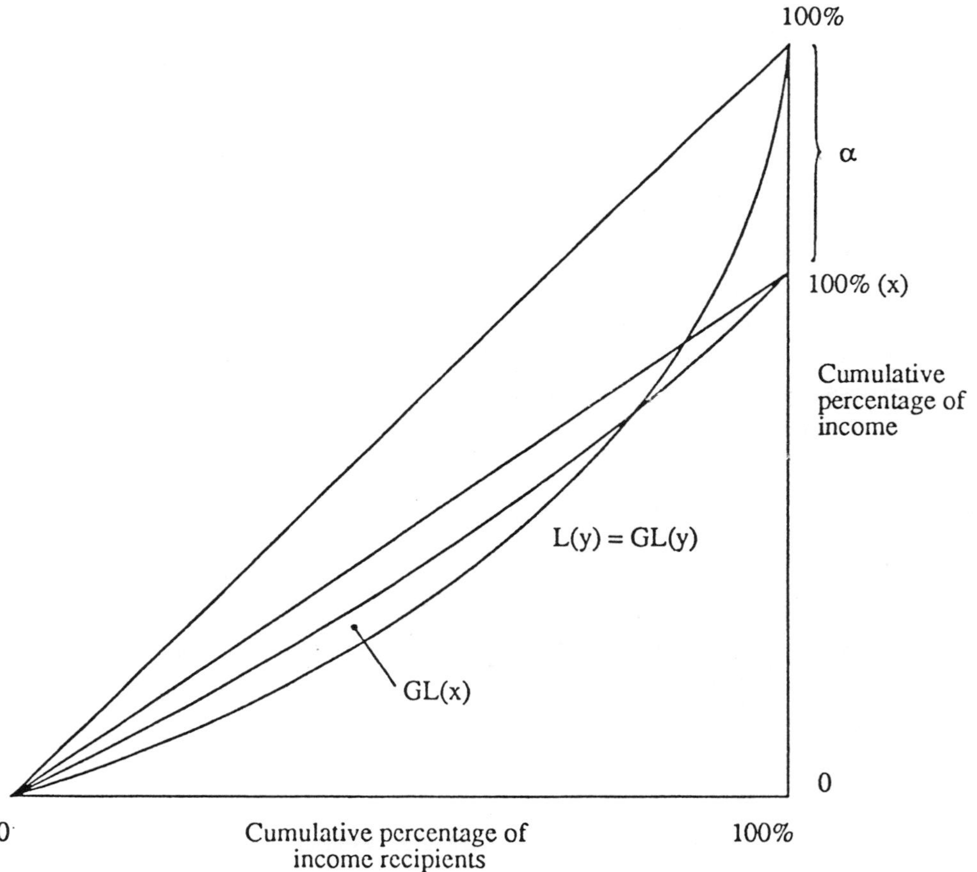

The unit of analysis

Reference has been made above only to the distribution of income between individuals—this is simply for convenience of exposition. The unit of analysis, whether it is the individual, the family, or the household, is important. Each alternative has disadvantages which require conclusions based upon them to be qualified. In particular, it is always difficult to take properly into account the extent of income transfers between family and household members and their impact on inequality. The choice of unit is also important when attempting to compare income with needs—as in poverty studies—given that needs vary with family and household size. A common practice is to focus on income per adult equivalent.

Concept of equity

It is usual to distinguish between vertical equity and horizontal equity when discussing income distribution. **Vertical equity** relates to the relative treatment of individuals (families or households) at different income levels. **Horizontal equity** relates to the way in which individuals at the same income level are treated. Vertical equity tends to be the focus of income distribution studies. It turns out, however, that often the combined impact of taxes, transfers, and benefits results in individuals at different income levels being treated very unequally, and it is not uncommon for the **ranking of individuals** in similar circumstances in the income distribution to be markedly affected by fiscal policy. This often reflects well-defined objectives of fiscal policy, such as a desire to encourage particular patterns of consumption, to promote home ownership or saving for retirement, or to foster regional development. It may, however, reflect inadequate administration or capricious discrimination. Most analyses of income redistribution take no account of rerankings, be they intentional or unintentional. However, studies that have attempted to reflect reranking have revealed a tendency for redistribution, especially through taxation, to be overestimated by the standard procedure.

Behavioral responses

Taxes, transfers, and benefits affect economic behavior—the supply of labor, together with consumption, savings and investment are all influenced by fiscal policy variables. A fully articulated redistribution study would compare the distribution of income taking into account fiscal policy with one that would prevail in its absence. At the very least, this would require knowledge of the relevant behavioral coefficients, and the adjustment of certain economic variables to reflect the impact of fiscal policy on them. Ideally, however, account should also be taken of the full general equilibrium implications of fiscal policy on the economy to specify properly the counterfactual that is being used as a baseline for comparison purposes.

Lifetime and intergenerational redistribution

Redistribution as discussed above is a contemporaneous concept, occurring at one particular point in time. However, many public programs—for example, social security—are directed toward redistributing income over individual lifetimes and have implications for redistribution between successive generations. The dynamic issues raised by such programs are difficult ones, but progress is now being made in recasting distributional analyses to reflect these more complex equity objectives.

The Efficiency of Redistribution

An implication of the pattern of redistribution shown in Chart 1 is that there is a large gap between the amount of gross redistribution associated with government programs and the resulting net redistribution. A significant proportion of the benefits resulting from expenditure programs flow back to those who pay the taxes to finance them. It has been argued that the disincentive effects associated with unnecessarily high taxes and the payment of benefits to those who do not need them imply that the efficiency cost of the net redistribution that actually takes place is unjustifiably high. **Middle class capture** has become one of the most powerful arguments used by those who push for less government intervention. To the extent that the same amount of net redistribution, or more, can be achieved with smaller gross income flows, proponents of this view argue that policies should be put in place to reduce gross income flows, and work effort, saving, and risk-taking will increase as a result. While it is difficult to deny the existence of some inefficiency associated with redistribution, the notion that net and gross income flows can be brought reasonably closely into line may be both inappropriate and unrealistic. As noted above, contemporaneous redistribution is only one aspect of redistribution policy, and to the extent that lifetime and intergenerational redistribution, for example, are important, a large mismatch between gross and net income flows may be justified. Moreover, **universality** in benefits has advantages where there are difficulties or high costs involved in identifying potential benefit recipients. These and other issues related to reducing gross income flows while fulfilling distributional objectives are discussed in the note on *Poverty and Social Security*.

Country Illustrations

Because fiscal incidence studies are more commonplace in industrial countries, the United Kingdom example is included to illustrate the type of analysis that is possible. The Bangladesh example is among the more detailed available for developing countries, but is still fairly rudimentary compared to its United Kingdom counterpart.

Fiscal incidence in the United Kingdom

The results of a fiscal incidence study for the United Kingdom are summarized in Table 1. A number of assumptions and simplifications were necessary to arrive at these results, which together tend to overstate the progressivity or redistributive impact of the tax and benefit system. These include: an assumption that all taxes are borne by those who formally pay them; in-kind benefits are valued on a cost basis, while they tend to be worth more to the rich; and public goods and other general expenditures are not included. Table 1 shows that although taxes rise sharply with income, in relative terms taxes are mildly regressive. Cash transfers, which are targeted toward the poor, are strongly progressive. In-kind transfers are also progressive. The net effect of taxes, cash transfers, and in-kind benefits is that the first few income deciles receive more in benefits than they pay in taxes, and vice versa at higher income levels; as a result the tax and benefit system appears fairly progressive.

Table 1. United Kingdom: Fiscal Incidence 1981
(Multiple of household average)

Income decile	Original Income	Taxes	Cash Transfers	In-kind Transfers	Final Income
Lowest	—	0.20	2.14	0.93	0.48
Second	0.05	0.21	1.91	0.81	0.47
Third	0.25	0.39	1.76	0.87	0.58
Fourth	0.56	0.63	1.10	1.01	0.72
Fifth	0.80	0.81	0.71	1.07	0.83
Sixth	1.00	0.98	0.59	1.06	0.94
Seventh	1.21	1.16	0.50	1.06	1.08
Eighth	1.48	1.37	0.48	1.07	1.27
Ninth	1.81	1.71	0.42	1.04	1.45
Highest	2.83	2.55	0.38	1.13	2.18

Source: Saunders and Klau (1985).

Fiscal incidence in Bangladesh

The fiscal incidence analysis for Bangladesh summarized in Table 2 is based upon far less detailed data than those available in the United Kingdom. The tax incidence assumptions are uncontroversial, and the incidence of the tax system reflects the offsetting effect of progressive import duties on luxuries and income tax—from which the poor are exempt—and regressive excise duties. Cash transfers—including food subsidies—are progressive at very low incomes but poor targeting results in some regressivity at higher incomes. In-kind benefits —comprising the imputed value of education, health, agriculture and water development expenditures—tend to be regressive, reflecting mainly the value of state education to the rich. While the ultra poor (with annual incomes below Tk 20,000) receive more in transfers than they pay in taxes, the poor (with annual incomes in the range Tk 20,000–24,000) on average make marginally positive net tax payments.

Table 2. Bangladesh: Fiscal Incidence 1986
(Multiple of household average)

	Percentage of Households	Taxes	Cash Transfers	In-kind Transfers	Net Taxes
Ultra poor	20.0	0.24	1.24	0.37	-0.19
Poor	32.4	0.33	0.98	0.44	0.04
Others	47.6	1.74	1.02	1.65	2.04

Source: World Bank.

Bibliography

Atkinson, A.B., and J.E. Stiglitz, *Lectures on Public Economics* (New York: McGraw Hill, 1980).

Saunders, P., and F. Klau, *The Role of the Public Sector,* OECD Economic Studies, No. 4 (Paris: Organization for Economic Cooperation and Development, 1985).

Sen, A.K., *On Economic Inequality* (Oxford: Clarendon Press), 1973.

XIX. Poverty and Social Security

Ehtisham Ahmad and Richard Hemming

How is poverty measured? Which groups are most vulnerable and why?
How instructive is industrial country experience for designing social security programs in developing countries?
To what extent do informal arrangements—based upon the extended family and local communities—provide an adequate safety net?
How can social security be targeted to the poor?

Concern about poverty in developing countries has two related aspects. Over time, a sizable reduction in poverty is important, both in its own right and as a first step in providing the means for the self-improvement of the most disadvantaged groups in society. The policies most likely to achieve these objectives are those that stimulate growth and employment, and in so doing provide incomes for the poor and use some of the resources generated to make adequate social provisions for people who cannot benefit directly from rising incomes. However, the macroeconomic stabilization and structural adjustment policies that are necessary for growth may adversely affect some poor groups in the short run. There is therefore a need to put in place policies to protect the poor from the immediate consequences of adjustment. Social security addresses both issues: the provision of safety nets is required by the short-term concern, while more comprehensive social protection meets longer-term objectives.

Assessing Poverty

Concepts

Poverty embraces material aspects that can be captured in terms of monetary indicators such as income or expenditure levels. It also includes nonmaterial aspects relating to quality of life, such as nutritional and health status and educational attainment. These are less easy to measure. Thus it is usual to supplement income-based measures of poverty with non-income indicators such as child or infant mortality, life expectancy, or educational status, to generate a more complete picture of poverty in a country. This may also have to be supported by sectoral (e.g., employment status) or regional (e.g., rural or urban) profiles of the poor.

The most common practice is to measure **absolute poverty** in relation to a subsistence level poverty line. Obviously, appropriately differentiated income or expenditure survey data have to be available, and it would normally be necessary to rely on data collected by national authorities or, in most cases, institutions such as the World Bank. Moreover, other UN agencies (UNICEF, WFP, and IFAD, for example) will also be a primary source of poverty estimates. However, such estimates have to be treated with caution. If the poverty line is defined with respect to minimum nutrition, clothing and shelter levels, serious problems arise in the definition of such a basket of goods given price changes, regional and cross-country variation, and household taste and composition differences. Additionally, when many people have an income close to subsistence level, minor variations in where the poverty line is drawn can make major differences to estimates of the incidence of poverty.

An alternative approach is to define **relative poverty** with respect to living standards that prevail in a particular society. An advantage of a relative poverty line is that it reflects changing perceptions of acceptable minimum living standards. Thus, while indoor sanitation or electricity may not be considered essential in very poor societies, these may constitute basic necessities in richer societies. A wider interpretation of relative poverty would also reflect nonparticipation in activities that are generally regarded as customary. In OECD countries, current practice is to define the poverty line as a proportion—usually 50 percent—of average income. However, in some instances the bottom 20-40 percent of households in the income distribution are defined as relatively poor. While this is generally difficult to defend, in developing countries with widespread poverty, the bottom 10–20 percent of households—all of which are poor in an absolute sense—may be an appropriate group to focus upon, since the ultra-poor rather than the poor are often the crucial target group.

Measurement

Having decided upon a poverty line, the most widely used measure of the extent of poverty is the number of poor, known as the **head count**. This has the shortcoming that it is insensitive to the actual income levels of the poor. Thus a transfer from the poorest to the least poor, which raises the income of latter above the poverty line, would reduce the head count. However, if account is taken of the **poverty gap**, that is the average deviation of the incomes of the poor from the poverty line, it is less obvious that poverty has fallen. But this still gives equal weight to all poverty gaps. If deprivation increases more than proportionately with individual poverty gaps, then **inequality among the poor** matters, and more weight would need to be attached to the poverty gaps of poorer individuals. More sophisticated poverty indices reflect each of these three aspects of poverty. For example, the **Sen poverty index** combines the head count, the poverty gap, and the Gini index of income inequality among the poor. Measures can also be based upon alternative inequality indices, some of which do not require explicit specification of the poverty line (see the note on *The Distributional Impact of Public Expenditure* for a discussion of inequality indices). Only in a very few cases will it be feasible to obtain estimates of these more sophisticated indices.

Characteristics of the poor

In industrial countries, poverty is closely linked to employment status. Thus the majority of the poor are elderly, disabled, sick or unemployed heads of household and their dependents. Women and children account for a significant share of the poor. Low pay tends to result in poverty only when it is associated with some other contributing household characteristic such as a need to support a disabled spouse, elderly dependents or large number of children. By contrast, in developing countries poverty is widespread among the working population. The emphasis on formal employment is far less, and landless rural workers and smallholders constitute the majority of the poor. Employment status is more important in urban areas; however, poverty incidence is often high in the low-wage informal sector. While the nonworking population in developing countries relies heavily on the family or community for financial support, in South Asia and some other rapidly growing parts of the world, widows, orphans, the disabled, and the aged are among the poorest segments of society.

Social Security in Industrial Countries

Social insurance, income maintenance and child benefits

If there were perfect insurance markets, people would be able to protect themselves against many of the contingencies that result in poverty. However, insurance markets are subject to market failure, to which social insurance is a response (see the notes on *Public Expenditure and Resource Allocation* and *Pensions* for further discussion). In the majority of industrial countries, employees contribute to a social insurance program that pays retirement and disability pensions, sickness benefit, and unemployment benefit. Social insurance often provides a significant degree of **income replacement**, in that benefits are related to previous earnings.

For those who are not eligible for social insurance, or for whom it provides inadequate benefits, income maintenance is usually available. This takes the form of **means-tested income supplements**, which guarantee a minimum income close to the poverty line. In recognition of the vulnerable position of children, child benefits are often paid outside the social insurance and income maintenance programs. Moreover, these tend to take the form of **universal benefits**, paid to every family with children. However, in some countries child tax allowances (or tax credits) are available instead. These have the disadvantages that they offer no benefit to families where the head is not employed and that they confer greater benefits to the rich, who face higher marginal tax rates. **Minimum wage legislation** can also be regarded as part of the social security system.

The social security systems in industrial countries have evolved in line with varying needs, and consequently differ in major respects across countries, and over time in a given country. Thus improved provision for the aged in the United States has been instrumental in reducing poverty among this group since the 1960s. However, unlike in France and Britain, there is no comparable system of (universal) child benefits in the United States, which has a much greater incidence of child poverty as a consequence. Changing needs are also reflected in the widespread introduction of unemployment insurance after the Great Depression and widows' pensions during World War II.

Problems and suggested solutions

The fact that poverty is not widespread in industrial countries can be viewed as a measure of the success of social security provisions. At the same time they are subject to criticism. These include the potentially adverse effects of unemployment compensation on voluntary unemployment, of sickness benefits on attendance at work, and of pensions on savings and the participation of the elderly in the labor force, although the evidence is far from unanimous. However, perhaps the most worrisome feature of social security programs in industrial countries is the persistence of significant pockets of poverty despite the availability of income support. The fact that this affects the elderly and children especially—groups who are least able to provide for themselves—is of particular concern. The principal shortcoming of social security programs in this regard concerns the operation and impact of means testing. First, the existence of the means test and the investigative manner in which it is often administered leads to stigma, with the result that not all the poor take up the benefits to which they are entitled. Second, the means test often implies that benefits are withdrawn at a high rate as other income rises. This benefit withdrawal rate is equivalent to a marginal tax rate that can be as high as 100 percent; moreover, even if it is lower, the combined impact of the withdrawal of a number of different benefits with income tax rates that are sometimes levied on very low incomes can impose effective income tax rates well in excess of

100 percent on the poor. Such punitive tax rates provide little incentive for the poor to work their way out of poverty; they therefore risk falling into a **poverty trap**.

To improve the effectiveness of social security in industrial countries, attention has focused on alternatives to means testing and the elimination of high marginal tax rates. The most radical proposals require the introduction of **integrated tax-benefit schemes** whereby benefits are paid to everybody—thus eliminating the means test—and then recouped through the tax system from those who do not need them. This avoids **unintentionally** high marginal tax rates on low incomes. However, the problem is that if the minimum income guaranteed under the scheme is to be sufficient to prevent poverty, general tax rates may have to be high. There is therefore a trade-off between equity (which is best served by universal provision of a high guaranteed minimum income) and efficiency (which requires low tax rates).

Social Security in Developing Countries

Constraints on social security policy

In addition to the different characteristics of the poor described above, social security policy in developing countries is constrained by a number of other factors. One important difference between industrial and developing countries relates to the severity of poverty in the latter and widespread failure to secure minimum food requirements. Other constraining factors include the limited range of activities in the formal sector, resource availability, and administrative capacity in developing countries. These differences have a number of implications for the design of social security in developing countries. Since employment status provides a poor guide to poverty risk, the primary focus will not be on providing social insurance. Instead, the combination of extensive poverty and limited resources suggests that the focus should be on establishing a **safety net** that guarantees access to minimum requirements, in particular food. In this connection, the targeting of benefits should be attached considerable importance. Administrative difficulties both in identifying beneficiaries and delivering benefits—together with cost considerations—suggest that existing community-based arrangements should be an integral part of the social security system.

Lessons from industrial countries

Insofar as the focus of social security policy in developing countries is on the provision of safety nets, the industrial country experience is of only limited relevance. In the early stages of development, there will be little overlap between social security systems in developing and industrial countries. However, one objective of developing countries should be to shift eventually from the direct provision of food and other goods and services to income maintenance, which is preferable from an allocative viewpoint. Also, as the formal sector grows, social insurance will become increasingly important. As the social security system develops in these directions, industrial country experience becomes more relevant.

Targeting

Perfect targeting occurs when only the target group is covered by a program **and** each member of the target group receives the benefits to which they are entitled. These two aspects of targeting come into conflict. Attempts to target too precisely result in **errors of exclusion**, as deserving beneficiaries are denied coverage.

However, efforts to improve the delivery of benefits invariably lead to **errors of inclusion**, as coverage widens beyond the target group. The first type of error reduces program effectiveness while the second type adds to the program's financial cost.

Means testing ensures that only the poor benefit from social programs intended to help them. Moreover, if all the poor took the means test they would receive appropriate assistance. However, as the industrial country experience illustrates, means testing is stigmatizing, which leads to low take-up, and can give rise to high marginal tax rates, which have disincentive effects. Taking into account also its steep administrative costs, extensive means testing is probably neither feasible nor desirable in developing countries. Reliance will have to be placed instead on self-targeted forms of social security and targeting based on proximate indicators of need. There are discussed below.

Role of community-based provision

The extended family is still the basis of support for contingencies such as old age, disability, or widowhood in most developing countries. This may be augmented by community (i.e. local) arrangements, for those with inadequate family support, and such measures often replicate provisions of formal social security. Local communities are relatively efficient in identifying and providing for those in need, and therefore targeting is fairly close. There is often also a greater willingness to pay for what is readily seen to be mutual insurance. However, these arrangements may not be adequate when a particular adversity affects entire communities; for example, in drought-prone regions there is clearly a role for government in transferring consumption across regions. Moreover, as social insurance becomes more important, the role of local communities will necessarily recede. Indeed, it should be noted that while the origins of social security systems in industrial countries can be traced to charitable giving at the local level, private sector involvement is now modest and tends to be employer based. Because of insurance market failure, the government is always likely to play an increasing role as development proceeds.

Policies

As indicated above, a primary objective of social security in developing countries is to provide a safety net, not only for the aged and those unable to participate in the labor market, but also for large groups of the working poor. **Food relief**—in the form of food subsidies, rations, or more targeted provisions like food stamps—is usually the principal form of assistance for vulnerable groups. General subsidies are self-targeting if they apply to inferior marketable commodities, but examples are not easy to find (see the note on *Price Subsidies* for further details). Rations approximate universal benefits in kind, and may be preferable to general subsidies for most normal goods, both on budgetary grounds and from the nutritional point of view if the rationed commodities would otherwise be priced out of affordable range for the poor owing to excess demand by the better-off consumers. Food stamps allow more precise targeting, but inevitably involve means testing. Supplementary feeding programs are often used to address severe malnutrition, providing food directly to those groups which face the greatest health risk, such as pregnant women, children, and the aged. However, because malnutrition often reflects not only food shortages but also the presence of disease, such programs have to be closely coordinated with the delivery of primary health care.

Public employment programs are also a commonly used form of social security. Poverty is reduced by providing employment to those in need, usually on labor-intensive infrastructure projects such as water and soil conservation, irrigation, flood control, roadworks, and reforestation. To be a cost-effective means of poverty relief, such programs should pay only subsistence wages, and so effectively target the poor through self-selection. Moreover, if importance is attached to food provision, the programs can be partly a form of **food-for-work**. Public employment programs offer the additional advantage that they often create infrastructure and other capital that can have second-round effects on the incomes of the poor.

Notwithstanding the availability of private transfers, food relief, public employment opportunities, and whatever more formal social security arrangements are in place, a number of people will be inadequately provided for. It is important to try to isolate the characteristics of the remaining poor. These may be fairly general (related to age, gender, or landholding, for example) or country specific (related to location, religion, race, or class, for example). If the most vulnerable and unprotected groups can be identified by such characteristics, this can provide the basis for a targeted safety net. Indeed, where finer targeting is impractical, such proximate indicators of poverty risk may have to be mainstay of affordable social security provision.

Country Illustration

Employment programs in Chile and Tunisia

Despite the fact that Chile has one of the oldest and most advanced social insurance systems in Latin America, the use of self-targeted employment provision at low wage levels played an important role in supplementing unemployment insurance during two major crises in 1974–77 and 1982–84. The Programas de Empleo (EEP) were instituted in 1974, and by 1976 employed around 6 percent of the labor force. At that stage, open unemployment was 16 percent. By the end of 1982, when the second major adjustment was forced, open unemployment was 16 percent. By the end of 1982, when the second major adjustment was forced, open unemployment rose to 31 percent. EEP was doubled in 1983 to cover just under half of the unemployed. However, because of the self-selecting nature of EEP, the total budgetary cost was 1.4 percent of GDP at the height of the crisis in 1983. The majority of workers in two of the main EEP schemes were in the lowest quintile of the income distribution. The EEP was gradually run down with a subsequent tightening of the labor market, and was withdrawn completely in 1988 as unemployment returned to around 6 percent. Not all public works programs are as effective in providing a relatively cheap social safety net. For example, one such program in Tunisia during the 1950s and 1960s paid such high wages that employment was rationed on a rotational basis. While the program covered up to 39 percent of the unemployed, its cost reached 5 percent of GDP. The contrast between the Chilean and Tunisian experiences emphasizes the desirability of targeting through low wages, which not only limits overall cost but also makes it easier for the scheme to be wound down when not needed.

Bibliography

Ahmad, Ehtisham, "Social Security and the Poor," *World Bank Research Observer* (Washington, World Bank, 1990).

Atkinson, A.B., "Income Maintenance and Social Insurance," in *Handbook of Public Economics*, Vol 2, ed. by A.J. Auerbach and M. Feldstein (Amsterdam: North-Holland, 1987).

Besley, T., and R. Kanbur, "The Principles of Targeting," in *Poverty in Developing Countries*, ed. by M. Lipton and J. van der Gaag (Washington: World Bank and IFPRI, 1990).

Kanbur, S.M. Ravi, "Measurement and Alleviation of Poverty: With an Application to the Effects of Macroeconomic Adjustment," *IMF Staff Papers*, 34 (Washington: International Monetary Fund, 1987).

Policy Issues

XX. Privatization

Richard Hemming and Kenneth Miranda

How does privatization affect economic efficiency? Does it result in goods and services being produced at lower cost? Is the private sector more responsive to consumer demand?
Is the impact of privatization different in competitive and monopolistic markets? Should public monopolists be privatized, exposed to competition, or both?
What forms can privatization take? Are there limits to the size and scope of a privatization program?
Does privatization have beneficial consequences for public finances?

Privatization is a term used to describe a wide range of policies designed to effect a transfer of activity from the public sector to the private sector. However, its most notable manifestation is the sale of public enterprises to private buyers, and in particular the sale programs undertaken in France and the United Kingdom, and now planned on an ambitious scale throughout Eastern Europe. However, privatization does not necessarily require total divestiture; franchising, contracting out and leasing, whereby public sector activities are undertaken by the private sector, are widespread forms of privatization.

The note is organized as follows. In the first section the link between privatization and efficiency is outlined. To a significant degree, this depends upon whether privatization is associated with increased exposure to competition. Therefore the relationship between privatization and competition is also discussed. After a description of some of the practical constraints facing successful privatization, the fiscal impact of privatization is considered. An attempt is made to distinguish between the characteristics and implications of asset sales as compared to less drastic forms of privatization.

Privatization and Economic Efficiency

There are two possible sources of increased economic efficiency that can be derived from privatization: gains in **productive efficiency**, when a given level of output can be produced at a lower cost; and gains in **allocative efficiency**, when resources can be reallocated to better meet economic and social objectives—see the note on *Public Expenditure Productivity* for further discussion of these efficiency concepts.

Productive efficiency

Proponents of privatization argue that it will reduce productive inefficiencies arising from public ownership and management. First, by limiting the scope for political interference, privatization will result in higher-quality managerial decision making. Second, the number of objectives that the public sector usually pursues will be reduced. Often these multiple objectives are inconsistent with one another, and this reduces the ability of managers to minimize costs. Third, privatization can impose the discipline of private financial markets, which leads to more rational managerial decisions. Fourth, privatization may improve managerial incentives by making managers responsible to profit-seeking shareholders rather than to civil servants.

The merits of the above arguments need to be examined closely. Privatization may indeed improve productive efficiency under certain circumstances, but this need not be the case universally and privatization may not necessarily be the best method of securing such improvements. For example, reducing political interference in the operations of a public enterprise could also be accomplished by creating a political structure that discourages interference. Substituting the single goal of profit maximization for multiple objectives can also be achieved without privatization. However, the central issue is whether the noneconomic objectives pursued by the government are compelling. Certainly some simplification of goals will often be desirable and feasible. But it is inevitable that efficiency will have to be judged relative to objectives that are wider than those in the private sector. As regards the discipline of the financial marketplace, a government can itself impose greater financial discipline on public agencies, making them compete with other firms on equal footing for scarce financial resources. This would force public enterprises to rationalize their operations along commercial lines. Finally, the argument that privatization will improve managerial incentives depends critically on whether or not privatization in fact increases the accountability of managers. The type of bureaucratic failures that give rise to **principal-agent problems**—where the principals (governments) cannot provide effective incentives or adequate monitoring to guarantee that their agents (managers) pursue the principals', as opposed to their own, interests—may also arise in the private sector.

Allocative efficiency

Improvements in allocative efficiency will in general only be achieved when privatization goes hand in hand with extending the exposure of firms to competition. Under such circumstances, increases in allocative efficiency can be expected to the extent that the monopolistic or quasi-monopolistic position of public agencies and enterprises is weakened. It is the discipline imposed by the product market—which determines profits—and the capital market—which determines whether sufficient profit is made to stay in business—that promotes allocative efficiency. However, since gains in allocative efficiency reflect mainly a change in the competitive environment, they can potentially emerge without any change in ownership structure. In the case of a public enterprise that is a natural monopoly (see the note on *Public Expenditure and Resource Allocation* for further discussion of natural monopoly) privatization can worsen allocative efficiency to the extent that the resultant private firm takes greater advantage of opportunities to restrict output and raise prices than the public enterprise. In such an instance, it may be necessary to regulate the newly privatized firm in order to maintain allocative efficiency. The issue then turns on whether public ownership is a more effective form of regulation than other alternatives.

The principal conclusion of the preceding discussion is that privatization cannot guarantee *a priori* an increase in economic efficiency. Increased competition is not only the key to improved allocative efficiency—which is generally independent of which sector undertakes an activity—but it may also provide the strongest incentive to seek improvements in productive efficiency by introducing the risk of bankruptcy or takeover. The questions that then arise are: (i) whether privatization makes it easier to increase exposure to market forces; and (ii) whether a government pursuing such a policy option will be in a position to complement it with a judicious choice of other policies, most notably liberalization to promote competition and regulation to prevent anti-competitive practices.

Privatization and Competition

Privatization is unlikely to result in increased efficiency unless it is accompanied by a dismantling of protective barriers that restrict competition. However, for a variety of reasons—such as the need to generate maximum revenue or to secure the compliance of management and workers—it may be thought appropriate to restrict competition at the time of privatization . Not only does this call into question the motives of a privatization program, it also makes it difficult to believe that liberalization will ever take place. The maximum efficiency gain will result from privatization accompanied by liberalization. Efficiency considerations also suggest that where conflict is likely to emerge, liberalization should precede privatization.

To the extent that public ownership reflects circumstances in which markets do not work well or produce outcomes that are considered socially or politically undesirable, removing barriers to competition would be insufficient or inappropriate. Natural monopoly, for example, is a market outcome; to introduce competition in a natural monopoly setting, the market has to be redefined. One solution is to make the right to run a natural monopoly the object of competition, by **auctioning franchises** to the private sector. This approach has been most widely adopted in the areas of local broadcasting and transportation. Also, some activities associated with natural monopoly, such as maintenance, are likely to be contestable, and these can be contracted out to the private sector. **Contracting out** has been successfully employed in a wide range of public services, such as street cleaning and garbage collection. Although extensive in the private sector, **leasing** is an option that is only now beginning to be explored in the public sector.

Certain social objectives may also be left unmet in a private market. The public sector can support loss-making activities of social value through cross subsidization by profit-making activities; in a liberalized market, the private sector will undertake only profitable activities (so-called cream skimming) and leave social needs to be met by the public sector. Certainly, the private sector can be induced, for example through the payment of subsidies, to provide essential services to sparsely populated areas and to employ people even when it is unprofitable to do so. The issue should then be one of cost-effectiveness of different types of intervention. In all likelihood, however, a wide range of priority social objectives will remain the responsibility of the public sector.

Constraints on Privatization

In designing a privatization program, especially for a developing country, a number of practical constraints will have a bearing on the type of program that can be introduced and, in the limit, on whether privatization is feasible or desirable. Of considerable importance is a policy environment and an administrative (especially legal) framework that is conducive to private initiative. If trade and industry are heavily regulated—through administered access to foreign exchange, quantitative import restrictions, entry and exit barriers, labor market controls, etc.—the scope for increased competition will be severely limited. This in turn will reduce the likelihood that privatization will be associated with increased efficiency.

To the extent that privatization involves the sale of public sector assets, the weak or nonexistent capital markets in many developing countries will restrict this option. On the other hand, some modest sales could be instrumental in expanding a fledgling capital market, and pave the way for more extensive privatization at a later date. The government must also have the administrative capacity to manage a privatization program, especially if asset sales are involved. Many ambitious privatization programs have failed to get off the ground because of the lack of specialist skills to implement them.

There may also be a resource constraint to privatization, particularly in the short term. Clearly there will be initial start up cost; consultants must be hired, government employees need to be trained, the public must be educated, and the privatization program needs to be administered. There may also arise a need to restructure public enterprises prior to sale, although this is probably best left to the new private owners. Afterwards, if privatization leads to the anticipated efficiency benefits, there may be a need to compensate for social costs such as increased unemployment, plant closures, and reduced services. Only in the medium term is privatization likely to yield the financial benefits to offset these initial costs. And even if there are the resources to get enterprises onto the selling block, there may not be sufficient domestic savings available to buy them and resistance to purchases by foreigners. The above constraints all provide reason to believe that privatization should not be embarked upon lightly. However, overriding all these considerations is the importance that must be attached to political commitment. Without it, none of these obstacles can be overcome and privatization is unlikely to work.

On these issues, developing countries may eventually be able to learn from the experience of countries in Eastern Europe, which plan rapid and extensive privatization. The intention in Poland, for example, is to privatize about a half of state industry, which dominates the economy, in as little as three years. While the political commitment to privatization as a means of effecting the transformation from a planned to a market economy is not in doubt, the institutional obstacles are immense. There are no capital markets, adminsitrative capacity is weak, the legal infrastructure hardly recognizes private property, price distortions make valuation difficult, and domestic savings are a small fraction of enterprise worth. To resolve the conflict between bold ambition and weak implementation capacity, a combination of every available privatization technique is being adopted, including mass privatization based upon the free disposal of shares to the population. At the same time, privatization is being supported by wide-ranging price and trade liberalization, appropriate competition policy, and fiscal and monetary reform.

Fiscal Impact of Privatization

Privatization is often ascribed objectives that extend beyond efficiency improvements. Diluting the strength of public sector trade unions and achieving wider share ownership are sometimes mentioned. However, it is in connection with reducing public sector deficits that privatization is most frequently associated. This is especially so where the sale of public sector assets, mainly public enterprises, is concerned.

Privatization and fiscal stance

As recommended in the Fund's *Manual on Government Finance Statistics*, proceeds from enterprise sales are treated as capital revenue or a loan repayment in the government accounts, which will lead to a once-and-for-all reduction in the fiscal deficit, assuming that the sale price obtained is greater than the net income generated for the government by the enterprise in the year of the sale. The change in the deficit, however, may not necessarily reflect a fundamental change in the fiscal policy stance. To gauge such a change, an analysis of the income flows and changes in the government's net worth arising from privatization is necessary.

Assume that a public enterprise is sold to a private buyer at a price equal to the present value of the stream of after-tax earnings of the enterprise. Moreover, assume that the public and private sectors face the same taxes, are equally efficient, and discount future income at the same rate. Then the reduction in the fiscal deficit in the year of the sale will be counterbalanced by larger deficits in all future years, reflecting the government's loss of revenue in the form of remitted profits. These larger future deficits, however, can be exactly offset if the government uses the sale proceeds to purchase financial or physical assets, or to retire a portion of its own debt. Under such a scenario, the government and private sector have simply exchanged assets, and this should not affect the demand for real resources at the time of the sale, or in the future. However, if the government uses the sale proceeds to finance an expansion of current expenditure or a reduction in taxation (or both), the deficit in the year of the sale would be unaffected, while future deficits will be larger. In such a case, the fiscal policy stance is affected by the sale. The resulting fall in government net worth signals the expansionary impact of the transaction, and the possible need for subsequent contraction to reastablish a sustainable fiscal stance. Thus, while privatization receipts may be formally treated as revenue, their economic impact is the same as financing.

The above line of reasoning holds for a loss-making enterprise, too. In such a case, the government may have to pay an up-front lump-sum subsidy. As such, a larger initial deficit in the year in which the public enterprise is transferred to the private sector will be counterbalanced by lower fiscal deficits in the future as a result of the government shedding its responsibility for future losses of the now-private operation. However, the service on debt accumulated to finance the initially higher deficit will return future deficits to their higher original level. Again, the public and private sectors have simply exchanged assets, and the fiscal stance will not be affected. This example also illustrates that a permanent improvement in fiscal performance will not necessarily be brought about simply by selling enterprises that are heavily subsidized; interest payments on debt accumulated to pay the private sector to take over the operations will offset any apparent fiscal gains.

Privatization can permanently improve fiscal performance only if large efficiency gains, both productive and allocative, result from the transfer of ownership from the public to the private sector. In such a case, the government will benefit from privatization to the extent that it can capture part of the expected efficiency gains in its sale price and/or additional taxes. Thus, in examining the fiscal impact of privatization, it is necessary to distinguish between cases in which privatization is likely to have a significant impact on productive and allocative efficiency and those in which such an outcome is unlikely. From the budgetary perspective, cases in which large efficiency gains can be expected should be the focus of a privatization exercise.

Privatization and financial policy

The design of financial policy is increasingly having to address the issue of the treatment of uncertain privatization proceeds when the price of enterprises and the timing of sales cannot be predicted. In principle, this uncertainty should not be a problem. The appropriateness of a government's fiscal stance is determined by financing needs. Therefore, if one starts from a budget that assumes no privatization revenue, fiscal stance will be unaffected if privatization revenue is forthcoming (from either domestic or foreign sources) and net credit to government is correspondingly reduced. Less obviously, if the budget makes allowance for privatization revenue that does not materialize, a compensating increase in net credit to government does not affect fiscal stance. In particular, there is no additional inflationary pressure owing to the increased money supply, which is matched by increased money demand because, contrary to initial expectations, privatized assets are not substituted for money in individual portfolios.

The usual practice is to assume no privatization revenue and to reduce net credit to government by the amount of actual receipts. In some cases, part or all of privatization revenue is earmarked to investment, especially if high-quality programs are pre-specified. A more cautious approach should perhaps be adopted when privatization revenue is assumed in the budget. If there is a shortfall, an offsetting increase in net credit to government is generally judged to be too risky because money demand cannot be tied down with any degree of precision. Instead, revenue has to be raised in its place or spending has to be reigned in. However, this approach can result in bad taxes being levied and fairly arbitrary expenditure cuts, with damaging consequences for efficiency. Hence the preference for assuming no privatization revenue in financial policy design.

Country Experiences

Problems with divestiture in Ghana and Sierra Leone

Past employment practices in Ghana led to significant overstaffing in the public enterprise sector. At the same time, collective bargaining agreements granted extremely generous severance pay arrangements. In an attempt to maximize proceeds from the eventual sales, pre-privatization efforts have focused on rationalizing manpower levels at many of the firms to be divested. However, in the absence of a political will or desire to repudiate past ill-conceived policies, part of Ghana's privatization program has been hindered and delayed by a lack of budgetary resources to cover the **contingent liabilities** of the firms to be divested, and in particular severance pay.

Public choice theory suggests that since the benefits of privatization will be spread out over a large number of people—but the costs will be borne by a small number, especially civil servants and public managers—the small group may voice strong opposition to the reform effort. In the case of Sierra Leone, however, members of the civil administration were the most interested prospective buyers of assets under a World Bank coordinated privatization program. Because of **limits on foreign ownership** as well as a **weak private sector** and **poor financial intermediation**, it appeared that the government might end up receiving less than a fair price for privatized enterprises. As a result, the privatization program is currently being restructured, with a view to raising the income the government derives from privatization and improving the government's fiscal position.

Experience with other forms of privatization

Franchising

In Thailand, the Bangkok Metropolitan Mass Transit Organization (BMMTO) began franchising bus routes in the late 1970s. The results have been mostly positive, as the BMMTO was able to increase the number of buses on crowded routes and was able to sell off many of its used buses at attractive prices. However, some evidence exists that the franchises were underpriced, and that the BMMTO did not maximize its financial gain.

Contracting out

In Australia, the government, in an effort to improve road sealing, town sweeping, and other activities at the city council level, decided to contract out these various functions. Contract specifications and conditions with built-in safety clauses to maintain the quality of service were developed. Regular review procedures and monitoring systems were also introduced. Competitive tendering resulted in a reduction in costs and an improvement in services offered.

Bibliography

Hemming, Richard, and Ali M. Mansoor, "Privatization and Public Enterprises," Occasional Paper No. 56 (Washington: International Monetary Fund, 1988).

Mansoor, Ali. M. "The Budgetary Impact of Privatization", in *Measurement of Fiscal Impact: Methodological Issues*, Occasional Paper No. 59, ed. by Mario I. Blejer and Ke-young Chu (Washington, International Monetary Fund), October 1987.

Shirley, Mary, "The Experience with Privatization," *Finance and Development* (Washington: International Monetary Fund, 1989).

XXI. Pricing and Cost Recovery

Richard Hemming and Kenneth Miranda

What is the scope for marginal cost pricing in the public sector?

What deviations from marginal cost pricing are needed to meet revenue and distributional objectives?

Can optimal pricing rules be implemented? What are the alternatives?

Are there advantages to earmarking revenues to particular expenditure programs?

Expenditure issues cannot be discussed independently of the way in which expenditure is paid for. Both taxation and borrowing have possible adverse consequences for efficiency and growth (see thé note on *Public Expenditure and Sustainable Fiscal Policy*). To the extent that the public sector can recover at least part of the costs it incurs in providing goods and services through charges, there is scope to reduce taxation and/or the fiscal deficit. Moreover, if publicly provided goods have private characteristics, and charges can be levied to reflect private benefits, this will improve efficiency.

Principles of Public Sector Pricing

Marginal cost pricing

Efficient resource allocation generally requires that prices be set equal to marginal cost. If consumers are willing to pay a price above (below) marginal cost for a particular good (or service), resources could be transferred to (from) the production of this good and thereby raise consumer welfare (see the note on *Public Expenditure and Resource Allocation*). In the end, prices will reflect the opportunity cost of the resources used to meet consumer demand.

Public sector production ranges from public goods to private goods. A public good is nonrival in consumption, and the cost of accommodating an additional consumer is zero; the marginal cost pricing principle implies that there should be no charge for such goods, and that the costs of provision should be met from general revenue. Private goods should be priced at their positive marginal cost, and the losses of decreasing-cost industries such as public utilities (for which marginal cost is below average cost) should also be met from general revenue. Strictly speaking, the only goods that fall in between these two extremes are group goods and local public goods, which are nonrival among identifiable beneficiaries; air traffic control and flood prevention have these characteristics. Such goods should be provided to the group or locality free of charge, but the same group or locality should finance their provision. However, goods that are associated with externalities are often thought to fall between public and private goods. For goods characterized by large external benefits, prices can be set below those that would prevail in a free market, with the resulting subsidy—designed to bring marginal social costs and benefits into line—financed from general revenue. Part of the revenue can be derived from taxes on goods characterized by large external costs.

Revenue objectives

If the government could impose nondistortionary lump-sum taxation, it could cover the cost of providing public goods, the losses of decreasing cost industries, and subsidies to internalize externalities without inducing distortions. The case for marginal cost pricing is then a first-best argument. However, lump-sum taxation is not feasible, and, in a second-best world where taxation is distortionary, departures from marginal cost pricing may be desirable. A special case is where the public sector has a revenue target that it cannot meet through taxation, owing to a narrow tax base or weak administrative capability. If the public sector is responsible for a significant share of total output and can control the price of that output—which realistically assumes a significant degree of monopoly power in the public sector—then public sector pricing can be used to generate revenue.

Ramsey pricing

Determining the second-best set of public sector prices that meets a revenue target but minimizes the efficiency loss as a result of deviations from marginal cost pricing is formally equivalent to deriving optimal commodity taxes. In their simplest form, the **Ramsey rules** imply that prices deviate from marginal cost in inverse proportion to demand elasticity. The intuition is that goods in relatively inelastic demand can bear high (implicit) taxes because taxation does not significantly affect consumption. More complex interpretations of the Ramsey rules have a similar intuition. An implication of Ramsey pricing is that it is generally inappropriate to impose financial targets as a means of setting prices in subsectors of the public sector. In particular, activities characterized by decreasing costs should not be subject to break-even constraints, as is the common practice. Rather, prices should be raised above marginal cost only insofar as demand conditions dictate, and if losses persist, they should be cross-subsidized.

Departures from efficient pricing

While Ramsey pricing assumes a monopolistic public sector, if the private sector exhibits elements of monopoly, marginal cost pricing may not be an appropriate basis for pricing in the public sector and the imposition of Ramsey prices to meet a revenue target may no longer be optimal. Moreover, even with a competitive private sector, the need to generate revenue is not the only justification for departing from marginal cost pricing. If there are difficulties in effectively imposing taxes, then the government's ability to redistribute through progressive taxation is also constrained. While public sector pricing may generate sufficient revenue to finance redistributive transfers and other social expenditure programs, some prices can also be subsidized for redistributional purposes. Although this is generally an inefficient way of pursuing distributional objectives—it is better to redistribute income—price subsidies may be justified when the scope to use other instruments is limited.

Limitations

The preceding discussion illustrates some of the limits to the marginal cost pricing principle. While desirable departures from marginal cost and Ramsey pricing may be described in some cases, when one takes into account the full range of market imperfections in the private sector, and the combination of multiple objectives and limited instruments of the public sector, optimal pricing is virtually impossible to characterize. Moreover, even in the simple cases, pricing rules may not be operational. In many cases marginal cost is not observable, although techniques are available to approximate it from other market or cost data. And if marginal cost can be calculated, the information required to compute optimal departures from marginal cost is often unavailable. For example, the demand elasticities on which Ramsey prices should be based are rarely estimated, nor is it straightforward to make such estimates. As a consequence of these limitations, pricing policy in the public sector is by necessity somewhat *ad hoc*, the objective being to push pricing policy in what is likely to be the right direction on the basis of clearly defined principles.

Public Sector Pricing in Practice

The notion that public goods should be provided free of charge is widely accepted. Similarly, that the public sector should charge market prices for private goods in competitive markets is uncontroversial. In both cases, there is consistency with the marginal cost pricing principle. Where the only source of competition is imports, border pricing is widely practiced. This will approximate marginal cost pricing only with unrestricted international competition in all markets; otherwise, border pricing is adopted to avoid smuggling to which market imperfections may give rise. Beyond these rather straightforward cases, pricing policy has to be considered on a case-by-case basis. In this connection, however, utility pricing and the scope for user charges in the social sectors—especially health and education—are issues that often arise.

Utility pricing

The natural monopoly characteristics of most utilities—which arise from the extensive use of networks such as electricity grids—make them clear candidates as a group for the application of Ramsey pricing to generate the revenue to cover their losses. Moreover, it is in industries such as electricity, water, and telecommunications that marginal cost is easiest to measure. Clearly, the standard problem about whether prices should be based upon short-run marginal cost or long-run marginal cost has to be resolved. Generally speaking, the former is preferable from a resource allocation viewpoint but produces large price variations, which are administratively costly, politically inconvenient, and create uncertainty among consumers and investors. But the main problem is that estimating the demand elasticities to calculate Ramsey prices for a group of industries is difficult. However, this does not preclude the use of a rule of thumb—water is more inelastically demanded than telephone services, for example—to get appropriate qualitative deviations from marginal cost.

If the scope for system-wide application of Ramsey pricing is limited, it may nevertheless be possible to apply it to one industry to meet a revenue target. Thus a breakeven constraint could be placed on the electricity industry, with a higher prices for lifeline services which are inelastically demanded and lower prices for more discretionary uses. The shortcoming of this approach—and the Ramsey rules in general—is immediately apparent. Goods and services in inelastic demand are often necessities, and charging a high price for necessities hurts the poor. This would not be a problem if there are other means of helping the poor, ideally by raising their incomes, but there may be few alternatives. If redistribution justifies a departure from marginal cost pricing, lifeline electricity should perhaps be provided at below marginal cost, and the revenue constraint will imply that some other inelastically demanded service—for example a specified minimum amount of electricity used by middle-class residential and commercial consumers—should be highly taxed. Peak-load pricing, which is intended primarily to match demand to available capacity, may serve the same purpose if the poor have the flexibility to switch their consumption to off-peak periods.

User charges in health and education

Distributional concerns take on particular significance in the case of social goods such as health and education. The principal issue is how to introduce an element of cost recovery through user charges without conceding distributional objectives. At the same time, there is a trade-off between the desirable implications for resource allocation of imposing some charges and the possible failure to internalize the external benefits of health and education provision if charges are pushed to too high a level. These are complex issues. However, a feature of both these services that facilitates charging is that they are nontransferable, and therefore they are amenable to **personalized prices**.

From the distributional point of view, personalized prices would allow the poor to be charged less than the rich if these groups can be distinguished. Moreover, if the external benefits of health and education are less appreciated by the poor, or if the poor are less likely to make well-informed decisions, this pattern of prices is consistent with efficiency objectives. However, the fact that governments usually provide universal access to health and education services of a certain quality, and in the latter case make consumption compulsory, suggests that pricing policy alone cannot compensate for market failure. These issues are discussed further in the notes on *Health* and *Education*.

Other user charges

User charges are not restricted to social goods, and can be applied quite widely in the public sector. However, because marginal costs are difficult to measure and distributional concerns usually are less compelling, different considerations are brought to bear upon their design. They are often applied to postal, civil aviation, coast guard, and port services, for example. However, perhaps their most common application is to road use.

Generally, user charges can be either **specific fees** or **system-wide fees**, depending upon the extent to which **metering** is possible. If consumption can be metered, fees can be charged that reflect the costs of different categories of demand. Thus a toll road can differentiate fees by distance travelled, and charge trucks more than cars because the former do more damage to the road. Fees can also be high for relatively congested roads. If metering is difficult, and in the case of roads this might be a reflection of high administration costs, a less differentiated fee structure may be used instead. For example, a uniform licence fee can be used to recover costs, but it does not distinguish between different users or the intensity of their use. **Indirect charges**, such as fuel taxes that distinguish between gasoline and diesel fuel, may more successfully internalize road damage externalities, while subsidizing alternative forms of transportation may reduce congestion.

Earmarking

An issue that arises in connection with user charges relates to whether the revenue raised should be used exclusively to pay for the expenditure that gives rise to them. Thus road user charges would be used to pay for road construction and maintenance. Because there is a close link between the payment of the user charge and the associated expenditure, this is an example of **strong earmarking**. This contrasts with **weak earmarking**, where the benefit link is weak. The use of lottery proceeds to pay for public education or a specified share of government revenue to pay for investment spending are examples of weak earmarking.

If the benefits derived from an expenditure program are purely private, expenditure should be **fully funded** by strong earmarked charges. In effect, private activities undertaken by the public sector should be indistinguishable from similar activities in the private sector—the private sector functions entirely on the basis of fully funded earmarking. In practice, earmarked public sector activities, like road construction and maintenance, are only **partially funded** by earmarked charges. In many cases, however, this extends beyond the level of earmarking that can be justified by reference to the strength of the benefit link, and is usually associated with extensive use of weak earmarking.

The earmarking debate

The most widely held view is that in the absence of a strong benefit link earmarking is not justified. It is argued that the level of expenditure on a particular program becomes significantly dependent upon the revenue generated to pay for it, which limits government discretion over those funds and leads to a misallocation of resources. Expenditure decisions are not dictated by efficiency criteria but more by the ability of politicians and bureaucrats to put in place earmarking arrangements that protect their favored programs. However, proponents of earmarking argue that even without earmarking, expenditure decisions reflect state failure that arises from the detrimental influence of politicians and bureaucrats. Under such circumstances, the fact that earmarking introduces rigidity into the budget reduces the scope for such influence, and this leads to an improved allocation of resources. In other words, while earmarking may be inefficient, it is more efficient than not earmarking.

The scope for earmarking

Resolving the earmarking debate is not easy since it largely depends upon identifying the extent to which public sector activity is impaired by political and bureaucratic interference and the relative effectiveness of earmarking in compensating for this. These judgements are difficult to make. However, even without being able to make such judgements, there may be some limited role for earmarking under certain conditions. For example, during periods of fiscal adjustment, the earmarking of revenue to essential programs that are relatively easy to cut—such as operations and maintenance—may be appropriate despite a weak benefit link. But in general, it is a strong benefit link combined with a desire to impose the discipline of the private sector on public sector activities that provides the main justification for earmarking.

Country Illustrations

Toll roads in Indonesia

The government justifies toll roads as part of its medium-term road development program on the grounds that where roads are congested and road capacity expansion is required, users should finance road construction through tolls that should not be higher than avoided congestion costs. The government finances the initial construction costs, generally through foreign loans, and retains ownership of any new toll road. However, it delegates administrative functions to one or more state corporations. Toll rates are set by presidential decree and in general provide for cost recovery over a defined payback period. Tolls are differentiated by vehicle type and weight and by traffic density on particular routes. Rates are periodically increased more or less in line with inflation.

In designing its strategy, the government integrated equity objectives into the policy. Not all new roads are financed through tolls. While the strategy generally calls for beneficiaries to bear the costs of an expansion in the current road network in order to reduce the burden on public finances, the policy allows for budgetary allocations to be set aside to finance road projects in the less-highly developed areas of the country and so promote more geographically balanced development. As a result, the government has purposely avoided the allocation of budgetary resources for the construction of high-cost roads in already highly developed areas, but continues to finance nontoll roads in rural areas of the country.

Earmarked fees in Ecuador

Revenues generated by charges levied on visitors to the Galapagos Islands are earmarked for national park maintenance across the country. The government introduced the fees in part to reduce damage to these ecologically fragile islands. The political appeal of introducing such fees was enhanced by dedicating their revenues to environmental concerns. The benefit link is, however, weakened to the extent that foreign visitors to the Galapagos Islands provide much of the revenue while local visitors to other national parks benefit from much of the expenditure it pays for.

Bibliography

Bos, D., "Public Sector Pricing," in *Handbook of Public Economics*, Vol. 1, ed. by A.J. Auerbach and M. Feldstein (Amsterdam: North-Holland, 1985).

Heady, Christopher, "Public Sector Pricing in a Fiscal Context." Country Economics Department Working Paper Series 179 (Washington: World Bank, 1989).

Jimenez, Emmanuel, "Social Sector Pricing Policy Revisited: A Survey of Some Recent Controversies," *Proceedings of the World Bank Annual Conference on Development Economics* (Washington: World Bank, 1989).

Newbery, David M., "Charging for Roads," *World Bank Research Observer* (Washington: World Bank, 1988).

XXII. Public Expenditure and the Environment

Richard Hemming and Kenneth Miranda

Does economic activity degrade the environment?

What are the least-cost methods of moving an economy toward a sustainable development path?

Who gains and who loses in the implementation of a program of environmental protection?

What issues arise when one country's economic activities give rise to transnational or global environmental problems?

In recent years, increasing attention has been paid to the importance of proper management of environmental resources in both industrial and developing countries. For the most part, this concern has reflected the emerging view, championed by both ecologists and economists, that economic policies should be directed toward achieving **sustainable development**, that allows the present generation to meet its needs without compromising the ability of future generations to meet theirs. As such, environmental resources are viewed as national assets that should be utilized in a manner consistent with maximizing their value across generations.

Fiscal instruments are central to proper and prudent environmental management, and can influence directly or indirectly such things as the rate at which natural resources are depleted, the extent to which air and water are polluted and soil is eroded, and whether or not entire species of animal and plant life are threatened. This note describes the role of fiscal instruments in general, and public expenditure in particular, in the design of policies to promote growth and development consistent with appropriate conservation of environmental resources.

Objectives of Environmental Policy

Environmental degradation is a **production or consumption externality**—see the note on *Public Expenditure and Resource Allocation*. Thus, the standard approach to the design of economic policy toward the environment is to attempt an evaluation of the costs associated with this externality and then reflect them in resource allocation decisions. The problem is summarized in Chart 1. The intersection of the demand curve DD and the free market supply curve SS generates equilibrium price and output combination A. However, the market will not take into account the fact that the use of resources in this way imposes costs elsewhere—these **external costs** imply that the supply curve should be SS', resulting in an equilibrium B, where price is higher and output lower compared to the case where external costs are ignored. The market therefore underprices and overuses resources, and the objective of environmental policy is to effect a move from an equilibrium like A to one like B.

Chart 1. The Impact of External Costs and User Costs

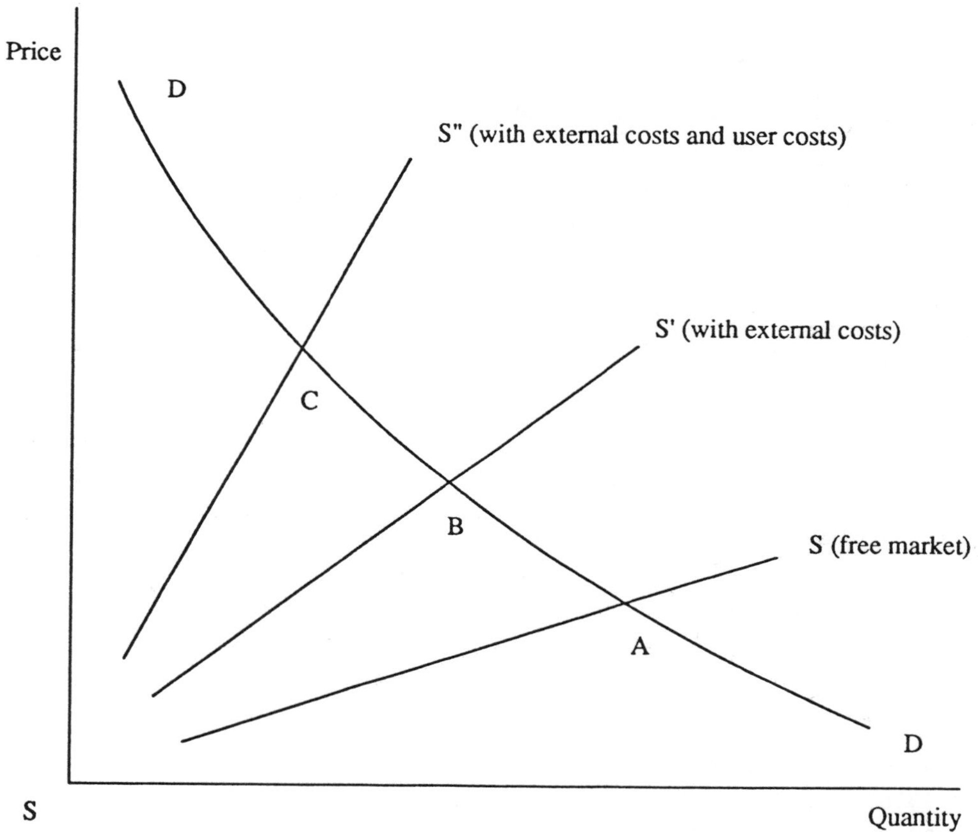

The fact that the development process may often involve the adoption of technologies involving negative environmental externalities does not necessarily imply that all such technologies should be avoided and environmental damage should be halted. Indeed, if the objective was to stop further damage, let alone return the environment to its initial state, few economic activities would take place and development would cease. Rather, the benefits and costs of such damage have to be compared and activities undertaken only to the point where (usually decreasing) marginal social benefits are equated with (usually increasing) marginal social costs. Thus, from an economic perspective, an optimal degree of environmental degradation can be established. This will be related to the **carrying capacity** of the ecosystem, that is its ability to repair ecological damage and to regenerate itself.

This optimal degree of environmental degradation is linked to the issue of sustainable development. In the absence of corrective measures, an activity may be undertaken that results in a reduction of the economic value of a country's environmental resources greater than the income stream the activity itself generates. In such an instance, development cannot be said to be sustainable; in essence, the economy is cannibalizing itself. With corrective measures, the activity may still be undertaken, but at a smaller scale. The net income flow generated by the activity must be at least as great as the reduction in the economic value of the country's natural resources and environmental assets—and hence net wealth at a minimum maintained—for development to be sustainable. The choice of the social discount rate is crucial in such comparisons, especially in cases of intertemporal externalities.

Much of the literature on **environmental economics** is concerned with estimating the direct costs associated with environmental degradation. Cost estimation in this area is tricky. The absence of **property rights** in respect of the environment means that external costs are often not recognized and that the benefits of reducing damage are generally non–appropriable. Ignoring these externalities may overstate the returns of damaging economic activities, and will understate the returns of undertakings with strong conservation components. Efforts to place a value on environmental damage rely either on indirect indicators—such as the extent to which housing prices are lower in the proximity of airports or factories—or are based on **willingness-to-pay** studies, where people are asked what they are willing to pay to prevent or repair environmental damage. At best, these estimates are only approximate, but it is generally better to have an appropriate qualitative guide to resource allocation decisions than to ignore the problem.

The failure to take account of **user costs**, that is the indirect costs of natural-resource depletion and of environmental degradation, is also a problem. The optimal degree of environmental degradation, taking into account external costs, could be consistent with the exhaustion of nonrenewable resources and the extinction of certain species. Advocates of sustainable development emphasize the irreversible character of much environmental damage, which makes it difficult or impossible to correct mistakes which, in retrospect, turn out to be inconsistent with long-run development policy. Recognition of user costs implies that the impact of current policies for the availability of environmental capital to future generations should be reflected in resource allocation decisions. User costs imply a supply curve such as S" in Chart 1, producing a new equilibrium C with a higher price and lower output than when external costs alone are considered. However, estimating user costs is especially difficult, since determining how much environmental capital any generation should consume is not a question with a clear answer in either principle or practice. For the moment, the importance of the user cost concept again lies in its qualitative implications—resource allocation decisions should at least reflect an awareness of the future ramifications of those decisions. In this connection, much recent attention has focused on the implications of economic and environmental policies in the **M–7 megabiodiverse** countries (Australia, Brazil, Colombia, Indonesia, Madagascar, Mexico, and Zaire), which contain more than half of the world's species.

Instruments of Environmental Policy

The environment is a classic public good (see the note on *Public Expenditure and Resource Allocation*). It is therefore the proper role of government to encourage the preservation of the environment. The government has at its disposal a wide range of instruments. The choice of instrument or combination of instruments depends upon a number of factors. Insofar as it is possible to ensure a better quality environment by altering the behavior of consumers and producers, the range of instruments includes the regulatory and legal framework, moral suasion, environmental subsidies and taxes, and other expenditure measures. There is also a need to correct policy failures which have led to the implementation of measures that do unintended damage to the environment.

Regulation, legal framework, and moral suasion

When **metering** is difficult—that is, pollution cannot be measured—**regulation** in the form of pollution standards (including the prohibition of particularly hazardous activities), specification of acceptable techniques of production, the issuance of pollution permits, or the use of refundable deposits may be the only alternatives. **Pollution permits** convey the right to pollute up to some agreed maximum level, and may be initially allocated or auctioned to firms. Furthermore, so long as they are marketable after being initially allocated or auctioned, pollution permits can be dynamically efficient. Politically, however, the sale of "licenses to pollute" may be unpopular. Where metering is possible but for technical reasons is not viable, **refundable deposits** have the advantage that they shift the burden of proof about pollution control to the claimant. In cases where the problem of externality derives from the ill-definition or lack of property rights, the assignment or clarification of property rights by the government, most notably through the legal system, and the subsequent development of mechanisms to establish legal liability, may also be an efficient instrument to preserve the environment. The efficacy of such an approach depends on, among other things, the enforceability of the rights themselves and the transaction costs associated with civil litigation. **Moral suasion—**that is, efforts to educate and otherwise persuade the public about the benefits of environmental protection and conservation—is appropriate where effective monitoring of regulations is difficult, as in the case of forest-fire prevention.

Environmental subsidies and taxes

When metering is economical, fiscal measures in the form of environmental subsidies and environmental taxes may have the clear advantage on efficiency grounds, because they have the potential to affect resource allocation decisions at the margin. Conservation or environmental **subsidies** are aimed at compensating those who voluntarily reduce the amount of pollution they generate. Examples include subsidies for installation of solar-generation capacity, for planting trees as windbreaks against soil erosion, and for taking marginal, highly erodible soil out of production or converting such land into permanent grasslands. However, only if there are strong political objections to charging are subsidies a substitute for **taxes (or fees)**, since the latter have advantages. While in principle there is an equivalence between subsidies and taxes in terms of cost per unit of pollution reduction, a tax penalizes a polluter; not only could a subsidy protect an otherwise unprofitable firm from bankruptcy, it also has adverse implications for the fiscal balance. There is a case for cutting back on environmental subsidies that are clearly less efficient than viable alternative policy measures, as well as subsidies that encourage environmental degradation (e.g., subsidies on pesticides, chemical fertilizers, gasoline, etc.). The principal shortcomings of taxes relate to the uncertainty of their impact and their inflexibility, both in terms of the possible need for change over time and differences between localities (see the note on *Transfers to Local Government* for a discussion of the advantages of centralized tax collection). Fiscal control of the revenues generated by environmental taxes is also an issue, with the main debate concerning whether such revenues should be used for general funding or earmarked to pollution abatement and conservation programs (see the discussion of earmarking in the note on *Pricing and Cost Recovery*).

Other expenditure measures

While all of the above measures have expenditure implications—they have to be administered—only subsidies are a direct expenditure measure. However, public expenditure policy is not limited to subsidies. The government can give **grants** to producers to install equipment to control pollution—the problem with grants of this sort is that they do not address the pollution problem directly. A grant provides little incentive to reduce emissions to an appropriate level or to use the most efficient method of achieving such a reduction; indeed, there is no guarantee that pollution will be reduced at all. Because grants share many of the same shortcomings as subsidies, only in exceptional cases are they likely to be an effective element of pollution-control strategy.

Government expenditure also has a clear role in **investment activity**. This is especially true where the public good characteristics of investments make private supply inefficient and/or there are scale economies—water purification is a case in point. Mounting evidence also indicates that many environmental projects have very high rates of return when economically correct forms of cost-benefit analysis are employed. This is especially true in energy and agricultural land conservation projects (see the discussion of shelterbelts in the note on *Public Investment*). However, a lack of institutional capability on the part of country authorities to evaluate environmental projects and/or to incorporate evaluation of environmental impact into project analyses prevents many governments from recognizing this potential benefit. Numerous countries, with the assistance of nongovernment organizations and multilateral lending agencies, are now addressing these deficiencies, with a view to improving investment allocation decisions and promoting sustainable development.

Government expenditures on **operations and maintenance** can also serve to promote environmental objectives. Thus, a well-maintained road network may improve vehicle fuel efficiency, thereby saving scarce resources and reducing the emission of harmful exhausts. Operations and maintenance expenditures to preserve water resources can play a critical role in the maintenance of natural ecosystem balances. Finally, operations and maintenance expenditures that ensure efficiency in electricity generation and transmission reduce energy losses, are thereby environmental degradation through harmful emissions.

The design of effective environmental policy involves the appropriate use of available instruments in pursuit of clearly specified objectives. In this sense, it is no different from economic policy making in general. It does, however, differ in one significant respect. If one looks at the way economic policy is made, there is at least a semblance of an effort to match targets and instruments in a way broadly consistent with well-established principles of policy formulation. In the case of environmental policy, the evidence suggests a strong reluctance to put principle into practice. In part, this reflects inadequate institutional capabilities referred to above. However, distributional considerations and problems involved in securing international agreement on environmental issues are the main constraints.

Constraints on Environmental Policy

Distributional impact

Environmental protection produces gainers and losers, and the distribution of these gains and losses has a significant bearing on the willingness to adopt effective environmental policies. This issue has a number of aspects. In industrial countries, there is a view that environmental protection is a luxury good, and its benefits are biased toward the rich. They have the time and education to lobby effectively; they make more intensive use of recreational facilities; and they have more resources and options to compensate for any adverse economic impact of environmental policy. In developing countries, the same argument can be interpreted as implying a pro-poor bias associated with environmental degradation. These countries are under severe pressure from rapidly growing populations and endemic poverty. The poor cannot afford to postpone consumption, and the rapid depletion of natural resources is necessary for subsistence. Politically, it is difficult for governments of industrial countries to resist the wishes of the large middle class and for the governments of developing countries to ignore the needs of the poor. The political difficulties in implementing environmental policy are compounded by the fact that those who must bear the costs of environmental protection—mainly industry—have been able to oppose policy measures effectively.

International dimension to environmental policy

The evidence of environmental damage across national boundaries is overwhelming. This takes two forms: transnational spillovers, as for example when acid rain affects the environmental quality in a bordering country, and international spillovers, as for example when oceans are overfished and polluted, or when there is global warming and depletion of the ozone layer. In the former case, property rights may be well-defined, but transactions costs associated with bilateral or multilateral negotiations hinder the effective resolution of the problem. In the latter case, property rights for **international common property** are not clearly allocated, and transactions costs are very high because all the countries of the world should theoretically be party to a negotiated settlement. Effective control, which is difficult at the national level, has proved almost impossible at the transnational and international level. The particular problems that arise are easily demonstrated. Any country that imposes a penalty on a polluting industry will raise its costs and affect its ability to export, with adverse balance of payments consequences; if other countries impose such penalties, a country that does not follow suit can benefit from the resulting terms of trade advantage. One solution may be for affected countries to impose trade restrictions on polluting nations. From other viewpoints, such measures have little to recommend them and, unless internationally coordinated, would not be effective.

Country Illustration

The national environment program in Madagascar

Recent estimates have placed the annual costs of environmental degradation in Madagascar at between US$100 million and US$290 million, roughly equivalent to between 5 and 15 percent of GNP. Deforestation accounts for about 75 percent of the cost, while decreased productivity in agricultural and pasture lands due to soil erosion accounts for another 15 percent. Increased operating costs and reduced life spans of infrastructural investments, especially irrigation and road networks, account for the balance. In an effort to address these environmental and economic problems, and in recognition of the unique biological diversity of the country, the government has recently strengthened its national environmental program in concert with foreign official donors as well as with nongovernmental organizations.

In August 1989, the Central Bank of Madagascar completed a **debt-for-nature swap**—the first of its kind in Africa—with the World Wildlife Fund (WWF) for an amount of US$3 million. In the first phase of the operation, the WWF used US$950,000 to purchase approximately US$2.1 million of eligible Malagasy debt at a price of US$0.45 on the dollar. The domestic currency counterpart provided by the central bank in exchange for the debt is currently being used to protect Madagascar's biodiversity, large tracts of undisturbed rain forests, and several critical watersheds. The proceeds are also being used to protect and manage Madagascar's high-priority protected areas and to train, equip, and support 400 park rangers. The budgetary programming of these expenditures was jointly agreed upon by the WWF and the government. In 1990 and 1991, the WWF will seek to convert the remainder of the debt for additional conservation efforts through the budget.

In collaboration with the World Bank, the government has also developed the first five-year segment of a 15-year **Environmental Action Plan (EAP)**, again the first in Africa. The EAP consists of seven components: (i) protecting and managing the unique ecological system together with the development of peripheral zones; (ii) promotion of soil conservation, agroforestry, reforestation, and other rural development activities in priority zones, including several large watersheds; (iii) development of maps and geographic information for program-related areas; (iv) improvements in land security through titling; (v) the training of environmental specialists and the promotion of environmental awareness and education; (vi) the initiation of environmental research programs on land, coastal, and marine ecosystems; and (vii) the development of support activities, including institution building and the adoption of environmental-assessment procedures. In terms of fiscal impact, the program is expected to be neutral in the short term, but substantially positive over the long term. The positive fiscal impact over the long term stems from improvements in land-tax collections due to titling efforts, greater rural tax collections as a result of improvements in agricultural productivity, the development of **eco-tourism** and the collection of tourist fees, cost-recovery efforts in park areas, and larger royalty payments resulting from a more effective management of resources.

Bibliography

Baumol, W.J., and W.E. Oates, *Economics, Environmental Policy, and the Quality of Life* (Englewood Cliffs: Prentice Hall, 1979).

Baumol, W.J., *The Theory of Environmental Policy* (Cambridge: Cambridge University Press, 1988).

Tisdell, C., "Sustainable Development: Differing Perspectives of Ecologists and Economists, and Relevance to LDCs," *World Development*, 16, 1989.

XXIII. Expenditure Arrears

Jack Diamond and Christian Schiller

What is the fiscal and monetary impact of arrears? How do they affect the behavior of the private sector?
At which stages of the budgetary process can arrears arise?
How can arrears be monitored? Does the accounting system matter?

The emergence of government expenditure arrears, indicating delays in a government's payments to its suppliers and creditors, has become an important fiscal issue in many developing countries. Given accounting conventions, the presence of arrears may lead to an underestimation of expenditure, the impact of government operations and the size of the fiscal problem facing a country. Since arrears are a form of **forced financing,** the government's borrowing requirement is understated, yielding a distorted picture of the sources of credit expansion in an economy. Arrears also raise issues related to fiscal adjustment. This note focuses on domestic arrears; arrears on external debt payments are discussed in the note on *Debt Relief.*

What Are Arrears?

In principle, the concept of arrears appears uncomplicated. They are the total outstanding obligations due for payment that the government has failed to discharge. Normally, claims that have been referred to adjudication, or are found wanting in documentation, should be excluded. Similarly, arrears arising from pay revisions with retroactive effect are also excluded. The aim is to isolate those payments for which claims have been established but which are kept pending for prolonged periods, usually for lack of necessary funds. The only obvious discretionary issue is the definition of when the time lag between the creation of a payment obligation and its discharge becomes so abnormal as to imply the existence of an arrear, or in the case of a prolonged delay, a default. In reality, the identification and measurement of arrears based on the notion of a greater than normal delay is rarely straightforward. Although legal requirements usually fix the date for payment, there can be considerable administrative lags in processing and recognizing the legal obligation to pay.

The Economic Impact of Arrears

The emergence of government arrears is likely to have implications for the allocation and distribution of resources within the economy, both through its effects on input prices and incomes, and through its macroeconomic effects. Two factors are important: the extent to which arrears are anticipated and the extent to which creditors can neutralize the impact of arrears. The most obvious **allocative effect,** in the short run, is that arrears constitute an alternative form of deficit financing. If forced taxation through money creation is not feasible, the government's claim on total output is limited by available foreign financing and by the amount the domestic economy is prepared to release to the government by paying taxes or by extending credit. The buildup of arrears increases the government's absorption of resources above this level. This initial effect, however, may be offset if the rest of the economy responds to the arrears by holding back tax payments and other fees and charges. At the same time, it should not be forgotten that there are often other transactions offsetting the accumulation of arrears to certain suppliers, for example, the prepayment of goods to other suppliers. There may also be important **distributional effects** of a buildup in arrears arising from the government being able to delay payment to one group of claimants much more easily than another. Finally, the accumulation of government arrears may have a serious impact on the confidence of private enterprises and households in the soundness of government financial operations. Private consumers and investors might anticipate increases in the nominal tax rate, inflation, or more generally, a deterioration in the financial situation of the country over the medium term.

Macroeconomic consequences

Goods and services

When arrears first emerge as a means of more than temporary government financing of purchases, the effective interest cost of financing arrears is wholly borne by the suppliers of goods and services (be they producers, importers, or wage earners), as the forced financing is presumably unanticipated. Over time, and in the face of further likely arrears by the government, those economic agents providing goods and services to the government may begin to adjust their pricing and production behavior to take account of such payment delays. Vendors dealing with the government may begin to charge higher prices to make up for refinancing costs, to reflect their risk premium, or to pay the bribes needed to speed up the payment process. Thus the government may have to pay prices above the market price and, with limited budgetary outlays, be forced to reduce the quantities of goods and services purchased.

The implicit interest costs of arrears are independent of whether or not providers of goods and services bid up prices to account for the delays in payment. The degree to which prices are increased only determines the distribution of the financial burden of the payment delay, for example, as between the government, by paying increased prices (and ultimately the consumers of its services through reduced services or higher taxes or fees), or the vendors, through a squeeze in their profit margins. To the extent that arrears are reflected in higher prices of those expenditure items on which arrears are frequently incurred, existing fiscal data provide a biased picture of the true weight of interest costs in the budget, not taking account of the implicit interest costs included in expenditure on goods and services.

In its normal purchases of goods and services from vendors, the government sets in motion an income-creating process that increases aggregate demand. The effects of the government incurring arrears on payments will depend upon the way vendors initially finance the production of the goods and services to be supplied to the government. If this financing takes the form of borrowing from the banking system, the impact will be no different than if the government had made the payment on time with proceeds borrowed from the commercial banks, except that the vendors will pay the interest costs; however, as noted earlier, the fiscal incidence of these costs is likely to be on the government. Thus the overall effect on aggregate demand will be very similar to that arising from bank-financed government expenditures. Alternatively, vendors might perceive the incurrence of government arrears as only a temporary phenomenon and thus reduce their cash balances below the level warranted by the prevailing interest rates and their volume of transactions. A strong effect on demand may also be expected if vendors satisfy their financing needs by external short-term indebtedness. While domestic arrears are usually passed on to other domestic suppliers, companies have adjusted to the government's inability to meet its obligations by creating arrears to the foreign parent company. In the latter case, the government has indirectly financed its expenditure by what amounts to an inflow of foreign short-term capital.

Wages and transfers

The change in aggregate demand brought about by the creation of **arrears in wage payments** to government employees will depend largely upon their perception of the postponement of wage payments and their underlying consumption behavior. If, for example, the spending decisions of government employees are determined by their actual cash income, and if the government stretches out the period between paydays such that the civil servants receive only 11 monthly salaries in a 12-month period, then their private consumption will drop by 1/12 = 8 1/2 percent. But, if their underlying consumption behavior is more accurately described by a permanent income model of consumption behavior, and if government employees regard delays in salary payment as only transitory, civil servants may perceive only the interest foregone on the deferred payment as a cut in permanent income. Their consumption outlays would then drop only marginally, and the temporary cash shortage would be made up by dissaving. In reality, civil servants may not have confidence in being able to recover the loss in cash income incurred by the payment delay, the drop in their permanent income will be considerably more than just the foregone interest. A similar analysis can be applied to arrears in other government payments to private households. **Delays in transfer payments** and in **interest payments on government bonds** held by the private nonbank sector will tend to reduce private consumption. The fall in consumption will be determined by the relevant consumption function and the perception of the household as to whether the payment delay represents a transitory or permanent change in government policies.

Principal repayments

The macroeconomic effects of amortization arrears are likely to be less than those arising from expenditure arrears, since the former do not set in motion an income-generating flow of goods and services from the rest of the economy to the government or engender any expectation of accrued income. To assess the effects of amortization arrears is difficult, since much depends on the response of creditors, which in turn hinges on whether such arrears were anticipated. In the extreme case of the creditor not anticipating the arrear, it could be argued that if the government fails to make a domestic amortization payment on time, the only immediate effect will be a substitution of a formal claim on the government by another one. The total amount of claims of the private sector on the government remains unchanged. This argument assumes that the government will continue to pay interest on the loan, and that the portfolio owner believes that the government will finally repay the loan. Typically, creditors might try to raise the interest rate somewhat in order to compensate for the higher risk now associated with this part of their portfolio. If, however, the government stops paying interest and so increases the perceived probability of default, a domestic amortization arrear may lead to a fall in private sector wealth, which will reduce consumption.

Arrears and inflation

At first glance, it appears likely that government arrears have an impact mainly on relative prices. As described above, suppliers are likely to react to the incurrence of government arrears by bidding up the prices at which they are prepared to sell goods and services to the government. In more general terms, in an environment characterized by financial instability, as reflected by the government's inability to make payments on time, economic agents will include high risk premiums in the calculation of the price at which they are prepared to render goods or services. But, where the provider of goods and services is able, within the overall credit ceiling, to bridge the delay in payments by borrowing from the banks, this may add pressure to the credit market, and as in the case of additional government borrowing, push up interest rates. If this effect induces the central bank to relax monetary policy or attracts capital inflow, the outcome would also be pressure on prices. When arrears are accumulated against public enterprises, as is often the case, and are of sufficient magnitude, the financial position of the public enterprise sector may worsen. If this results in higher credit from the central bank, arrears will end up creating inflationary and balance of payments pressures. Where the creation of arrears takes place at a very late stage of the expenditure process by increasing the stock of outstanding checks beyond the normal check float and beyond the government's short-term capacity to honor them, then significant monetary effects can be expected. Because government checks are normally highly liquid, an increase in broad money takes place, and if the demand for money does not grow at the same pace, a continued overhang of check float can be destabilizing.

Identifying and Monitoring Arrears

Controlling arrears requires a clear definition of an arrear, an inventory of arrears based on this definition, and a means of monitoring changes in this inventory. In identifying arrears, there are difficulties arising from dubious obligations that have yet to be regularized. Interlocking arrears also create problems, especially where the parties involved dispute their validity. Generally, net arrears are more relevant than gross arrears; an exception would be where tax payments are held back. Even if arrears can be identified, monitoring the subsequent discharge of arrears is often difficult. Developing an appropriate control mechanism is very much a function of existing budgetary procedures. The characteristics of the British and French types of accounting systems suggest that the monitoring of arrears is likely to be easier in francophone countries (see Chart 1). In these countries, there is greater possibility of gaining a more complete picture of the movement in government arrears by tracing the changing stock of outstanding commitments, through the stock of payment orders, to checks issued and cashed and having a reporting system at different stages of the expenditure process. In this way, the French type of budgetary system, when functioning properly, offers a direct indicator of arrears relatively early in the expenditure process. The British-type system, on the other hand, is less centralized and does not offer intermediate indicators of changes in arrears, since there is generally no centralized consolidation of payment orders issued to compare with checks issued and cashed.

Country Illustration

Monitoring arrears in Zambia

The identification and eventual resolution of a persistent government arrears problem requires the development of effective budgetary monitoring and control procedures, including adequate accounting and reporting requirements for government ministries, departments, and other specialized agencies. In the case of Zambia, weaknesses in these procedures have made it difficult to monitor the financial operations of the government, and hence the emergence of domestic budgetary arrears. Under procedures that were in effect in 1990 and earlier years, ministries and departments were required to report expenditures for which vouchers (i.e., payment orders) had been issued. Commitments entered into, but for which vouchers had not been issued, were not reported. As such, the existing reporting system did not provide an adequate early warning system to indicate

Chart 1. Arrears and Time Lags in the Stages of the Expenditure Process

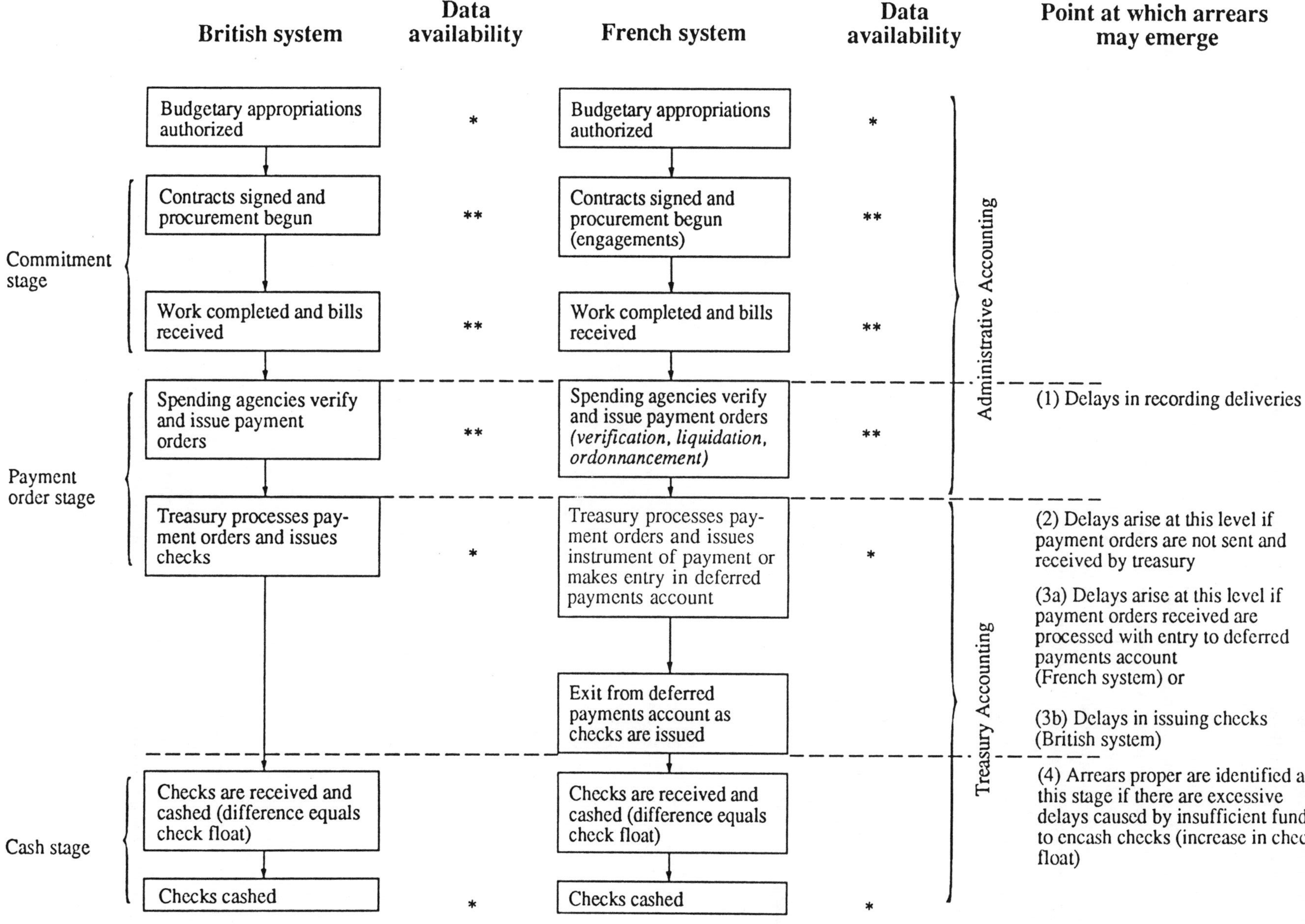

* Data are usually available in consolidated form.

** Data are only available on a disaggregated basis.

whether, by how much, or in what areas budgetary commitments were accumulating, and thus creating an arrears problem. A substantial but undetermined accumulation of arrears thus occurred in 1990 and earlier years.

To address these deficiencies, the Budget Office of the Ministry of Finance undertook a review of the government accounting and reporting procedures, and developed revised procedures that would allow the budget to be monitored on commitment, vouchers-issued, and cash bases. These revised procedures are now in the process of being implemented. The four largest ministries (in terms of budgetary appropriations) were the first to begin adopting the new procedures, with the view that effective implementation will take a number of years and that it was essential to cover the greatest proportion of the total budget as quickly as possible. As part of the overall effort, the government is also verifying the stock of domestic arrears from 1990 and previous years, with a view to programming a phased reduction as quickly as possible.

Bibliography

Diamond, Jack, and Christian Schiller. "Government Arrears in Fiscal Adjustment Programs," in *Measurement of Fiscal Impact: Methodological Issues,* Occasional Paper No. 59, ed. by Mario I. Blejer and Ke-young Chu (Washington: International Monetary Fund, 1988).

XXIV. Debt Relief

Richard Hemming and Claire Liuksila

How are debt rescheduling and debt reduction reflected in fiscal accounts?

In what ways are official debt and bank debt relieved?

Does the distinction between government and central bank liabilities matter?

An inability to service external debt indicates that macroeconomic policies have been unsustainable and that a policy adjustment is unavoidable (see the note on *Public Expenditure and Sustainable Fiscal Policy*). However, adjustment measures may be incapable of restoring sustainability without either temporary or permanent debt relief. The purpose of this note is to outline the fiscal implications of alternative ways of restructuring debt to provide such relief.

The Accounting Framework

The conventionally defined fiscal deficit measures the gap between revenue and expenditure. The cash deficit refers only to transactions for which cash has been disbursed or cash revenues have been received. The commitment deficit measures the government's planned net use of resources resulting from budgetary decisions. The government's inability to meet its expenditure commitments on a timely basis is reflected in an accumulation of payments arrears, producing a difference between the commitment deficit and the cash deficit. While an unsustainable debt burden may manifest itself in a variety of ways—including a need to levy bad taxes or cut essential spending programs—it is often associated with an accumulation of arrears to external creditors. Assuming that the government plans to service its debt in full, its interest obligations would be reflected in the commitment deficit and its actual interest payments in the cash deficit. Where the government has no intention to fully service its debt, it is sometimes useful to distinguish an accruals-based concept of the deficit to reflect the gap between its contractual obligations and its budget commitment. Rather than making this distinction, the term "commitment" tends to be used rather flexibly. The build-up of amortization arrears affects other financing needs. The alternative deficit concepts give rise to different accounting frameworks:

Cash basis

Revenue
- Noninterest expenditure
- **Actual** interest
= Cash deficit
= (-) Financing
= New external borrowing
- **Actual** amortization
+ Net domestic borrowing

Commitment basis

Revenue
- Noninterest expenditure
- **Scheduled** interest
= Commitment deficit
= (-) Financing
= New external borrowing
- **Scheduled** amortization
+ Change in arrears
+ Net domestic borrowing.

Alternatively, the two accounting frameworks can be combined as follows:

Revenue
- Noninterest expenditure
- **Scheduled** interest
= Commitment deficit
- Change in interest arrears
= Cash deficit
= (-) Financing
= New external borrowing
- **Scheduled** amortization
+ Change in amortization arrears
+ Net domestic borrowing

This framework—which ignores nondebt related payment arrears—will be used below to describe the impact of the main debt restructuring options.

The distinction between the commitment and cash deficit has a significance that extends beyond the implications discussed in the note on *Expenditure Arrears*. In particular, where there are external arrears, it is the commitment deficit that often needs to be reflected in macroeconomic analysis. Since the commitment deficit is defined analogously to the external current account deficit, which is always defined on a commitment basis, a comparison of the two will lead to correct inferences about the implied private sector savings-investment balance. See equation (2) of the note on *Public Expenditure and Sustainable Fiscal Policy*.

Official Debt

Debt rescheduling and debt reduction

Official debt restructuring has focused primarily on the **rescheduling** of debt service payments in respect of medium- and long-term debt to governments and multilateral lending agencies. Terms are normally agreed in the context of Paris Club negotiations between creditors and debtors. These terms vary on a case-by-case basis, with exceptional, more favorable, rescheduling (Toronto terms) granted to the poorest and most heavily indebted countries. There is a menu of rescheduling options which allows for changing the maturity structure of debt, extending grace periods, canceling some portion of debt service, and the use of concessional interest rates. Arrears are usually consolidated under Paris Club agreements. Rescheduling changes the time profile of debt service payments, giving a country breathing room in which it can get an economy back on track so that it can eventually discharge its debt service obligations. It is for this reason that a Paris Club rescheduling is often linked to the strength of adjustment policies in general, and Fund conditionality in particular. With exceptional rescheduling terms the present value of the debt is also reduced. But in some cases, the debt burden is so great that even rescheduling on exceptional terms is not enough, and a significant **reduction** in the stock of debt is required. This would be the case where the debt overhang discourages investors, who see the future need for an unacceptably large diversion of resources to meet debt payments.

Fiscal impact

Debt rescheduling alone has no impact on the fiscal deficit measured on a commitment basis. The accounts would simply record the following:

Revenue
- Noninterest expenditure
- **Originally** scheduled interest
= Commitment deficit
- Rescheduled interest
= Cash deficit
= (-) Financing
= New external borrowing
- **Originally** scheduled amortization
+ Rescheduled amortization
+ Net domestic borrowing

By contrast, the cash deficit will likely fall, depending upon how much of the interest obligation was previously being discharged. Similarly, amortization payments will probably fall, implying an even smaller need for new external borrowing and domestic borrowing than implied by the fall in the deficit alone. With lower domestic borrowing, domestic interest and amortization could also fall by a modest amount in the same year, but by more over the medium term. Only where a country is accumulating large interest and amortization arrears is debt rescheduling likely to place an additional burden on the budget, as debtors are required to share some of the cost of debt relief.

In the case of debt reduction, the government is relieved of the obligation to repay part of its debt. Official debt reduction can take a variety of forms—debt can be canceled, interest and amortization payments can be forgone—which can be compared on a present value basis. Whatever method is adopted, the deficit measured on a commitment basis should fall. The cash and commitment deficits are brought into line (or closer into line if nondebt-related payment arrears persist), as follows:

Revenue
- Noninterest expenditure
- **Newly** scheduled interest
= Commitment deficit
= Cash deficit
= (-) Financing
= New external borrowing
- **Newly** scheduled amortization
+ Net domestic borrowing

The new cash deficit may be higher or lower than the preceding cash deficit, depending upon the cash flow implications of the debt reduction operation. But countries that require debt reduction are probably servicing rather little of their debt, and a requirement that the debtor is expected to bear some of the costs of debt reduction could again lead to increased interest and amortization payments. Debt reduction operations also have some transactions costs. The advantage of accepting this deal is that relations with creditors are regularized, access to foreign capital is reestablished, and the burden of debt service—relative to capacity to pay—will hopefully be reduced.

It should be clear from the preceding discussion that the distinction between debt rescheduling and debt reduction is blurred, since debt rescheduling on exceptional terms embodies an element of debt reduction. Moreover, debt rescheduling and explicit debt reduction will often go hand-in-hand. There is therefore a need for flexibility in the application of the accounting procedures suggested above to describe the fiscal impact of debt relief.

The debt reduction case nevertheless demonstrates rather clearly the macroeconomic importance of the commitment based definition of the fiscal deficit. Debt reduction is intended to close external financing gaps, and is normally reflected in a reduction in the external current account deficit. With given investment plans, the implied reduction in foreign saving must be offset by higher domestic saving. Since there is no reason to believe that private saving will be immediately affected, this offset must be seen in government saving, if properly defined. This is indeed what happens, as the commitment deficit will reflect exactly the same amount of interest relief (net of transactions costs) as the external current account deficit, while the cash deficit could rise and the cash-based measure of government saving would fall correspondingly.

Bank debt

Bank debt restructuring is more ad hoc than its official debt counterpart, although there is a significant element of commonality to the agreements that have been concluded. In part, this reflects efforts to ensure **burden sharing** between the banks and official creditors in granting debt relief. A feature of bank debt restructuring agreements is that interest payments falling due or in arrears have in virtually all cases been excluded from rescheduling. As part of these arrangements, short-term debt is sometimes rolled over or converted into medium-term loans. Medium-term loans are also refinanced. Like agreements with official creditors, bank debt restructuring is linked closely to the strength of adjustment being undertaken. Stronger policies usually attract longer maturities and grace periods, reduced fees, and have favorable terms for refinancing. The principle of burden sharing has also been extended debt reduction. The fiscal impact of bank debt restructuring is much as described above for official debt restructuring, except that there are usually additional transactions costs involved, which depend upon the nature of the debt reduction operation.

Modalities of bank debt reduction

Debt buybacks

The secondary market price of developing country private debt is often substantially less than its face value—Peruvian debt, for example, has traded at a 95 percent discount. It has been argued that these discounts can be exploited to reduce debt cheaply. With a 95 percent discount it would cost only 5 cents to reduce debt by $1. However, if debt is reduced by this method, capacity to service remaining debt will likely increase and the price of that debt—and its market value—will rise. The debtor country could find itself worse off as a consequence, since it has incurred the costs of debt reduction but its debt remains largely unaffected. The external creditor is correspondingly better off. In essence, the debtor is repurchasing marginal debt at its average price rather than its lower marginal price. The cash flow repercussions for the debtor can, however, be alleviated if the buyback is paid for externally, which is the essence of the Brady Plan. But if the debtor incurs new debt in the process, there remains a sizable transfer from the debtor to its creditors which must be paid for out of the budget.

Debt exchanges

It is sometimes argued that exchanging new debt for old debt offers a costless way of reducing debt. With a 95 percent discount a government could buy back $100 million of old debt with $5 million of new debt if the new debt sells at par. But unless the perceived riskiness of debt is affected, the discount on the new debt will be the same as on the old, and debt cannot be reduced by this method. This can happen only if it can be established that new debt is senior to old debt. Whether it is then in the creditors' interests to allow debt exchanges depends upon how the creditor translates seniority into an expected flow of debt service payments.

Debt equity swaps

Debt equity swaps are alleged to have the additional advantage that they reverse capital flight and attract capital inflows, as well as reducing external debt. But swapping debt for equity involves no more than an exchange of liabilities. Whether this is beneficial depends upon the efficiency consequences of having **additional** equity owned by foreigners. If this is not the final effect—because foreigners sell equity domestically (and then use it to purchase foreign exchange, for example) or foreign equity owners cannot exercise effective control over their assets—then there is no benefit and possibly some harm resulting from the exercise. Some more innovative debt swap operations are illustrated below by reference to country experiences.

Role of the Central Bank

It has been assumed that all external debt is a liability of the government, and debt service transactions take place directly between the debtor government and its foreign creditors. However, in many cases, foreign financing is channeled through the central bank. It is the Fund's recommended practice that in such circumstances the benefits of debt relief be treated as general balance of payments support, and obligations of the government (and private debtors) to the central bank arising from the onlending of external borrowing continue to be serviced in domestic currency. This preference arises from a desire to ensure that the benefits of debt relief are not lost through a loosening of fiscal policy. If the central bank lends on the same terms it receives, there is macroeconomically no difference between debt relief granted to the government and the central bank. Debt relief to the central bank will have no effect on government finances; it would, however, affect public sector finances if central bank and government financial operations are consolidated. Without consolidation, care is needed in interpreting fiscal data, since the central bank may be bearing costs otherwise borne by the government, such as foreign exchange losses (see the note on *Fiscal Activities of Public Institutions* for further discussion.)

Country Illustrations

Innovations in debt swap operations

In recent years, a number of new modalities have been developed for the purpose of debt reduction. **Debt-for-nature** swaps have tended to take the form of an acquisition of developing country debt, at a discount, by conservation organizations; the debt is then converted into local currency instruments to fund conservation programs. A program was launched in **Bolivia** in July 1987, which exchanged US$0.7 million of claims—obtained in the secondary market at an 85 percent discount—for local currency to fund the management of ecological resources and to demarcate an area of tropical forest around the Beni Biosphere Reserve as a protected area. In **Costa Rica**, the Central Bank authorized the conversion of up to US$5.4 million of debt. Conservation organizations can redeem such debt, obtained at a discount, for local currency bonds. Interest earned on these bonds may be used to finance conservation programs approved by the Ministry of Natural Resources, Energy, and Mines. The use of bond financing of conservation programs as a means of extinguishing external indebtedness reflected, in part, the authorities' concern with limiting the domestic liquidity impact of conversions. A similar program has been in place in **Ecuador** since October 1987. Under this program, up to US$10 million of debt claims purchased on the secondary market at a discount may be converted into local bonds to be held by the Fundacion Natura. The bond principal will provide an endowment, and the Fundacion Natura will use the interest proceeds from the bonds to finance a variety of conservation programs. In the case of the **Philippines**, the authorities agreed to redeem up to US$2 million of debt obtained by the World Wildlife Foundation (WWF) for local funds to implement a conservation strategy focusing primarily on management of protected natural areas, conservation training, and support of conservation groups.

Other recent innovations include **debt-for-charity** swaps. These arrangements usually involve the outright donation of commercial bank claims by the commercial bank itself (usually reflecting the existence of a tax break for charitable donations), which in turn are exchanged, through an intermediary, for local currency used to support charitable programs. In late 1988, the Midland Bank in the United Kingdom donated US$0.8 million to UNICEF; in 1989 Deutsche Bank donated another US$2.9 million worth of claims. Proceeds from the conversion of the claims into local currency at a discount are currently being used to finance health care, water supply, and tree-planting projects in central **Sudan**. Similar operations have also been undertaken in **Bolivia** and **Zambia**.

Bibliography

Dornbush, Rudiger, John H. Makin, and David Zlowe (eds.), *Alternative Solutions to Developing-Country Debt Problems* (Washington: American Enterprise Institute for Public Policy Research, 1989).

XXV. Fiscal Activities of Public Institutions

Henri Lorie and Kenneth Miranda

Which monetary activities of central banks have an expenditure dimension?

Do other public institutions undertake similar activities?

How are these activities reflected in fiscal accounts?

Conventional accounting methodologies may seriously misrepresent the size and composition of public expenditure. While the consolidation of expenditure by local and central governments is routinely undertaken, the consolidation of expenditure by nonfinancial and financial public institutions (including public enterprises) with that of the general government is not common practice, because such expenditure is assumed to be akin to private sector expenditure. For purposes of public sector consolidation, only the cash balances of public institutions are consolidated into the general government accounts. This is appropriate for gauging the financial policy implications of government operations, but—because many public institutions do not operate along solely commercial lines—may understate the full scope of general government activities. In many cases, such institutions are charged with important public policy objectives which require them to undertake **quasi-fiscal expenditures.**

As the same time, public institutions, like the government, may also undertake certain activities which, though not involving an immediate cash outlay, expose the government to potential future spending. Such noncash policies, generally in the form of explicit (**contingent**) or implicit (**conjectural**) insurance or loan guarantees, which can have important economic effects, are not adequately captured under conventional expenditure or deficit measures.

Quasi-Fiscal Expenditures

Central banks

Central bank activities have various quasi-fiscal aspects. Revenue generation by central banks is commonplace. For example, the administration of a multiple exchange rate system under which the central bank has a monopoly over the purchase and sale of foreign exchange (the exchange rate being more depreciated for the latter than the former) is tantamount to an export-import tax scheme, the revenues from which will be captured in the profit/loss account of the central bank. The collection of seignorage revenue and the inflation tax, whose proceeds eventually benefit the government, is another example.

A central bank may also undertake a wide range of quasi-fiscal expenditures. The following are the most important:

Credit subsidies

Provision of subsidized credit to priority sectors such as agriculture or export, either directly or indirectly (through rediscounting of commercial banks' bills at a subsidized rate), is a major implicit expenditure which in many cases seriously weakens the income position and balance sheet of central banks.

Support of financial institutions

It is common for central banks to assist financial institutions in difficulty by injecting capital or lending at subsidized rates (for instance, to development banks), assuming their liabilities, or taking over some of their nonperforming assets on nonmarket terms. The subsidy element would be reflected in the income position of the central bank.

Foreign exchange subsidies

Foreign exchange subsidies on particular types of transactions such as essential imports or debt service payments are often provided. In the case of forward cover (exchange rate guarantees) granted on subsidized terms to enterprises for import bills or external debt service payments falling due in the future, the impact consists of revenue forgone in the current period (lower than actuarial insurance premia) and higher expenditure in the future, when the exchange rate loss cannot be covered by the insurance funds set aside earlier.

Foreign exchange swap arrangements

Central banks often acquire foreign exchange reserves from domestic commercial banks with a commitment to sell them back later at a predetermined and agreed exchange rate. Of course, the more the commercial banks perceive the exchange rate to be overvalued in comparison with market signals, the more they will be inclined to participate in such a transaction. When the foreign exchange acquired is sold to an importer at an obviously overvalued exchange rate, an implicit subsidy is involved. If the exchange rate depreciates before the swap arrangement is fully undone, the central bank then buys foreign exchange at a more depreciated exchange rate. The transfer of that foreign exchange back to the commercial banks at the earlier exchange rate leads to a swap loss which is matched by an income transfer to the commercial banks.

Foreign exchange revaluation

When the central bank revalues its positive (or negative) holdings of net foreign assets, an unrealized revaluation gain (or loss) ensues. Because this revaluation has no impact on private sector purchasing power, the usual practice is to block it separately in a revaluation account. Clearly, though, such unrealized revaluation gains or losses have significant implications. Consider, for instance, the case of a country that has had severe balance of payments difficulties which led to a negative net foreign assets position. A devaluation would involve offsetting adjustments in net foreign assets (becoming more negative) and the revaluation account (becoming more positive) on the asset side of the central bank balance sheet. This asset is obviously nonperforming, while interest accrues in domestic currency terms on larger negative net foreign assets. Recognition of the burden occasioned on the income position of the central bank by large revaluation losses, whether realized or not, is one reason why arrangements are often made to transfer unrealized revaluation losses from the central bank to the government. Such transfers would not directly affect the government deficit. However, to the extent that they involve increasing central bank net claims on the government, interest payments of the government would increase.

External debt rescheduling

Nonblocking at the central bank of public sector external debt payments falling due, but subject to rescheduling, may weaken the income position of the central bank. Assuming that current domestic interest rates are higher than foreign interest rates, and that an expected exchange rate depreciation does not cover this differential, the government may find it advantageous to assume the servicing of rescheduled obligations, although it may still try to shift the exchange risk to the central bank. To the extent that the central bank reduces the resulting excess liquidity in the banking system by selling (or buying fewer) domestic securities at higher domestic interest rates, this has an expenditure impact. The reverse argument applies when domestic interest rates are artificially low while the exchange rate is expected to depreciate; in this case, one may expect the government to rush to make payment of external obligations falling due, with the central bank inheriting the burden of servicing the rescheduled amounts and the exchange rate risk.

Other public institutions

While it is commonly recognized that central banks undertake numerous quasi-fiscal activities, many other financial and nonfinancial public institutions are also involved in such activities, and especially quasi-fiscal expenditure. Financial institutions, such as development banks, may also provide loans at below-market interest rates to priority sectors of the economy. Nonfinancial public institutions undertake quasi-fiscal expenditure, insofar as they do not operate strictly along commercial lines. In developing countries, such institutions may provide certain essential goods (especially food) and services at prices below cost-recovery levels, in order to meet social objectives. Nonfinancial public institutions may also create employment at levels higher than are justified on commercial terms, pay wages at above market-clearing levels, or provide certain goods and services to employees. The costs of attaining these noncommercial objectives could be met through explicit budgetary subsidies or transfers, and are therefore equivalent to expenditures.

Fiscal impact

Since quasi-fiscal activities are generally reflected in a public institution's profits, if these are remitted to the government it can be argued that such activities are also reflected in the government surplus or deficit. Their impact on aggregate demand and the public sector sector's claim on private saving are therefore also taken into account. However, the level and structure of revenues and expenditures of the public sector are misrepresented, and hence the role of the government in the economy is not clearly reflected in the data. When the net income position of a public institution turns out to be negative, there is no established mechanism through which its deficit is reflected in the government accounts, since no profit transfer occurs. As a result, the government surplus or deficit does not reflect the impact of its activities on aggregate demand or on savings flows in the economy. Moreover, even if profit transfers occur, numerous methodological issues arise in assessing whether the true impact of a public institution's activities has been adequately consolidated into the public sector accounts. These issues relate to differences in accounting practices between public institutions, which are likely to calculate profit transfers on an accrual basis, and general government, which generally uses cash-based accounting systems. To the extent that the profit transfer of a public institution differs from its cash surplus in a given year, the economic impact of its activities will not be correctly gauged.

Contingent and Conjectural Liabilities

While conventional accounting methodologies can be modified in a fairly straightforward manner to account for quasi-fiscal expenditures, it is more difficult to modify these procedures to account appropriately for noncash policies. Contingent policies, such as loan guarantees, deposit insurance, and social security, commit a public agency (or the government) to a potential future cash flow. In other words, in comparison to a noncontingent liability (such as interest-bearing debt), the contractual obligation of the government for a contingent liability is dependent, in its timing and amount, on the occurrence of some discrete event. From an income statement point of view, contingent liabilities do not appear when the obligation is incurred, but rather only when the actual expenditure is made. Nonetheless, such transactions expose the government, directly or indirectly, to potential expenditures that should be reflected on the public sector's balance sheet. In practice, however, most contingent liabilities are not treated as potential liabilities, and are *de facto* treated as "off-balance sheet" activities.

Whether on- or off-balance sheet, the provision of such contingent claims to the private sector can affect economic behavior—especially if the claims are valued by the private sector more highly than any fees or charges levied in exchange for their provision. Thus, the conventional practice of accounting for expenditures only when a cash outlay is incurred may seriously understate the government's current fiscal impact. Moreover, when such liabilities are not carefully monitored (and put "on balance sheet"), it may be difficult to control public finances.

Unlike contingent liabilities, which are explicit in nature, conjectural liabilities are implicit in nature, and are not in general enforceable. Conjectural liabilities may, however, affect economic behavior substantially. Examples include provision of relief in the event of a natural disaster, or the saving of a bankrupt financial or nonfinancial private institution (such as a large bank or manufacturing firm) in instances where the potential consequences are deemed too large not to intervene. While not legally callable, the perception that such guarantees or insurance exist can fundamentally alter private sector economic behavior. For example, if it is expected that the government will provide relief in the event of a natural disaster, individuals may make inappropriate location, insurance, and savings decisions. In cases where public institutions are assumed to be backed up by the full faith and credit of the government, the private sector may extend loans to them on preferential terms. Finally, large private institutions, especially banks, may undertake more risky business activities if it is perceived that the government will ultimately be forced to rescue them from insolvency.

Country Illustrations

Social expenditure by the central bank of the Islamic Republic of Iran

Conditioned in part by the exigencies of the civil and economic dislocation resulting from the revolution and war, the Central Bank of the Islamic Republic of Iran has administered a multiple exchange rate system since the early 1980s which effectively acts as an export tax scheme coupled with a social expenditure policy. Under the system, oil is exported at an exchange rate of rials 70 per U.S. dollar, while government imports of certain essential foods, consumer, and capital goods are valued at the same rate. This rate compares to an officially sanctioned free market rate of about rials 1,400 per U.S. dollar at end-1990. In essence, the central bank uses the official exchange rate as an instrument of resource taxation and of subsidization of essential commodities—rather than as an instrument of macroeconomic management. Analysis of central government fiscal operations is also complicated by the quasi-fiscal operations of the central bank—because public sector revenues are understated by the amount of the implicit subsidies. While estimates for the full set of implicit taxes and subsidies under the current multiple exchange rate system are not available, an analysis of central bank operations reveals that the cost of implicitly subsidizing 13 essential consumer commodities (sugar, chicken, eggs, tea, cheese, butter, vegetable oil, lamb, beef, rice, wheat, detergent, and soap) amounted to rials 1, 579.3 billion in 1990/91 (or about 4.3 percent of GDP) calculated on the basis of a notional equilibrium unified exchange rate. The budgetization of these activities would not, *ceteris paribus*, affect the overall fiscal balance of the consolidated public sector, and would allow the central bank to use the exchange rate as an instrument of macroeconomic management.

Deposit insurance in the United States

The provision of deposit insurance to savings and loan institutions represents a major contingent liability on the part of the U.S. government. The Federal Savings and Loan Insurance Corporation (FSLIC) was created in 1934 to insure the deposits of savings and loan institutions, and was intended to create depositor confidence and to prevent runs on S & Ls. For nearly 50 years, until about 1980, such federal insurance operated successfully, with relatively few S & L failures and no runs. As a result, the liabilities were never called, and hence general budgetary support for the operations of the FSLIC was never needed.

Beginning in the 1980s, however, the situation began to change. Because S & Ls held mainly long-term fixed assets (such as mortgages), deregulation of interest rates in an inflationary environment had adverse financial implications on the profitability of the industry as a whole. High and rising interest rates increased the costs of attracting deposits, and also created capital losses on the existing portfolio of assets. Together, these were enough to wipe out the net worth of many S & Ls. Numerous S & Ls failed, requiring the FSLIC to compensate depositors. Since insurance premia charged by the FSLIC were not actuarially rated, reserves were not sufficient to cover these costs. Once it became evident that reserves would be exhausted, the contingent liabilities of the government, extended through the FSLIC, were called, and hence the costs of cleaning up the S & L crisis were placed "on-budget." Currently it is estimated that the total (net) costs of meeting called deposit insurance obligations will reach nearly US$500 billion (at 1991 prices). While the liabilities of the government were accruing over a fairly lengthy period of time, the actual cash outlays and financing needs will be condensed into a fairly short time period.

Bibliography

Robinson, David J., and Peter Stella, "Amalgamating Central Bank and Fiscal Deficits," in *Measurement of Fiscal Impact*, Occasional Paper No. 59, ed. by Mario I. Blejer and Ke-young Chu (Washington: International Monetary Fund, 1988).

Towe, Christopher M., "The Budgetary Control and Fiscal Impact of Government Contingent Liabilities," *IMF Staff Papers*, 38 (Washington, International Monetary Fund, 1991).

Biographical Sketches

Ehtisham Ahmad, a Pakistan national, is a senior economist in the Government Expenditure Analysis Division of the IMF's Fiscal Affairs Department. Prior to joining the IMF, he was a senior economist with the World Development Report '90 in the World Bank and Director of the Development Economics Research Program - London School of Economics, and Deputy Director, Development Economics Research Center, Warwick. Mr. Ahmad holds degrees from Cambridge, Punjab, and Sussex universities. He has published extensively in development and public finance.

Ke-young Chu, a Korean, is Chief of the Government Expenditure Analysis Division of the Fiscal Affairs Department. Before joining the Fiscal Affairs Department, he was in the IMF's Research Department. Mr. Chu received a doctorate in economics from Columbia University and has published in fiscal policy issues in developing countries and world primary commodity markets.

Jack Diamond, a U.K. national, is a senior economist in the Budget Expenditure and Control Division of the Fiscal Affairs Department. Mr. Diamond received a doctorate in economics from the University of York, has lectured on economics, and has published in public finance and development economics.

Peter Heller, a U.S. national, is Assistant Director and Chief of the East Africa I Division in the IMF's African Department and was Chief of the Government Expenditure Analysis Division of the Fiscal Affairs Department. Before joining the IMF, he was Assistant Professor of economics at the University of Michigan. Mr. Heller holds degrees from Harvard University and Trinity College and has published in government expenditure policy, economics of operations and maintenance, and economics of health care in developing countries.

Richard Hemming, a U.K. national, is Deputy Chief of the Government Expenditure Analysis Division of the Fiscal Affairs Department. Prior to joining the IMF, he was a university lecturer, a senior research officer at the Institute for Fiscal Studies in London, and an administrator at the OECD in Paris. Mr. Hemming holds degrees from the Universities of Sussex and Stirling and has published in taxation, social expenditure, poverty, and privatization.

Daniel Hewitt, a U.S. national, is an economist in the Government Expenditure Analysis Division of the Fiscal Affairs Department. He received a doctorate from Columbia University and has published in fiscal federalism and analysis of government expenditure.

Robert Holzmann, an Austrian, is an associate professor at the Economics Department of the University of Vienna and Director of the Ludwig-Boltzmann Institute for Economic Policy Analysis in Vienna, as well as a consultant for the IMF, the Organization for Economic Cooperation and Development (OECD), the World Bank, the International Labor Organization, and the ISSA. Mr. Holzmann was a senior economist in the Government Expenditure Analysis Division of the Fiscal Affairs Department when he prepared his contribution to the Handbook. Prior to joining the IMF, he was a principal administrator at the OECD in Paris. Mr. Holzmann studied economics at the Universities of Graz, Grenoble, and Bristol and received a doctorate in economics from the University of Vienna. He has published in various areas of public finance, in particular on social security, expenditure and tax policy, and most recently on economic policy issues of economies in transition.

Kalpana Kochhar, an Indian national, is an economist in the Asian Department. She was an economist in the Government Expenditure Analysis Division of the Fiscal Affairs Department when she prepared her contribution to the Handbook. Ms. Kochhar has a doctorate in economics from Brown University and has published in the areas of fiscal policy and growth.

Claire Liuksila, a U.K. national, is a senior economist in the Fiscal Review Division of the Fiscal Affairs Department. She was in the IMF's European Department before joining the Fiscal Affairs Department. Mrs. Liuksila has a doctorate in economics from Cambridge University and has published in labor economics and agricultural pricing policy, as well as on poverty issues.

Henri Lorie, a Belgian, is Deputy Chief of the Fiscal Review Division of the Fiscal Affairs Department. Before joining the IMF, he held academic positions in the United States and the United Kingdom, including at the University of Pennsylvania and the London School of Economics. He holds a Masters degree in Economics from the Catholic University of Louvain (Belgium) and a Ph.D. in Economics from Northwestern University and has published in macroeconomic and monetary theory, fiscal policy, and international economics.

G.A. Mackenzie, a Canadian, is Deputy Chief of the Special Fiscal Studies Division of the Fiscal Affairs Department and was a senior economist in the Government Expenditure Analysis Division. He was formerly an economic analyst with the Canadian Department of Finance. Mr. Mackenzie holds degrees from Dalhousie University in Canada and Oxford University and has published on fiscal policy of oil-exporting countries, taxes and economic growth, indicators of the stance of fiscal policy, and social security issues in Latin America.

Kenneth Miranda, a U.S. citizen, is an economist in the Government Expenditure Analysis Division of the IMF's Fiscal Affairs Department and was an economist in the African and Asian departments before joining the Fiscal Affairs Department. Mr. Miranda received his doctorate from the University of Chicago.

Jerald Schiff, a U.S. national, is an economist in the Government Expenditure Analysis Division of the Fiscal Affairs Department. Prior to joining the IMF, Mr. Schiff was an assistant professor of economics at Tulane University and financial economist with the U.S. Department of Treasury. He received a doctorate from the University of Wisconsin and has published in the areas of tax and expenditure policy and nongovernmental organizations.

Christian Schiller, a German national, is the IMF's resident representative in Madagascar. Formerly with the IMF's Fiscal Affairs Department, he has published on government expenditure and the crowding-out effect and on the fiscal consequences of privatization.